THE WESTERN FRONT THEN AND NOW

FROM MONS TO THE MARNE AND BACK

December 1991

My dear husband wrote this book with great love and feeling for all those soldiers of World War One. He read the final proofs just two days before he died. I like to think that he is now at peace with those brave soldiers for whom he started the Western Front Association and who he admired so much.

Margery Giles

THE WESTERN FRONT THEN AND NOW

From Mons to the Marne and back

JOHN GILES

AN
AFTER THE
BATTLE
PUBLICATION

AFTER THE BATTLE

**THE WESTERN FRONT
THEN AND NOW
From Mons to the Marne and back**
ISBN: 0 900913 71 1
© John Giles 1992

Printed in Great Britain by
Plaistow Press Ltd, Church House,
Church Street, London E15 3JA.

Published by Battle of Britain Prints
International Ltd, Church House,
Church Street, London E15 3JA.
Telephone: 081-534 8833

FRONT COVER
The Canadian Memorial on Vimy Ridge, on a misty autumn afternoon in October 1991.

BACK COVER
German graves are honoured at the German Military Cemetery at Fricourt in the mid-1970s.

FRONT ENDPAPER LEFT
Canadian troops come out of the front line for a rest during the November battles of 1916. (IWM)

FRONT ENDPAPER RIGHT
British walking wounded receiving food at a dressing station in Aveluy Wood during the Battle of the Ancre, during the Somme battles of November 1916. (IWM)

REAR ENDPAPER
How the Armistice was reported in *The Evening News* of Monday, 11th November, 1918.

FRONTISPIECE
Canadian troops search captured German trenches on Vimy Ridge whilst prisoners are escorted to the rear, April 1917. (IWM)

PAGE 4
Troops of the 3rd (Tyneside Irish) Brigade of the 34th Division advancing on La Boisselle on 1st July, 1916, on the first day of the Battle of the Somme — they were wiped out by artillery and machine-gun fire. (IWM)

PAGE 8
The original caption to this tragic picture reads simply 'Canadians buried where they fell in the barbed wire, October 1916.' (IWM)

PAGE 11
Troops of 2nd Battalion The Scots Guards rest by the roadside during the march from Thielt to Roulers, 13th October, 1914. (IWM)

PAGE 83
Troops of the Scots Guards mending their trenches in the front line, December 1915. (IWM)

PAGE 131
German dead outside their dugout in a front-line trench during the Battle of the Somme, July 1916. (IWM)

PAGE 136
Stretcher-bearers and German prisoners bring in wounded British troops from the battlefield at Vimy Ridge, April 1917. (IWM)

PAGE 190
Huge 'bag' of German prisoners arrive at a PoW 'cage' near Amiens during the battle there in August 1918. (IWM)

CONTENTS

LIST OF MAPS

INTRODUCTION

This volume completes a planned trilogy dealing with the 1914–1918 battlefields of France and Flanders on a photographic 'Then and Now' basis — a theme I adopted more than two decades ago — my other two books having concentrated specifically on the Ypres and Somme sectors. In this book the coverage has been extended to take in all the other main British battle areas of the old Western Front in France and Belgium, beginning with Mons and ending with the final march to victory.

Although the book is concerned with the operations of the British forces — and not, obviously, with those that appear in the other two — I have included brief coverage of the fighting at Verdun on the French part of the line, and of the two initial independent actions fought by the Americans. As in my other books, I have taken the present-day photographs myself, except for a few exceptions which are credited. This also applies to the aerial photographs. These originate from an aerial project that I undertook in 1982 financed by contributions from members of The Western Front Association, based on an idea I initiated.

Because there are more photographs and captions required to cover a much wider area, a change has become necessary in relation to the amount of extracts from eye-witness accounts compared with the other two books. Here, this aspect comprises pages from an officer's diary and short items on four old soldiers, one of whom is still living as at April 1991.

A topic that has purposely been avoided in this book is that of British military leadership in the Great War. Suffice it to say that undoubtedly both strategic and tactical mistakes were made — in war that is inevitable and sadly it also means the loss of lives — but our opponents, and our allies, also committed major errors: a fact that should not be overlooked by anyone attempting to arrive at a conclusion on that subject. Whatever, judgement should not be passed in hindsight without first trying to understand the enormous difficulties confronting those in command who had to wage war with the limited facilities that were available at the time. The fact remains that the once all-powerful German Army *was* finally defeated *in the field*, with British forces being well to the fore.

Neither is there any intended emphasis on the 'Beastly Hun' aspect which was so dear (not surprisingly) to the propagandists of the period. The introduction of flammenwerfers (flame throwers) and poison gas by the Germans in 1915 were of course barbarous deeds in an already bloody war, but they in turn considered that our use of tanks was a shameful act of brutality. War is brutal and ugly, but it is felt that few, if any, of those still alive who fought in the First World War would disagree with the contention that the German soldier of that era was a formidable foe who was not lacking in valour.

The real object of this book is to emphasise the courage and stoicism, and humour, of the front-line soldiers of 1914–1918 who fought in the most appalling conditions and suffered accordingly. Coupled with that is a deep appreciation of the extraordinary miracle of nature which even the worst extremes of man failed to eliminate, as proven by the now-lovely acres that once were zones of utter desolation.

JOHN GILES 1991
Guilton Mill,
Nr. Canterbury, Kent

FOREWORD

Major The Rt Hon. The Earl Haig, OBE, K.St.J, DL

Some years ago my wife and I were members of a party from The Western Front Association on a tour of the Somme battlefields. We were fortunate in having John Giles as our chief guide and mentor and were given most graphic descriptions of the battles, which included hand-to-hand fighting, in the setting of a landscape relatively unchanged since 1916.

As Mr Giles's father had been a member of the 1st Battalion The Queen's Own Royal West Kent Regiment and had been severely wounded at the Battle of Le Cateau in 1914, it is that battle which is particularly meaningful to the author. The descriptions of the fighting at the beginning of the campaigns in Belgium and France which have not been included in his two other books *Flanders Then and Now* and *The Somme Then and Now* are especially relevant.

It was in the early days of the First World War that our highly trained small army went over to help defend Belgium against a dangerous German attack, which threatened the Channel ports and to round up the Allied forces, as happened later in 1940. After the German forces under von Kluck had been held up at the Battle of Mons, at a cost of some 1,600 British casualties, we retreated back into France and took part in the battles of The Marne and the Aisne, and the First Battle of Ypres. This phase of a long and terrible war was a vital part of its — and our — history. The part we played as a relatively small cog in the Allied war machine was of grave importance. Thanks to the defence of Antwerp by the Belgian forces we were allowed time for manoeuvre and to prepare to face the concentration of German forces in front of Ypres.

The stand at Le Cateau was not part of Sir John French's intentions, but it no doubt gave some respite to the marching men of II Corps and helped to slow up the German advance. It was an important part of our effort to support the Allied left wing at a time when the war might well have been lost. Unfortunately Sir Horace Smith Dorrien's decision to fight at Le Cateau lost him the confidence of his Commander-in-Chief, and incidentally failed to win the support of my father, who commanded I Corps at that time, either.

The story of the many hard-fought battles which took place during the four long years of war is retold without rancour or bitterness, and without any attempt to attribute blame. The ordeals of the British soldiers who fought amidst the awful conditions of trench warfare with courage and tenacity are described in simple terms.

We are reminded of the daily lives of those heroic men who are lauded in terms of deep thankfulness. To them thanks are rendered for a victory which had a powerful effect on the future of mankind. As a result they maintained the freedom which we enjoy today.

The writer of these citations himself deserves our praise for recording them in spite of his own physical illness.

Haig of Bemersyde
May 1990

The frontiers of Europe before the lights began to go out.

1914

THE ROAD TO WAR

THE TRAGEDY OF SARAJEVO

On 28th June 1914 a tumultuous event occurred which altered the course of European history when the heir to the sprawling eleven-nation Hapsburg Empire, Archduke Franz Ferdinand, visited its southernmost province of Bosnia to attend military manoeuvres. With him was his wife, Sophie, partner in a morganatic marriage, who had been a Bohemian Countess before being granted the rank of Duchess of Hohenburg following a union which had caused something of a constitutional crisis.

Bosnia had been annexed by Austria only six years before, and nationalistic undercurrents constantly swirled beneath the surface. During the visit these feelings erupted into actual violence which not only ended the lives of two high-ranking people, but much else besides. It was, in fact, the spark which ignited the fuze that led to a world-wide explosion and resulted in millions of people losing their lives, in the map of Europe having to be redrawn, and in the dismantling of three empires — including the Hapsburg Empire which, at the end of the war, dissolved into separate republics.

Although the cauldron of European affairs had been simmering and bubbling for some years, nobody could foretell on that summer day in 1914 what would stem from that visit, or how the world would be plunged into chaos by the action of a young 19-year-old fanatic by the name of Gavrilo Princip who, with several others, had come to Sarajevo with the express purpose of trying to murder the Archduke. Indeed, they had almost succeeded in their aim earlier that same morning, for one of the conspirators had thrown a bomb at the Archduke's car, but it had exploded on the ground, wounding a number of people, some seriously.

Archduke Franz Ferdinand and his wife about to enter the car which was to carry them to their doom. [IWM]

The car came along the quay on the far side of the river from the right. Princip was standing outside the three-storey building before the bridge. The car turned right at the bridge, reversed to continue straight on, and the Archduke and his wife were then right in front of him. [IWM]

Because a muddle occurred over the route which their car was to follow when taking them out of the capital, fate decreed that the vehicle would stop and reverse outside a delicatessen opposite Latin Bridge (afterwards to be called Princip's Bridge). By pure chance, Princip was standing at that precise spot and he seized the opportunity and fired his pistol twice. The first shot killed the Duchess almost immediately; the second hit the Archduke, who died shortly afterwards, but not before he had pleaded with his wife to live 'for the sake of the children'. Sadly his plea went unanswered, as by then the Duchess was dead. Princip was immediately arrested; but the damage had been done, and five weeks later, following numerous threats and counter-threats between various nations, the Great War began. Princip died through illness before the war ended.

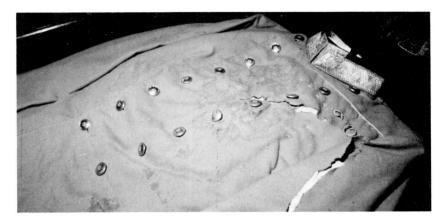

Exhibits in the Heeresgeschichtliches (Army) Museum, Vienna.
Above: The car in which the Archduke and his wife were assassinated. Princip fired his revolver from the nearside.
Above right: The Archduke's bloodstained tunic.
Below right: Painting of the Archduke in better times, below which are the death masks of the murdered couple.
[Photographs on this page by Paul Foster]

A CHRONICLE OF EVENTS

28th June 1914 — Assassination of the Archduke Franz Ferdinand, heir to the Austrian throne, and his wife, by Serbian conspirators.

23rd July — Austria-Hungary presents Ultimatum to Serbia which demands cessation of Serbian agitation.

25th July — Russia seeks more time for Serbia, but Austria refuses.

26th July — Serbia sends reply to the Ultimatum which Austria-Hungary considers to be evasive. The Austrian Ambassador leaves Belgrade. Serbians mobilise.

27th July — Sir Edward Grey, British Minister for Foreign Affairs, proposes mediation by France, Germany, Italy and Great Britain to prevent a quarrel between Austria and Russia that could embroil all Europe.

28th July — Austria-Hungary declares war on Serbia. Russia begins partial mobilisation. British First Fleet ordered to preliminary war station in the north.

29th July — Belgrade bombarded. Russia threatens full mobilisation. Kaiser holds all-night council. British regular officers and men on leave recalled. Belgian Government places army on reinforced peace footing.

30th July — Austrian troops occupy Belgrade. Russia orders mobilisation of her four southern armies. Germany threatens to mobilise in view of Russian action.

31st July — Austria, Russia and Turkey mobilise. Germany proclaims 'imminent danger of war' and sends ultimatum to Russia demanding cessation of mobilisation.

1st August — France and Germany order general mobilisation. King George makes a final effort for peace by sending a personal telegram to the Czar. Germany declares war on Russia.

2nd August — German troops invade Luxembourg (the neutrality of which had been guaranteed by Prussia by the Treaty of 1867) and concentrate in the neighbourhood of Liège. They also violate the neutrality of Belgium and penetrate into France at four points. Germans send Utimatum to Belgium at 7 p.m. giving the Government until 7 a.m. Monday to agree to the passage of German troops over Belgian territory, and threatening to use force if their demand is not complied with, whilst promising that in the event of compliance Belgium's independence and possessions would be assured at the conclusion of peace.

3rd August — Belgium refuses to comply with German demand and declares that she would repel any aggression by all possible means.

Sir Edward Grey states in the House of Commons that the French Ambassador has been assured that 'If the German Fleet comes into the Channel, or through the North Sea, to undertake hostile operations against the French coasts or shipping, the British Fleet will give all the protection in its power.' He also said that with regard to Belgium the British Government was prepared for the consequence of having to use all the strength we had and never was confidence in the power of the Navy more justified.

Germany declares war on France.

The Italian Government declares that Italy would remain neutral in the impending struggle. Greece declares neutrality.

Article VII

La Belgique, dans les limites indiquées aux Articles I, II, et IV, formera un État indépendant et perpétuellement neutre.. Elle sera tenue d'observer cette même neutralité envers tous les autres États.

The Treaty of London. 'The Scrap of Paper'. [IWM]

The Quintuple Treaty of 1839, which guaranteed Belgium's perpetual neutrality, was signed by the Great Powers of Austria, France, Great Britain, Prussia and Russia. It was Germany's violation of this treaty, in August 1914, which brought Great Britain into the war, a decision that led to the German Imperial Chancellor, von Bethman-Hollweg, to make the historic remark to the British Ambassador in Berlin that 'Just for a scrap of paper Great Britain is going to make war on a kindred nation.'

As the British ultimatum to Germany expired on the night of 4th August, another famous comment was made, by the British Foreign Secretary, Sir Edward Grey, when he said: 'The lamps are going out all over Europe; we shall not see them lit again in our lifetime.' For millions of soldiers and others of the warring nations this prediction was to prove a tragic truth.

Before the storm broke. The crowned heads of Europe at Buckingham Palace at the time of the funeral of King Edward VII in 1910. From left to right, standing: King Haakon VII of Norway, King Ferdinand I of Bulgaria, King Manoel II of Portugal, Kaiser Wilhelm II of Germany, King Gustav V of Sweden, King Albert I of Belgium. Seated: King Alphonso XIII of Spain, King George V of England, King Frederick VIII of Denmark. [IWM]

15

Outside Buckingham Palace the crowds cheer. The King wrote in his diary: 'Tuesday August 4. I held a Council at 10.45 to declare war on Germany. It is a terrible catastrophe, but it is not our fault. An enormous crowd collected outside the Palace; we went on the balcony both before and after dinner.' [IWM]

The Kaiser goes on his balcony. The crowds cheer. [IWM]

4th August — The German Minister forwards a Note to his Belgian counterpart stating that as Belgium has declined Germany's well-intentioned proposal, Germany, with deep regret, is compelled to carry out by force of arms the measures considered to be indispensable in view of the French menace. The Belgian Minister for Foreign Affairs in London informs the British Government by telegram that Belgian territory has been violated.

The British Government protests to the Germans by telegram against the violation of Belgian neutrality, and in reply receives an assurance that, even in the event of armed conflict with Belgium, Germany will not under any pretext whatever annex Belgian territory. The British Government in turn replies that they cannot regard this telegram as in any sense satisfactory and requests a further response before midnight (German time).

At 11 p.m. Britain declares war on Germany.

In the House of Commons the Prime Minister, Mr Asquith, advises members of a message from the King saying that His Majesty was, by proclamation, about to order that the Army Reserve should be called out for permanent service and the Territorial Force was to be embodied.

5th August — Britain's declaration of war on Germany is read from the steps of the Royal Exchange, in the presence of cheering crowds.

6th August — Serbia declares war on Germany. Montenegro declares war on Austria-Hungary.

11th August — Montenegro declares war on Germany.

12th August — Britain and France declare war on Austria.

MILITARY BALANCE AT THE OUTBREAK OF WAR

The British had 11 infantry divisions and 3 cavalry divisions, all told; but the BEF could only muster 6 infantry divisions (4 of which initially went to France) and 1½ cavalry divisions. The Territorial Army consisted of 14 infantry divisions and 14 cavalry brigades.

The Germans had 7 armies totalling approximately 1,485,000 men. Germany was able to draw upon a reserve of 4,300,000 trained men. There were 136 German and Austrian infantry divisions and 22 cavalry divisions.

The French had 5 armies totalling 1,071,000 men (62 infantry divisions and 10 cavalry divisions).

The Belgians had 6 infantry divisions and 1 cavalry division (117,000 men plus 90,000 fortress troops).

In the air, Germany possessed 384 aeroplanes and 30 airships; France, 123 aeroplanes and 10 airships; Britain, 113 aeroplanes (of which 63 went with the BEF).

CALLED TO THE COLOURS

Volunteers for Kitchener's New Army passing under the Admiralty Arch, London, September 1914. [IWM]

Recruits in training. 'H' Company Post Office Rifles marching in column. Regents Park, September 1914. [IWM]

French troops receiving an enthusiastic send-off on their way to the front. [IWM]

A station farewell. Whole families and local town notables watch German troops depart for the front. [IWM]

In August 1914 a British infantry division comprised a total of 18,073 all ranks divided into 3 infantry brigades = 12 infantry battalions, together with divisional troops. A battalion consisted of approximately 1,000 men in 4 companies = 16 platoons, each of about 54 men. Two heavy (Vickers) machine-guns were an integral part of each battalion (thus making 24 machine-guns per division). It was not until July 1915 that the lighter, American-designed Lewis Gun became available in small numbers. In 1916 each infantry battalion was equipped with 16 of these. The main infantry weapon of the British soldier was the Short Magazine Lee-Enfield (SMLE) .303-inch rifle.

A vessel carrying troops of the BEF arriving in France. [IWM]

CAVALRY

In August 1914 the Regular Army contained 31 regiments of cavalry = 21,830 officers and men. A cavalry division comprised 4 cavalry brigades = 12 cavalry regiments together with divisional troops. The strength of a cavalry division was 9,269 all ranks, 9,815 horses, 20 13-pdr guns, and 24 machine-guns. Marching depth was about 11½ miles. When *dismounted* the rifle strength of a cavalry division was approximately that of an infantry brigade.

ARTILLERY

Royal Horse Artillery: brigade = 2 RHA batteries and brigade artillery column. (An RHA battery comprised 6 13-pdr guns and 12 ammunition wagons.

Royal Field Artillery: 3 RFA batteries and brigade ammunition column. (An RFA battery comprised 6 18-pdr guns (or 6 4.5 howitzers) and 12 ammunition wagons.

Royal Garrison Artillery: 4 60-pdr guns, 8 ammunition wagons and battery ammunition column.

THE FIRST MOVES

Immediately after Great Britain's declaration of war on Germany, the first steps were taken by the military authorities to put into motion prepared plans for the embarkation of the British Expeditionary Force. It was to be commanded by Field Marshal Sir John French and was to comprise four infantry divisions and one cavalry division, with embarkation to commence on 9th August. Two other divisions (4th and 6th) were to be held back for the time being, the possibility of a German landing on the British coast having to be taken into account. (Instructions for the 4th Division to join the BEF were issued on 19th August and it arrived just in time for the Battle of Le Cateau. The 6th Division embarked for St Nazaire on 28th/29th September.)

Mobilisation of the various units having taken place, the wheels began turning on the appointed date with remarkable smoothness as the embarkation plans were put into effect. In one five-day period 1,800 special trains were run, and from 12th to 17th August a daily average of thirteen large transports were despatched across the Channel under the watchful eye of the Royal Navy.

On 14th August the Commander-in-Chief crossed to Le Havre and reached Amiens just after 9 p.m. For the next three days he visited Général Joffre and other high-ranking French officials, from whom he learned of the dispositions of the French forces. Meanwhile an enthusiastic welcome was given to the British troops disembarking on French soil. Concentration of the British Army began on the 14th within a 25-mile area between Maubeuge and Le Cateau. The Royal Flying Corps, with 63 aeroplanes and 860 officers and men, was located at an airfield at Maubeuge. By the 20th the concentration was practically complete, marred only by the sudden death, in a train, of Lieutenant-General Sir James Grierson, commander of II Corps, whose position was taken over on 21st August by Sir Horace Smith-Dorrien.

On 19th August the RFC carried out its first reconnaissance to the north and north-west but saw no large bodies of troops. Next day, though, a long enemy column was sighted at Louvain, this being part of the German First Army. That same day, von Kluck's troops entered Brussels, whilst further north the Belgian Army retired into Antwerp. These events coincided with an order despatched by Général Joffre for a general advance, with the British moving north-east on the left of the French Fifth Army, which was commanded by Général Lanrezac. Orders were thus issued by Sir John French for the BEF to move forward, it being anticipated that on 23rd August its left would be on a line to the east and north-east of Mons. Events, however, caused a change of plan, with Mons and the Mons–Condé canal becoming the immediate objectives but with a continuing advance still the intention.

Field Marshal Sir John French (the BEF's first Commander-in-Chief) leaving HMS Sentinel on arrival at Boulogne, 14th August 1914. [IWM]

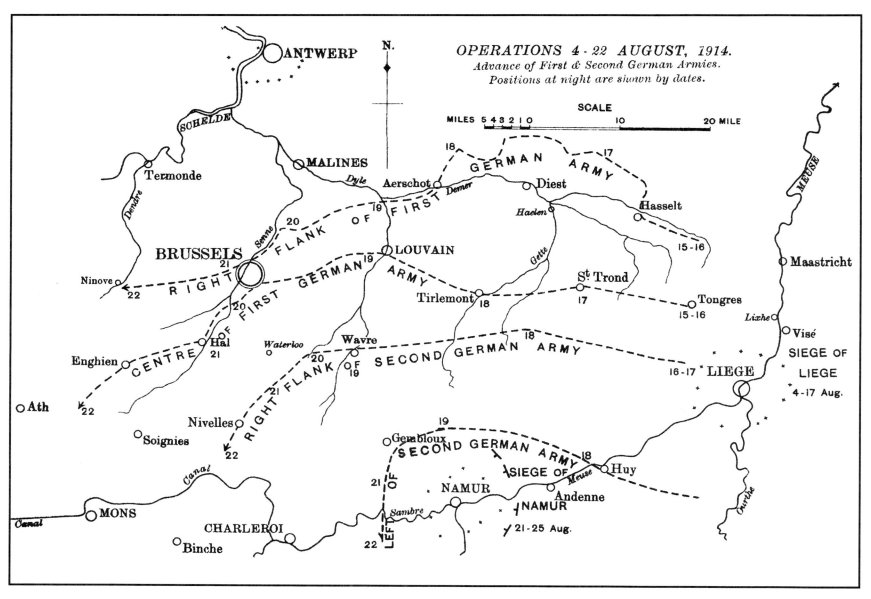

Map of the early operations showing the route of the invading German armies wheeling in conformance with the famous 'Schlieffen Plan' formulated by Count Alfred von Schlieffen, Chief of the German General Staff from 1892 to 1906.

Below: Entry printed in a small bible issued to troops at the beginning of the war. Field Marshal Lord Roberts, who was very popular, became ill during a visit to Indian troops in France and died on 14th November at St Omer. This town was the location of General Headquarters from October 1914 until April 1916.

25th August 1914

I ask you to put your trust in God. He will watch over you and strengthen you. You will find in this little book guidance when you are in health, comfort when you are in sickness, and strength when you are in adversity.

Roberts FM

German transport and soldiers in Brussels. The city was occupied by enemy troops on 20th August 1914. [IWM]

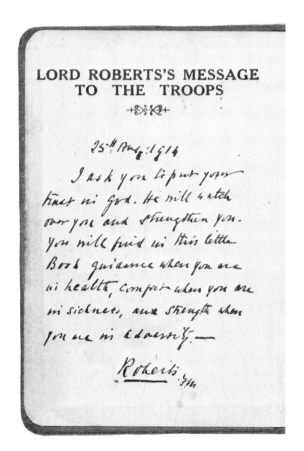

LORD ROBERTS'S MESSAGE
TO THE TROOPS

25th Aug: 1914

I ask you to put your trust in God. He will watch over you and strengthen you. You will find in this little Book guidance when you are in health, comfort when you are in sickness, and strength when you are in adversity. —

Roberts FM

The border between France and Belgium near Malplaquet, across which streamed column after column of British troops marching towards the foe in the hot, sunny days of August 1914. In the background is a French monument which commemorates the Battle of Malplaquet in 1709. Mons is about ten miles north of this point. After the Battle of Mons the British troops were streaming in the opposite direction, towards Le Cateau, where General Smith-Dorrien's II Corps turned and fought back.

The Château de la Roche (also known as Château de la Haie) at Sars-le-Bruyer, south-west of Mons, 1984. It was here that a War Council took place at 5 a.m. on the morning of August 23rd 1914 during which various military options were considered including that of retreat. On the step is the present owner of the château, the Comte d'Hendécourt, whose father was killed in action in the war.

A marble plaque at the entrance to the château which commemorates the momentous meeting of 1914 and gives the names of those attending. Close to it is the spot where a German soldier thrust his bayonet into the wall in a moment of anger after the British had retreated to the south.

At dawn on 22nd August the first British contact with the enemy was made by 'C' Squadron, 4th Dragoon Guards (2nd Cavalry Brigade). This skirmish occurred near Casteau, south of Soignies, on the Mons–Brussels road; it was the moment when the first British shot of the war was fired. Further east, at about 10 a.m., two squadrons of Scots Greys (5th Cavalry Brigade) came in contact with a German detachment which directed artillery and rifle fire at them, but fortunately with little effect. A troop of the 16th Lancers also engaged a party of Jäger west of Péronnes at little cost to themselves.

While the cavalry patrols pushed forward, very early on the 22nd the I and II Corps resumed their advance. Because of the need to fill a gap, the 1st Division of I Corps found itself faced with what turned out to be a long and tiring march, and therefore did not reach its billets until very late at night. The 2nd Division of I Corps was more fortunate and was not called upon to proceed beyond its original halting point west of Maubeuge.

The II Corps, after its early start, reached its destination around Mons at about 1 p.m. after a trying march over cobbled roads. Later in the afternoon its outposts were in place along the line of the Mons–Condé Canal, with those of the 3rd Division on the right and of the 5th Division on the left. Around Mons itself the canal formed a pronounced salient which created a major problem for its defence. From right to left, holding the salient and the line of the canal were battalions of the 5th Division's 8th and 9th Infantry Brigades; and from St Ghislain–Les Herbières–Pommeroeul, battalions of the 3rd Division's 13th and 14th Infantry Brigades. (The 4th Cavalry Brigade continued the line westwards to Condé at dawn on the 23rd, before being relieved that afternoon by two battalions of the 19th Infantry Brigade.)

As the afternoon wore on, disturbing news came in from the RFC of very large bodies of enemy troops approaching; also that the French were being driven back in the Sambre sector. It became clear to the British Commander-in-Chief that any further thoughts of continuing the advance were out of the question, especially in view of the somewhat isolated position of his forces, and this decision was confirmed at a staff conference at Le Cateau on the evening of the 22nd. Another problem was the nature of the terrain, which was unsatisfactory for defence, being broken by pit-heads, slag-heaps, numerous buildings and streams. It was close country which made things particularly difficult for the artillery, and the situation was not helped by the well-wooded ground to the north which gave good cover to the advancing enemy.

A warning was issued to all troops to expect to be attacked next morning.

A German infantry division comprised 3 (sometimes 4) infantry regiments, each of 3 battalions. Each battalion consisted of 4 companies (26 officers and 1,050 other ranks, plus transport). Two infantry regiments formed a brigade in an infantry division. The German Army fought by regiments (as compared to the British Army which fought by battalions). Total strength of a German Division was 17,500 all ranks, 4,000 horses, 72 guns, 24 machine-guns. (By including regimental replacement reserves, each German division effectively had 48 machine-guns.) Its main infantry weapon was the '98 pattern Mauser 7.9mm (.311-inch) rifle.

Below: German soldiers eating in a village during their advance. The faces of these men hardly conform to the propaganda image of 'the Beastly Hun'. [IWM]

22nd August 1914. Private Carter of 'D' Company, 4th Battalion, Middlesex Regiment, on guard at Mons. During the action that developed the following day the coffee house and six houses nearby were set alight by German shells. [IWM]

Above: The wide modern concrete bridge at Nimy. In the 1960s, before major reconstruction, it was a relatively narrow humped-backed structure of latticed iron girders. In 1914 a low swing-bridge was located here.

THE BATTLE OF MONS

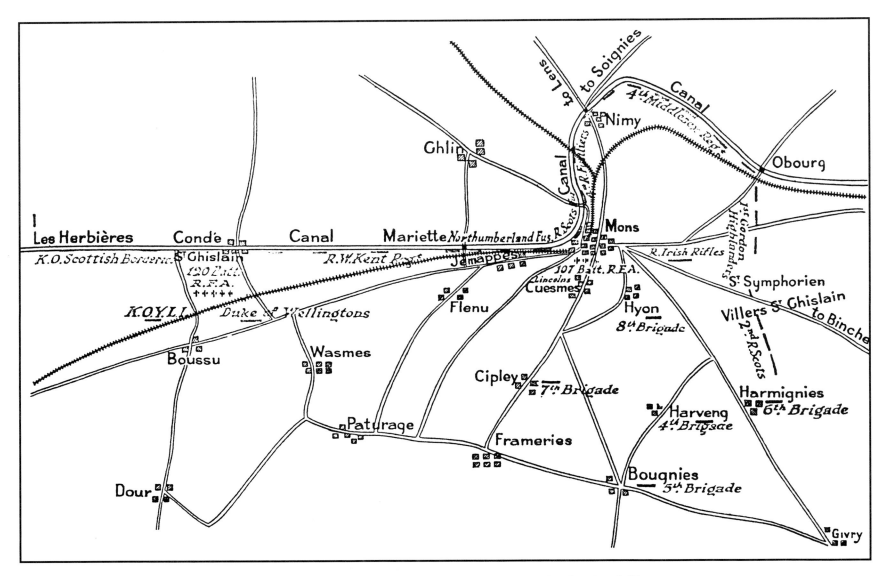

Map showing the disposition of British troops at the Battle of Mons.

Sunday, 23rd August, was a day that started off misty and rainy, but it cleared during the morning. Trains ran and church bells called the faithful to prayers as if the war were far away. Soon, however, this illusion of peace was to be shattered as the first cavalry encounters occurred at various locations in the vicinity of Bray, Havre and Obourg. Shots were exchanged at Obourg between the 4th Middlesex and German cavalry, and similar incidents happened at the apex of the salient and Nimy; also further to the west. Meanwhile, 'A' Company of the 1st Battalion, Royal West Kents moved forward to a point close to Tertre, north of the canal and beyond the bridge at St Ghislain, in support of 5th Division Mounted Troops (19th Hussars).

German guns came into action around 9 a.m., firing from high ground north of the canal, whilst hordes of German infantry pressed forward from Obourg to Nimy. Their massed formations made superb targets and this opportunity was made good use of by the Middlesex, Royal Fusiliers and Royal Irish, who poured rifle and machine-gun fire into the advancing troops. Under a hail of bullets — which introduced them to the renowned rapid fire of the British infantryman — the Germans hesitated and then began to work their way forward in small groups.

To the west of Mons things remained generally quiet until about 11 a.m. when Jemappes and its bridge came under German artillery fire. Here too the oncoming German masses were flailed by rifle and machine-gun fire which held them in check and caused them heavy losses. A similar situation prevailed at Mariette. In an attempt to overcome the defenders of that bridge, the Germans brought two field guns closer to the canal and opened fire with high-explosive shells, one of which wiped out a group of the 1st Northumberland Fusiliers holding out on the north side of the bridge. The Germans then took advantage of the presence of a party of little Belgian girls to get closer to the canal, the defenders being forced to cease fire to avoid hitting the children who, it is believed, had inadvertently come on the

The first clash of arms between British and German troops occurred here on the Mons–Brussels road at Casteau. The monument on the left records the first British rifle-shot of the war, fired at about 6 a.m. on 22nd August 1914 by Corporal (later Sergeant) E. Thomas, MM, during a sortie by a patrol of 'C' Squadron, 4th Royal Irish Dragoon Guards. It so happened that the Canadians had an outpost here on 11th November 1918 when the war came to an end.

The old route of the once-busy canal which created a pronounced salient at the apex of the British lines as it turned north towards Nimy. On the right is where men of the 4th Royal Fusiliers poured a withering fire across the canal at the advancing Germans. The famous Mons Belfry can be seen on the extreme right.

scene. Even so, the Northumberland Fusiliers continued to hold their own and to deny a crossing of the canal.

Further to the left the forward company of West Kents in front of the bridge at St Ghislain came under fire just after 11 a.m. Their opponents were the Brandenburg Grenadiers of the German 5th Division, and as these seasoned enemy troops moved forward in massed formation from Tertre the West Kents blasted them with machine-gun and rifle fire

which took a heavy toll. With enemy pressure growing all the time, the West Kents slowly withdrew towards the canal, but not before they had inflicted severe punishment on the Brandenburgers, at a cost of about half of the company.

Pressure against the main positions of the West Kents intensified. The Germans brought up more artillery and forced the withdrawal of a section of the 120th Battery guns from the towpath where they had been giving close support

LORD KITCHENER'S MESSAGE TO THE MEN OF THE BRITISH EXPEDITIONARY FORCE

[*This paper is to be considered by each soldier as confidential, and to be kept in his Active Service Pay Book.*]

You are ordered abroad as a soldier of the King to help our French comrades against the invasion of a common Enemy. You have to perform a task which will need your courage, your energy, your patience. Remember that the honour of the British Army depends on your individual conduct. It will be your duty not only to set an example of discipline and perfect steadiness under fire but also to maintain the most friendly relations with those whom you are helping in this struggle. The operations in which you are engaged will, for the most part, take place in a friendly country, and you can do your own country no better service than in showing yourself in France and Belgium in the true character of a British soldier.

Be invariably courteous, considerate and kind. Never do anything likely to injure or destroy property, and always look upon looting as a disgraceful act. You are sure to meet with a welcome and to be trusted; your conduct must justify that welcome and that trust. Your duty cannot be done unless your health is sound. So keep constantly on your guard against any excesses. In this new experience you may find temptations both in wine and women. You must entirely resist both temptations, and, while treating all women with perfect courtesy, you should avoid any intimacy

Do your duty bravely.
Fear God.
Honour the King.

KITCHENER,
Field-Marshal.

to the defenders. Fierce and accurate rifle and machine-gun fire was directed at the attackers by the West Kents, Yorkshire Light Infantry and Scottish Borderers, all of whom took full advantage of the excellent targets presented to them by the German infantry, and it stopped the advance several hundred yards short of the St Ghislain bridge. Unknown by the defenders at the time, they had given the Brandenburg Grenadiers such a drubbing that this regiment was withdrawn to the rear immediately after dark, having been shattered by the unexpected ferocity of the British defence which, according to German accounts, appeared to consist of massed machine-guns.

The railway bridge at Les Herbières (further left) also came under heavy enemy pressure, but here too massed infantry attacks were stopped short, with the East Surreys and the Suffolks mowing down the attackers at little cost to themselves and the German advance being brought to a complete standstill in that sector.

On the I Corps front things had been quiet until about 2 p.m. when German artillery opened up from a position near Binche, causing some casualties. German cavalry movements in that area were also noted. The main danger, though, still seemed to be further west, around the Nimy salient, where on the II Corps front the 4th Battalion of the Middlesex and 4th Battalion of the Royal Fusiliers were under severe pressure. At Obourg, the Middlesex were forced to fall back through the Bois d'Havre and attempts by the enemy to break through to Hill 93 were stopped by the accurate fire of the Royal Scots and Gordon Highlanders. The situation had worsened now that the Germans had forced the passage of the canal near Obourg, but the Middlesex and Royal Irish still continued to hold their own in spite of being under intense artillery fire. However, by 3.15 p.m. large numbers of German infantry were working around the Royal Irish, who then had to withdraw towards Bois-la-Haut, in the rear; and the Middlesex fell back too at about the same time.

The Grande Place at Mons; a photograph taken in 1984 on the 70th anniversary of The Battle of Mons. The Hôtel de Ville — the building with the British, French and Belgian flags hanging above its arched entrance — dates from the fifteenth and seventeenth centuries. At the rear is an interesting museum with a collection of exhibits of the 1914–18 period. Mons has been the scene of many battles throughout the centuries and was besieged six times between 1572 and 1792.

Below the modern Nimy Bridge, this was where the original swing bridge was situated in 1914. The bridge had been opened to create a major obstacle to the enemy but a German soldier named Niemeyer jumped into the canal and operated the bridge mechanism under British fire, thus closing the gap for his comrades. His bravery cost him his life, for he was shot dead by the British defenders, who early in the afternoon were given the order to retire as they were then in danger of being surrounded.

A group of First World War veterans at the 70th anniversary commemorative ceremony at Mons Town Hall, 23rd August 1984. Sadly, the ranks of these fine old soldiers become more and more depleted with the passage of time. On the right is ex-Captain Johnnie Morris (aged 87 in 1984), a Mons veteran who was wounded (temporarily blinded) on the Marne.

In accordance with orders, the Royal Fusiliers began retiring from Nimy at 2 p.m., and an hour later the Scots Fusiliers did likewise through Jemappes. Because the bridge there had not been destroyed, they were close-pressed by the Germans, which led to sharp fighting amongst the slag-heaps and houses near Frameries. At Mariette, attempts were made to blow the bridge and Captain T. Wright of the Royal Engineers received the Victoria Cross for his bravery. Two other VCs were won in defence of the railway bridge at Nimy by Lieutenant M. J. Dease and Private S. F. Godley. The bridges at Les Herbières and La Hamaide were blown by the Royal Engineers after the Scottish Borderers and East Surreys began their withdrawal. At St Ghislain, the West Kents still held their positions at dusk, thus foiling any attempt by the Germans to get over the canal at that point.

Left: A charming custodian at the Hôtel de Ville standing by a painting which depicts the famous legend of 'The Bowmen of Mons'. The story, which was first published in the 'Evening News' at the end of September 1914 and created much controversy, was based on British soldiers having claimed to witness angels or ghostly bowmen confronting the advancing German hordes. This apparition is alleged to have caused the enemy to break and run away, thus saving the British forces from annihilation. Years later it was divulged that the legend was a figment of the imagination of a well-known author and journalist, Arthur Machin, who was said to have concocted the story at a time of great trial in order to raise morale. Even as recently as a few years ago the controversy continued to be aired in the columns of national newspapers, in spite of Machin's admission that the tale was entirely without foundation.

Above left: The railway bridge at Nimy where Lieutenant Maurice Dease and Private S. F. Godley of the Royal Fusiliers won two of the first VCs of the war on 23rd August 1914. All this open ground was once swept by the machine-gun operated by these two men at the near end of the bridge. Lieutenant Dease was wounded several times before being taken away dying. He is buried in St Symphorien Military Cemetery. Private Godley took over the gun — all the other members of the gun-crew having been knocked out — and continued to fire into the advancing masses until, wounded and almost overwhelmed, he threw it into the canal before being taken prisoner. A total of four VCs were won on the first day of the battle. Since this picture was taken (in August 1974) the terrain has changed completely, the ground over which the Germans attacked in 1914 having been excavated and turned into a huge lagoon. The Mons–Condé Canal was converted from a waterway into a motorway in the late 1970s.

Above: Poppy wreaths and crosses beneath the railway bridge on the 70th anniversary of the Battle of Mons. Above the wreath is a memorial tablet commemorating the gallant action here.

Left: Photograph of Lieutenant Dease in Mons Museum.

The canal from Mons to Condé, at Jemappes (west of Mons), where it was bridged by the engineers of the 6th German Division under fire from the 1st Northumberland Fusiliers on 24th August 1914. [IWM]

The old iron girder bridge at St Ghislain before the canal was converted into a motorway. On the towpath here guns of the 120th Battery were located for a while during the Battle of Mons and two of them had to be abandoned to the enemy. Here too the 1st Battalion The Queens Own Royal West Kent Regiment (of which the author's father was a serving member) put up a stalwart defence against the Brandenburg Grenadiers, who were shattered by the rapid rifle-fire of the British troops, believing that they were actually faced with numerous machine-guns.

A remnant section of the old Mons–Condé Canal at Jemappes which has been bypassed by the motorway on its northern side.

Looking west along the former line of the canal, now covered in tarmac and concrete. Slow-moving barges have given way to fast-moving vehicles. The St Ghislain bridge has been replaced by a modern (but less attractive) structure. On the left, somewhere under there, was the towpath.

Gathering the hay bales west of Péronnes where a troop of the 16th Lancers came across a party of Germans, charged through them twice, and suffered only slight casualties. 'E' Battery unlimbered nearby.

The railway station at Obourg in August 1974 before the whole area was changed. One of the supports for a concrete bridge can be seen being built, and the station was shortly to be demolished. On 23rd August 1914 a resolute British soldier continued to fire at the advancing Germans from a flat roof of part of the station until he was killed, and the station was then captured. On the waiting room wall a plaque was put up which recorded the event.

In a field near Péronnes beside the Mons–Binche road this small tablet is set in the ground where 'E' Battery RFA fired the first British artillery shot of the war. The field is now part of the grounds of a large factory that was built close by.

The plaque at Obourg — now incorporated into a small brick structure on the modernised (open) station.

Above left: Part of the original canal at Obourg before the changes occurred, with the old lock gates in the centre. When this photograph was taken in August 1974 the ground on the left was being freshly excavated and this new stretch of the canal is now quite wide, as can be seen in the more recent picture. The motorway is just to the north.

Below left: Looking across the revised line of the Canal du Centre from the new bridge above Obourg station.

Below right: An explanatory plate on the modernised station.

The grave of Private J. Parr. Until 1987 the date of his death was recorded on the headstone as having occurred on 23rd August 1914 but further research confirmed that he was killed whilst on a cycling patrol two days before the Battle of Mons.

A circle of graves of forty-six men of the Middlesex Regiment. When the Germans laid out this cemetery after the Battle of Mons they mistakenly worded the obelisk in the centre to refer to the 'Royal' Middlesex Regiment.

The resting place of Lieutenant Dease, VC. To the right rear is the grave of Private J. Price, the last Canadian soldier to be killed in the war (see also pages 237–238).

Neat headstones in a German part of the cemetery. St Symphorien can rightly be claimed to be one of the most attractive of all the Great War military cemeteries on the Western Front.

By 5 p.m. the position on the right flank had worsened; the Royal Irish again had to retire, and parties of the Middlesex were overwhelmed by the attacking masses. Survivors marched towards Hyon and the Royal Irish then found that the Germans had got ahead of them, causing them to make a wide detour around the Bois-la-Haut. On the left flank the 13th Infantry Brigade began its retirement at nightfall — the West Kents still in position on the canal but with orders to fall back to south-east of Wasmes. Elsewhere on the left other units moved back, not without punishing the Germans with heavy fire as they endeavoured to cross the canal.

By midnight the canal positions had all been evacuated as the British troops fell back to a second position in the rear. The men remained in high spirits, having given a good account of themselves against superior numbers of a well-trained enemy. Overall casualties, with just over 1,600 killed, wounded and missing, had been comparatively light, the great majority of them incurred by II Corps. Only two guns had been lost (from the 120th Battery) and heavy casualties had been inflicted on the enemy.

Although the Battle of Mons was considered by the Germans to have been of minor importance, the stand of the BEF had delayed the enemy advance by a whole day and had interfered with his schedule. The fact that the Germans were still wary of what might be ahead of them was indicated by their reluctance to continue their advance after dark. Instead, all along the canal their bugles were heard to sound the 'cease-fire', after which all was quiet.

THE RETREAT FROM MONS

The night of 23rd/24th August passed with few signs of activity by the enemy and at dawn on the 24th the centre of the British line was located about three miles south of Mons. It was Sir John French's intention to withdraw to an east-west line through Bavai, about eight miles to the south, and I Corps began to do so at 4 a.m. Except for the extreme tiredness of the troops, little occurred in the I Corps sector to interfere with the retreat. On the II Corps front, though, it was a different story. A fierce German attack developed against the 9th Infantry Brigade at Frameries. Sharp fighting also occurred near Paturages, and at Wasmes heavy shelling by German artillery caused some losses to the 13th Infantry Brigade. At Elouges, too, a fierce little action occurred, and near Quievrain mounted troops charged advancing Germans but with only limited success. 'L' Battery, which was to become so famous at a later stage of the retreat, took a heavy toll of the German masses advancing from Quievrain, and heavy rifle and machine-gun fire by the Norfolks and Cheshires added to the carnage.

Photograph of a watercolour by R. Simkin depicting the Grenadier Guards (4th Guards Brigade, 2nd Division) in action at Mons, August 1914. The 2nd Division was on the left of I Corps and south-east of the town. [National Army Museum]

What had been intended as an enveloping movement by the Germans was completely foiled by the 5th Division, with the help of cavalry and the 19th Infantry Brigade. Then, as enemy pressure increased, the exhausted British troops continued to fall back as planned.

Total British losses on 24th August were greater than those on the 23rd and amounted to over 2,500, of which the great majority (some 1,650) occurred in the 5th Division. Nevertheless, the Germans had by no means had things all their own way and von Kluck's staff officer, von Kuhl, admitted later that 'the enemy put up a lively resistance so that we only advanced slowly'.

Meanwhile, the British Commander-in-Chief had anticipated von Kluck's intentions and ordered a continuance of the retreat on the 25th by a further fifteen miles, to a position in the vicinity of Le Cateau.

During the early stages of the Retreat from Mons, confusion reigned at these crossroads at Bavai as French troops, retreating on an east-west axis, crossed the line of march of the British forces.

Below: The unending road. The straight Roman road along which the footsore, thirsty and exhausted men of General Smith-Dorrien's II Corps staggered for mile upon mile during the retreat. To the left is the western edge of the Forest of Mormal, on the other side of which General Haig's I Corps endeavoured to keep abreast whilst heading for Landrecies. Apart from being constantly harried by the enemy at the rear, an additional worry for the corps commanders was the ever-present threat of German cavalry patrols getting ahead within the confines of the forest, and also possible ambushes from its dark depths.

Major-General Monro watching men of the 2nd Division passing during the retreat. [IWM]

Retreat from Mons. British cavalry retiring. [IWM]

MAROILLES

On the evening of 25th August 1914 the vital bridge over the River Sambre at Maroilles (above) was guarded by a troop of the 15th Hussars. The nearby village itself was full of men of I Corps. At about 6 a.m. Germans debouched from the Forest of Mormal (in the rear of the picture above) and engaged the Hussars with a field gun, forcing them to retire along a causeway leading to Maroilles. Shortly afterwards troops of the Royal Berkshire Regiment attacked the enemy, who had by then barricaded the bridge and had placed the field gun in a commanding position. The British attack failed, with the loss of sixty men. The Germans afterwards retired for a time and the British retreat once more got under way, with the village being evacuated.

LANDRECIES

At about 7.30 p.m. on 25th August, as dusk fell, this small town was the scene of a comparatively minor but not unimportant action by the 4th Guards Brigade when it was attacked by the advancing Germans.

A short while earlier the 3rd Battalion of the Coldstream Guards had established a piquet at the northern end of the town by the road junction close to the Forest of Mormal. They heard the sound of wheels and horses and, upon making a challenge, voices answered in French. Soon afterwards the outpost was attacked by French-speaking Germans who attempted to break through. Fierce fighting ensued, during which British reinforcements came up, and a number of casualties were suffered by both sides. Eventually the enemy was beaten back.

It was getting dark as the Germans advanced in strength from the northern approaches, and the I Corps commander, General Haig, believing the assault was being made by far superior numbers, sought help from II Corps. In the event it was not needed. There was a certain amount of turmoil as the town was hastily put into a state of defence. Then, in a fierce little battle in which artillery was used by both sides, the attackers were held; and when in the early hours of the 26th they pulled back, the British troops were able to withdraw from the town without undue hindrance. British casualties in the overall fighting came to about 100; the German figure was put at 127 though at first it was thought that they were much higher.

Across this road leading from the north a rope was stretched with a bell attached to it. The Germans, advancing in the darkness, caused the bell to be sounded, whereupon British troops opened up a brisk rifle fire, afflicting numerous casualties.

Above: The bridge over the River Sambre at Landrecies, which in 1914 was defended by the Guards.

Left: The road junction just north of Landrecies where fighting erupted at dusk on 25th August 1914. The Forest of Mormal is just beyond the car on the right.

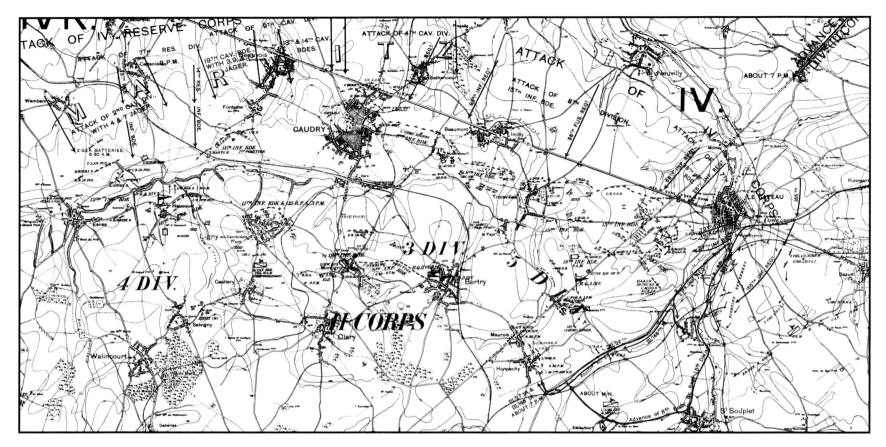

THE BATTLE OF LE CATEAU

26th August 1914

Because of misleading air reports which he received on the evening of the 24th and early morning of 25th August von Kluck fully believed that the British Army was retreating on the fortress town of Maubeuge. He was also convinced that such a move provided an excellent opportunity for his First Army to envelop and destroy the BEF, and then turn on the left flank of the French.

Shortly afterwards, however, he realised he had been mistaken, for a further air report informed him that the British were moving in almost the opposite direction. Fresh orders were immediately issued to his corps commanders, and these made the clashes that occurred at Maroilles and Landrecies (and also Solesmes) inevitable as his advance guards pushed south, with his III Corps marching southeastwards through the Forest of Mormal. While all this was happening the Belgian Army sought to assist the British and French troops fighting on the River Sambre by making a sortie out of Antwerp and striking at German communications. In this manoeuvre they were initially successful, but on 26th August they once more retired into Antwerp.

At 7.30 p.m. on the 25th Sir John French issued orders at St Quentin, where he had established his headquarters, for the retreat to be continued. Both corps commanders prepared to conform with these instructions, but in the early hours of 26th August, partly because of the exhaustion of the troops in general and partly because of the fact of General Allenby's cavalry being too scattered to be able to give immediate useful cover to the retreat, General Smith-Dorrien (who had taken command of II Corps only five days earlier) decided, with the agreement of his divisional commanders, that a stand should be made. Sir John French was informed of this decision and his somewhat ambiguous reply was later to lead to much acrimony between himself and Smith-Dorrien which subsequently led to the removal of the latter from his command. A plan to make a stand at Le Cateau had been mooted earlier, but for various reasons this had been ruled out by the Commander-in-Chief, one reason being the gap which existed between I and II Corps as a result of their passing on either side of the Forest of Mormal.

The 26th of August was the anniversary of the Battle of Crécy, fought in 1346; and as the day dawned, the military situation was somewhat similar to that famous day over 500 years earlier when the English force stood to repel an enemy whose numbers far exceeded its own.

The dispositions of the British troops were far from good. Most of the men were deployed in open ground, on a forward slope, along the line of the Le Cateau–Cambrai road and west of the town that gave the battle its name. To the north was high ground from which the Germans could flail the British troops with heavy fire, there being virtually no cover of any sort either for the men or the artillery. Indeed, several of the British batteries were practically in the actual infantry firing line; others were only a comparatively short distance to their rear.

The main street of Le Cateau, with the tower of the Hôtel de Ville on the left. On 25th August 1914 this area was full of exhausted British troops, some of whom were almost trapped on the morning of the 26th by the Germans advancing into the town at the northern end.

Part of the Le Cateau battlefield, looking north from near the crossroads to the west of the town covered by the 5th Division, and showing the ground over which the German 66th Infantry Regiment advanced towards the Cambrai road. The main dispositions of the British forces were just to the rear of where this photograph was taken.

The British section in Le Cateau Military Cemetery, looking south-west. The terrain beyond is the location of the British positions in August 1914.

The French section in the cemetery. Some Russians who served with the French are also buried here.

Because of the enemy pressure it had been possible to prepare only shallow entrenchments, and the inadequacy of these limited excavations became more and more apparent as the battle progressed. Also, much dead ground, small valleys and suchlike, permitted the enemy to approach without being observed. On the left flank advantage was taken of some trenches dug by local civilians just before the battle began.

The right of the line was held by troops of the 5th Division covering the crossroads to the west of the town where they were located on both sides of the Roman road leading to Reumont. On the 5th Division's left was the 3rd Division and then, on its left, came the newly-arrived 4th Division (not part of II Corps, but which placed itself under Smith-Dorrien's command for the battle). In reserve were the Cavalry Division and the 19th Infantry Brigade which had been placed under II Corps the previous night and had hardly got clear of the town before the first Germans arrived just after 6 a.m. (Two companies of the East Surreys and others of the Duke of Cornwall's Light Infantry were actually fired on before they got out of the town.) On the left of the Reumont road (facing north) were the 2nd King's Own Yorkshire Light Infantry with the guns of 122, 123 and 124 Batteries RFA close to them, and on the KOYLI's left the 2nd King's Own Scottish Borderers. Further south along the road, on the right, were the 1st East Surrey's, and to their left rear, in brigade reserve, were the 1st Queen's Own Royal West Kents. The guns of 52nd Battery, 37th (Howitzer) Battery, 80th Battery and 11th Battery were in position over on the right and in full view of the enemy on the high ground at Rambourlieux Farm, two miles to the north, north-west of Le Cateau. All of these batteries gave a very good account of themselves during the action in spite of their exposed positions.

The mist was still thick when the German guns first opened fire from the north-east of Le Cateau just after 6 a.m., while others joined in from Rambourlieux Farm soon afterwards. Shortly after 8 a.m. small-arms fire was directed at the British guns from the high ground north-west of Le Cateau and an attempt was made by the Germans to infiltrate on the right flank along the valley of the Selle under cover of the mist. In this they were foiled by enfilade fire from the DCLI and guns of 'D' Battery, and were forced to withdraw. Later it became obvious that it was on this flank that danger would arise, though it was at first thought that I Corps would be taking care of the area to the east. Unfortunately, this was incorrect, as the corps was in fact continuing its retreat.

At about 10 a.m. the German guns began enfilading the British guns and infantry positions with a storm of shells which caused considerable losses. The Suffolks, KOYLIs and the front line in general were literally pounded by high-explosives and shrapnel, and the Germans then began to advance en masse along a two-mile front from the valley of the Selle to Rambourlieux Farm, thus presenting an excellent target. Great execution followed, but at the same time many British troops fell to the unceasing artillery and small-arms fire. Only one of the 11th Battery's guns remained in operation. It, and those of the other batteries, continued to blaze away at the advancing masses. The 108th Battery, at the rear, added to the din and destruction, its sixty-pounder shells creating havoc amongst the German infantry. The 122nd Battery, which was well forward, wiped out a whole platoon of Germans as they broke cover and caused similar havoc each time the enemy endeavoured to advance from that direction.

The Suffolks came under devastating rifle and machine-gun fire and they were reinforced by some Argyll and Sutherland Highlanders and others from the 1st Middlesex, on their right rear. The last gun of the 11th Battery was finally silenced and the enemy steadily increased pressure all along the front in spite of suffering heavy casualties. Towards the left flank the Germans continued to be foiled by the splendid marksmanship of the British defenders, though some parties managed to work their way forward and got

The German section in Le Cateau Military Cemetery. The head-stones have replaced black crosses which were here until a few years ago. Near the entrance to the cemetery is a mass grave of German soldiers.

The central sector of the Le Cateau battlefield, looking north towards the high ground from which German guns pounded the British troops in their shallow trenches along the line of the Le Cateau–Cambrai road, which is just beyond the buildings on the right. The trees on the right mark the position of Le Cateau Military Cemetery. This photograph was taken from near the crossroads of the Le Cateau–Cambrai road and the Bavai–St Quentin road through Reumont.

across the Cambrai road, where they were engaged by machine-guns of the Royal Scots near Audencourt. Caudry was heavily shelled but until noon the enemy was held without too much trouble. On the extreme left, on the 4th Division's front, the King's Own (Royal Lancasters) were hit hard, first by machine-gun fire, then by a storm of shells from German batteries, but in spite of about 400 casualties they rallied and fought back with great determination. The Lancashire Fusiliers were enfiladed by the fire of numerous enemy machine-guns (there were twenty-one in that part of the battlefield alone) and suffered accordingly, and the Warwickshires also suffered badly from the intense shelling.

The story was similar all along the front: the Germans advancing first in mass formation, being repulsed, and then coming forward in open order before being cut down by the rapid fire of the British troops. For six hours the battle ebbed and flowed, but still the line held firm. However, just before 1 p.m. it became evident that the situation was becoming serious on the right wing. Soon afterwards gun teams of the 11th, 37th and 80th Batteries dashed forward and managed to bring out a number of guns and howitzers. Those of the 52nd Battery had to be abandoned. A while later the teams of the 122nd Battery galloped through the lines of the Royal West Kents, who stood up and cheered them loudly. Two of the guns were successfully recovered; a third team was shot down after limbering up. The guns of the 121st and 123rd Batteries also had to be left, making a total of twenty-five field guns and a howitzer falling into the hands of the enemy after having their breech blocks and sights removed.

At about 2 p.m. steps were taken for a general retirement. The Germans were increasing the pressure, particularly on the right, with intense machine-gun fire being directed along the whole ridge to the rear of the Suffolks and Dorsets. Elements of the 2nd Manchesters and the Argyll and Sutherland Highlanders were moved forward to help the Suffolks but themselves came under heavy fire and suffered severe losses.

Another gallant episode occurred early in the afternoon. Captain Reynolds of the 37th Battery, together with a handful of volunteers, dashed forward to rescue two howitzers that had been left in the open. One of the teams was shot down, but the other gun was safely retrieved. The Germans were only two hundred yards away. For this outstanding act of bravery Captain Reynolds and Drivers Luke and Drain received the Victoria Cross.

At 2.30 p.m. the end was near. The Germans had all but surrounded the Suffolks, who still continued to fight back fiercely in company with the Argylls, two of the Highland officers counting aloud as they claimed their victims. More enemy rushes tightened the noose and subsequently the Suffolks and the Argylls went down after nine hours of incessant bombardment.

The Yorkshiremen's turn came next. They had not actually received the order to retire and were attacked from the right rear and from the Cambrai road, although they at first drove back the Germans with rapid rifle and machine-gun fire, they were overwhelmed in a final rush. By their fine stand they helped to give the rest of the 5th Division a good start to their retirement. The West Kents fell back slowly and methodically, as did the Scottish Borderers, a number of whom were captured through not having received the order to retire. In the right centre, on the 3rd Division's part of the line, the Bedfords and the Dorsets also fell back slowly. Those of the 3rd Division's units that did not receive the order to retire included most of the 1st Gordon Highlanders, who held the ground north of Audencourt against continuous fierce attacks, some of the 2nd Royal Scots and two companies of the 2nd Royal Irish.

As the retirement proceeded, in some parts of the line there was some confusion and disorder, but no panic. By about 5 p.m. the bulk of II Corps had begun its retreat southwards and General Smith-Dorrien had moved his headquarters to St Quentin. The 4th Division now began to move off, its departure being helped by the appearance at about 4.30 p.m. of the French cavalry, which held the line to its left rear, and by the intervention of the cavalry's artillery firing into the Germans' flank, which provided a welcome diversion. North and east of Harcourt, some three to four

Above: Le Cateau battlefield. This photograph was taken west of the Roman road which leads to Reumont and by the location of the 1st Queens' Own Royal West Kent Regiment (in brigade reserve). It was here that the author's father, who served in that unit, was severely wounded. Here too the men of that battalion rose to their feet from shallow trenches and cheered as teams of horses galloped through their lines under heavy fire in an effort to save some of the guns.

hundred men of the Royal Warwickshires, two companies of the Royal Dublin Fusiliers and two of the King's Own fought on, unaware of the order to retire.

As darkness came down, with a drizzling rain falling, the enemy's pursuit slackened and died away. While the isolated detachments continued to hold out, the rearguards covering the retreat southwards fell back and the troops continued on their way, for the most part unharried other than by long-range artillery fire which caused a few casualties. The enemy had been struck a hard blow in spite of his numerical superiority. The II Corps had been neither overwhelmed nor enveloped, and although losses had been quite heavy, the battle had given the Allies a well-deserved breathing space.

British losses at Le Cateau amounted to 7,812 men and 38 guns. This included about 2,600 men who became prisoners of war. (One German account suggested that 12,000 prisoners had been taken.) A number of these prisoners were wounded who could not be evacuated owing to a lack of field ambulances in the 4th Division. The Germans too suffered heavy losses; but for reasons best known to themselves they tended to play down a battle which their Supreme Command described in an official bulletin as the 'Defeat of the English at St Quentin'.

Above: The right sector of the Le Cateau battlefield, with the town itself in the centre-distance. On the extreme right is a small monument to the Manchesters and other units engaged in the fighting. It was over this ground that the Germans carried out their successful outflanking movement which resulted in the near annihilation of the 2nd King's Own Yorkshire Light Infantry.

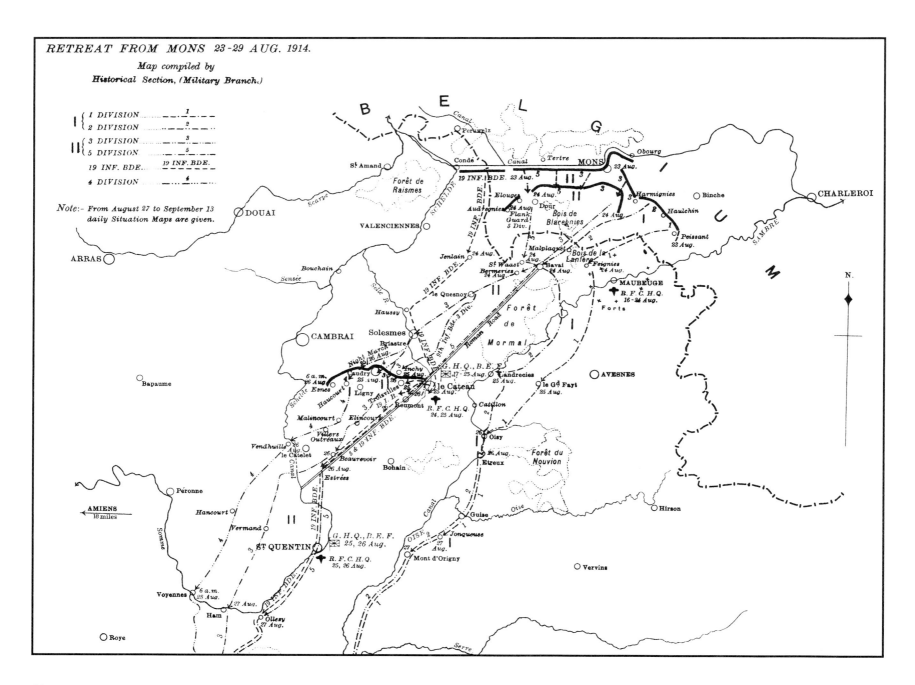

RETREAT FROM MONS 23-29 AUG. 1914.

Map compiled by
Historical Section, (Military Branch.)

1 DIVISION 1
2 DIVISION 2
3 DIVISION 3
5 DIVISION 5
19 INF. BDE. .... 19 INF. BDE.
4 DIVISION 4

Note:- From August 27 to September 13
daily Situation Maps are given.

N.

THE RETREAT CONTINUES

All told, some two thousand men had been left behind on the left flank, about half of whom made good their escape. An attack made shortly after nightfall was beaten off. The existence of these detachments of the 4th Division made the Germans jumpy, and for several hours this caused them to be wary of advancing, not knowing what might lie ahead of them in the darkness. On the 3rd Division's sector, too, the Germans showed caution, bringing down two heavy bombardments on Audencourt at 6.45 p.m. and 8.30 p.m.

At 11.00 p.m. the Warwickshires and Dublin Fusiliers set off southwards together, but became separated. The Warwickshires got back safely, and so did the King's Own, who started out at about the same time. The Dublin Fusiliers, however, ran into Germans and lost a number of men in sharp engagements. Only seventy-eight managed to get through the German lines, the remainder being killed or captured.

It was past midnight before the isolated groups of the 3rd Division marched off through Audencourt under the command of Brevet-Colonel William Gordon, VC. At a village called Montigny they ran into parties of Germans, and following a sharp exchange of fire it became obvious that they were completely surrounded. After further fighting they were overwhelmed and most were taken prisoner.

Meanwhile the main body of retreating troops pressed on through the dark night. Some confusion was inevitable on roads choked with transport. Half-dead with fatigue, the men and horses longed for rest, and in spite of the drizzling rain and the cold many of the dog-tired soldiers fell asleep on their feet at halts or, in the case of the cavalry, in their saddles. Eventually, as daylight broke on the 27th, the weary columns staggered into St Quentin. Rations were distributed and a short rest was allowed. Trains and carts had been laid on for those who were beyond marching any further.

The 5th Division marched into town as properly-formed bodies, some of them not arriving until the sun was well up, and after being fed and rested for an hour or so they went on their way. The food and the opportunity to relax for a while worked wonders, and whereas arrival in the town was mostly in silence, the march was resumed in a much more cheerful manner, with whistling and singing in the ranks. Before night fell on the 27th, the 5th Division had reached a position south of the Somme, having fortunately received no interference from the enemy.

1st Cameronians at a farm during the Retreat from Mons, with a cheerful looking group of officers in the foreground. The one using the binoculars is presumably looking at an aircraft flying overhead. Their apparent unconcern suggests that it is of British origin and not a German Taube. [IWM]

INCIDENT AT ST QUENTIN

Regrettably, there was one very disturbing incident at St Quentin, which marred what was an otherwise well-disciplined assemblage, when a mob of stragglers and disorganised soldiers from the 4th Division collected at the station demanding transport by train. The last train had already left some time earlier. The men were in a very truculent mood and several hundred more were sprawled around the Grande Place, obviously set on going no further. The Mayor of the town had apparently persuaded two British colonels to sign a surrender paper, so that it could be sent out to the approaching Germans and spare the town from bombardment. It meant, though, that many British soldiers would have been taken prisoner.

On the evening of the 27th there came upon the scene Major Tom Bridges, of the 4th Dragoon Guards, together with a small band of mounted Dragoons who had been acting as a cavalry rearguard. After summing up the situation he harangued the men at the station, at first to little avail. He then gave them an ultimatum and told them that no British soldier would be left alive in St Quentin; carts, he said, would be provided for anyone who could not walk. His tough stance and the promise of assistance had the desired effect. The men, who were in a sorry state, rallied round.

At the Grande Place, though, things were more difficult; little notice was taken of the major's exhortations. He then had a brainwave. In a nearby shop he obtained a toy drum and a 'penny whistle', and with these he and his trumpeter marched around the square playing 'The British Grenadiers' and 'Tipperary'. At that, men to all intents and purposes dead to the world sat up, laughed and cheered, and slowly fell in behind. Just after midnight, the major marched them out of the town and into the night before the Germans arrived. Thus a very delicate situation had been retrieved by the action of a gallant soldier who was eventually to become Lieutenant-General Sir Tom Bridges, KCB, KCMG, DSO. The good humour of the British Tommy also helped in what could have been a very nasty episode.

Both colonels involved in this incident were court-martialled and cashiered. One of them (Colonel Elkington) joined the Foreign Legion and regained a commission. He was badly wounded and received the Legion of Honour. He was reinstated into the British Army by His Majesty King George V, and was awarded the DSO. The other colonel disappeared into oblivion.

The main street of St Quentin, leading to the station at the bottom of the hill — and to where during the retreat a knot of troops were of a mind not to march another step of the way.

The Grande Place of St Quentin, with the Hôtel de Ville in the centre. This was the scene of the incredible exploits of Major Tom Bridges in getting recalcitrant men to fall in and rejoin the retreat.

BEYOND ST QUENTIN

Having left St Quentin well behind, the II Corps continued southwards — the heat and constant marching inevitably taking its toll on the weary troops.

On the I Corps front, meanwhile, a sharp rearguard action took place on August 27th at Etreux, where two companies of the Royal Munster Fusiliers (1st Guards Brigade of 1st Division) were trapped by enemy troops who had managed to get ahead of them. For nearly twelve hours this small band fought against overwhelming odds before finally being engulfed at around 9.15 p.m. By their sacrifice they held up the enemy in that sector by about six hours.

On 29th August the exhausted troops of I Corps enjoyed a limited rest, generally undisturbed by the enemy. The somewhat extensive gap between I and II Corps had by then been reduced to seven miles, thus bringing the columns of the BEF into closer proximity.

On 30th August, which was an intensely hot day, I Corps continued on its southward movement. II Corps, equally exhausted, also marched on, but in a south-easterly direction, which again reduced the gap between the two wings of the BEF. Apart from a limited cavalry rearguard action, little interference was caused to the troops by the enemy that day, von Kluck being convinced that the British Army was thoroughly beaten.

On 31st August, and in extremely trying conditions — the more so because of a lack of drinking water for both men and horses — I Corps crossed the Aisne near Soissons. The enemy kept his distance, though, enough for men of the 6th Infantry Brigade to manage to get a bathe in the Aisne — a welcome relief from the heat and dust.

The I Corps halted for the night on the northern side of Villers-Cotterêts; the II Corps south-west of the town and at Crépy-en-Valois. The newly constituted III Corps (formed on 30th August from the 4th Division and the 19th Infantry Brigade and commanded by General Poultney) marched through the Forest of Compiègne and reached its allotted area at Verberie, at the south-western corner of the forest. With it was the 4th Cavalry Brigade. The 1st Cavalry Brigade and 'L' Battery RHA, after keeping watch for enemy troops, moved to Verberie, thence on to Néry, a small village set in pleasant wooded countryside, where they arrived as dusk was falling. The 5th Dragoon Guards were located at the northern end of the village and the 11th Hussars were in farms and other buildings on the eastern side. The 2nd Dragoon Guards were in houses on the western side (with 'C' Squadron in a field), and 'L' Battery's guns were at the southern end close to a sunken road along which was a sugar factory where battery headquarters was installed. Reveille was to be at 2.30 a.m., with departure 4.30 a.m.

That day (31st August) aerial reconnaissance by the RFC had confirmed that von Kluck's First Army was no longer moving to outflank Paris from the west and was instead wheeling south-eastwards. This change of direction was later a cause of some acrimony between von Kluck and von Bulow, with each blaming the other for its consequences. It was, however, sanctioned (albeit reluctantly) by the German Supreme Command, based on von Kluck's belief that everything was going extremely well, with the British in full retreat and the French also in a bad way after a clash at Guise where they had fought a fierce rearguard action. A satisfactory result of a brush with outposts of the French Sixth Army led him to believe (mistakenly) that there was no real danger from that direction. To von Kluck the overall situation indicated an early and satisfactory end to the war.

The scent of victory was also in the nostrils of General Otto von Garnier, commander of the German 4th Cavalry Division, who in spite of the exhausted condition of his troops and horses, pressed on during the dark and rainy night in the belief that by doing so it would lead to the outflanking of the French. Directly in his path, though, were British troops who had spent the night unaware of the danger which was close at hand.

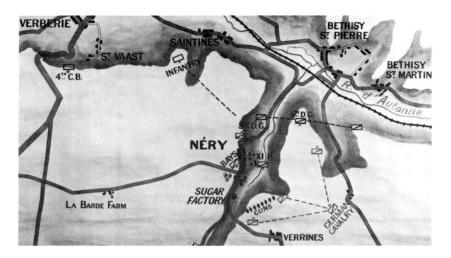

Left: Photograph of a sketch map of Néry, 1st September 1914. 'L' Battery is located at the lower end of the village opposite the Bays. [IWM]

Left: Photograph of a sketch map of Néry, 1st September 1914. 'L' Battery is located at the lower end of the village opposite the Bays. [IWM]

'L' Battery in happier days. Officers and men of this famous battery in 1913. Some of those seen in this photograph doubtless perished in the hurricane of fire from German guns during the 'Néry affair'. [Photo: John Tanner]

THE NERY AFFAIR

Dawn broke at Néry with a thick mist indicating that 1st September would be another very hot day. The troops in Néry had already begun preparations for the planned move but, because of the misty conditions, orders were given to stand fast until 5 a.m. It was thought that the Germans were still some distance away, so there appeared to be no need for undue haste. Breakfast was consumed and the horses were taken to the sugar factory for watering.

Two cavalry patrols were sent out before dawn and upon return reported having made no contact with the enemy. At 4.15 a.m. another patrol, from the 11th Hussars, set out. They had gone about a mile from the village when they ran into German Dragoons, who chased them some way before giving up the pursuit. The startling news of enemy cavalry in the vicinity was passed on to the Brigadier (Brigadier-General Briggs) and men were posted in firing positions along the east side of the village overlooking a steep ravine and rising ground beyond it. A short while earlier some horsemen seen on that ridge had been thought to be French cavalry who were believed to be in that area.

The northern end of Néry: the now-quiet village main street along which terrified horses of the 5th Dragoons galloped and were shot down in heaps by the German gunfire.

Suddenly, just after 5.30 a.m., with the mist still thick, the peace was shattered by a roar of guns and the rattle of machine-guns and rifles. High-explosive shells burst over the village and amongst the horses and guns of 'L' Battery. Horses of the Queen's Bays bolted northwards along the main street of the village, many of them being hit by the intense fire. 'L' Battery's commander, Major Sclater-Booth, was knocked out and blinded by a shell-burst as he was approaching brigade headquarters.

What had happened was that von Garnier had learned about a British cavalry brigade being at Néry and had immediately planned to attack. Under cover of the mist two batteries, each of four 77mm guns, were deployed on the heights east of Néry, together with machine-guns and cavalry. More cavalry and a third artillery battery were assigned to the south-east of the village, with other cavalry units being kept in reserve. When all the groups were in position, the artillery pieces opened up and almost immediately were joined by the machine-guns in pouring a concentrated fire on the village, and particularly on 'L' Battery. The sudden and totally unexpected bombardment had a disastrous effect on the horses, which were mostly tethered in the open. Like those of the Bays, many of the 'L' Battery teams were killed or maimed, although those of 'F' Subsection escaped through still being at the sugar factory.

Before he was hit, Major Sclater-Booth saw three of his guns coming into action as the British troops were rapidly galvanised into activity. Firing positions were hurriedly prepared along the eastern side of the village, horses were placed under cover and machine-guns were set up in the sunken road leading to the sugar factory. Because of the all-pervading mist, the machine-gunners aimed at the flashes of the German guns. The right flank was secured by men holding the sugar factory, and the left flank at the north-east end of the village by 'C' Squadron of the 5th Dragoon Guards with machine-guns. In the centre the 11th Hussars set up its machine-guns overlooking the ravine east of the church.

View of Néry from German gun positions. [IWM]

The location of 'L' Battery's famous 'fight to the death' action at the southern end of the village. The chimney belongs to the sugar factory. The hedge on the right marks the line of the sunken road leading to the factory.

Although taken by surprise by the ferocity of the German attack, the British troops quickly placed the village in a state of defence and Brigadier-General Briggs even arranged for the 5th Dragoon Guards to be ready for a counter-attack. Indeed, two squadrons that moved off for the counter-attack were instrumental in beating back an attack by dismounted Uhlans and other Germans who were endeavouring to get into the village from the north. In the fierce fighting that followed, the enemy suffered heavy casualties and gave up the attempt. In the south, too, an attack towards the sugar factory by German Dragoons was foiled by the Bays, who inflicted serious losses. More attacks in that sector were repulsed, although the Germans did occupy some of the factory outbuildings but were stopped from getting any further. In the centre, the steep sides of the ravine, combined with accurate British fire, prevented any incursions from that direction.

While all this was going on, 'L' Battery's situation had become desperate, with men and horses suffering very heavy casualties. Three of the guns had been brought into action by Captain Bradbury and what men were available, but almost immediately one gun had been put out of action by a direct hit. Another was quickly silenced, its detachment wiped out. Two remaining subalterns then joined Captain Bradbury on the third gun, which defiantly continued firing against twelve German guns. These poured concentrated fire on the one remaining British gun but failed to silence it. Captain Bradbury seemed to bear a charmed life amongst the storm of explosives. The two subalterns were struck down and he was then joined by Sergeant Nelson, who had already been wounded, and Battery Sergeant-Major Dorrell. Ammunition was almost expended and Captain Bradbury left the gun in the care of the NCOs to procure more shells. As he moved away an explosion blew off both his legs. In spite of these terrible wounds, and in great pain, he still endeavoured to act as observer to the gun. Ammunition finally ran out and at about 8 a.m. the last round was fired. 'L'

Battery at last fell silent, though the Germans still poured fire in its direction. Captain Bradbury was taken away to a First Aid post, but he was beyond help and died without knowing that his bravery was to be recognised by the posthumous award of a Victoria Cross.

Fresh attacks were mounted by the Germans but still the British defences held firm. The sun broke through at last and for the first time the defenders could clearly see the German gunners who had wrought such havoc in their midst. The opportunity was seized and heavy fire was directed at the gunners, causing some of the German artillerymen to abandon their guns to escape the hail of bullets.

Meanwhile, British reinforcements had come up, including 'I' Battery of 4th Cavalry Brigade, which opened fire from

The famous 'Néry' Gun — the 13-pounder of 'L' Battery. This gun is now on display at the Imperial War Museum's VC, GC exhibition, together with the three VCs awarded for this famous action. [IWM]

about two thousand yards away to the south-west — almost at the same time that 'L' Battery fell silent. The German artillerymen then attempted to remove their guns but were pounded by the heavy fire from 'I' Battery and the British machine-guns. Only four of the Germans' twelve guns were got away and even those were captured the next day. Men of the 1st Middlesex, followed by a squadron of the 11th Hussars, charged the enemy batteries only to find that there were no live Germans left on the scene. The Hussars then pressed on and captured seventy-eight prisoners.

Memorial at Néry erected to commemorate the 70th anniversary of 'L' Battery's famous action.

By 8.45 a.m. the battle was over. The village surrounds looked like a slaughterhouse. Amidst all the carnage, however, one of 'L' Battery's horses was seen to be standing, calmly eating his fodder in spite of having received eight wounds!

The Victoria Cross was also awarded to BSM Dorrell and Sergeant Nelson, both of whom were later commissioned. The Legion of Honour was bestowed by the French on Lieutenant Gifford, who had also fought his gun to the last before it received a direct hit and he had been wounded three times. (He was wounded yet again as he dragged himself to the shelter of a haystack.) The Médaille Militaire was awarded to Gunner Derbyshire and Driver Osborne, both of whom had done valiant work in feeding ammunition to the one remaining gun.

Casualties sustained by the 1st Cavalry Brigade at Néry came to about 135 officers and men (including Colonel Ansell of the 5th Dragoon Guards). Of this number, 5 officers and 49 men belonged to 'L' Battery. The Germans suffered at least as many casualties — and possibly more. Three of the German guns were brought home and exhibited on Horse Guards Parade. Over 300 horses were buried by the Néry villagers after the action.

There were two other rearguard actions on 1st September: at Crépy-en-Valois and Villers-Cotterêts. At Crépy, a few miles east of Néry, an outpost line of the 5th Division was attacked at 6 a.m. by mounted troops and German Jäger. The main weight of the attack fell on the 1st West Kents. The guns of 119th Battery were close to the firing line and these quickly came into action in support of the West Kents by firing 150 rounds in five minutes. The attack was stopped in its tracks and by midday the British troops had withdrawn to the south of Crépy without further harrassment, though German cavalry patrols had been sighted from time to time.

Further east, I Corps started off at 4 a.m. and marched through the forest of Villers-Cotterêts by two roads. Some miles north-north-west of Villers-Cotterêts the 3rd Cavalry

Brigade was attacked by numerous Germans and sharp fighting occurred in the woodlands. To the east, the 4th Guards Brigade came under attack; the Irish Guards were assaulted at about 10.45 a.m., and the 2nd Grenadiers and 3rd Coldstreams also became involved in fierce fighting. Other British units were drawn into the action, which did not end until 6 p.m. Two platoons of the Grenadiers were surrounded but fought until there were no survivors. The Germans also suffered heavy casualties and even fired at each other in the general confusion.

Above: Entrance to the village of Villers-Cotterêts, which is approximately sixty miles from Mons as the crow flies. The nearby forest was the scene of a fierce rearguard action by the 4th Guards Brigade during which they lost over 300 officers and men. The 6th Infantry Brigade also lost 160 men here.

Above right: A colossal monument north-east of Meaux which was erected by the Americans to commemorate the First Battle of the Marne.

Below right: Distant view of Meaux, on the River Marne, from the base of the monument. The town was on the line of the retreat and was reached by British troops on September 3rd, with the bridges being blown to hinder the advancing Germans. Beyond is terrain over which the British subsequently retraced their steps after the retreat ended. The right of the French Sixth Army rested on this flank during the severe fighting which led to the Battle of the Marne.

THE TIDE TURNS

Further clashes occurred as the British forces continued the retreat, and some anxiety arose as a consequence of the Commander-in-Chief's apparent aim to get as far away as possible from the Germans regardless of the need for co-operation with the French. This led to Lord Kitchener making a special journey across the Channel to meet Sir John French at the British Embassy in Paris on 1st September, where he emphasised the importance of the two armies working in conjunction with each other's movements. Faced with what amounted to a firm instruction, Sir John French cabled the Secretary of State for War on 3rd September confirming 'his full accord with Joffre and the French'.

By now the formerly separated I and II Corps had at last come together and, fearful of the nearby enemy mounting a night attack in strength, Sir John French ordered his corps commanders to get clear by a night march.

On 2nd September the last stages of the retreat began. The heat was intense throughout the day and this necessitated long halts. Fortunately the enemy failed to follow too closely, and although there were some exchanges of artillery and rifle fire the River Marne was reached on 3rd September and crossed, with bridges being blown to impede the enemy advance. The British Commander-in-Chief had actually suggested to the French that a stand be made on the Marne, but this was rejected by Joffre, who was not ready to change his plans and was even prepared to retreat behind the Seine if necessary.

On 4th September the British forces crossed the Petit Morin River and then the Grand Morin. That day, Général Gallieni visited the British headquarters at Melun and suggested that the British Army should cease its retreat and go over to the offensive in conjunction with the combined forces of the French Sixth Army and the Paris garrison which he had ordered to move eastwards. Sir John French, however, believing that he would be conforming to Joffre's plans, decided to retire further south, and on 5th September the march was continued for several more miles. This was the day when Général Maunoury's Sixth Army came into contact with the right flank of von Kluck's forces, and the time for a decisive change of strategy had arrived. By then the BEF had retreated for thirteen days and, with the enemy constantly snapping at their heels, had marched a distance of at least 200 miles by road from Mons (136 miles as the crow flies). Men and horses had undergone a severe ordeal, constantly short of food and sleep; yet the troops had remained an army, its morale intact. Losses had amounted to about 15,000 killed, wounded and missing; and, apart from general war material, forty-two guns had been lost.

Now the retreat was over. A new phase was about to begin.

Statue of Général (later Maréchal) Gallieni on the road to Paris and overlooking ground where his famous 'taxi-cab army' reinforced the French 6th Army at a time of crisis. Gallieni commandeered all the taxi-cabs in Paris and rushed 11,000 men to the battlefield in these vehicles.

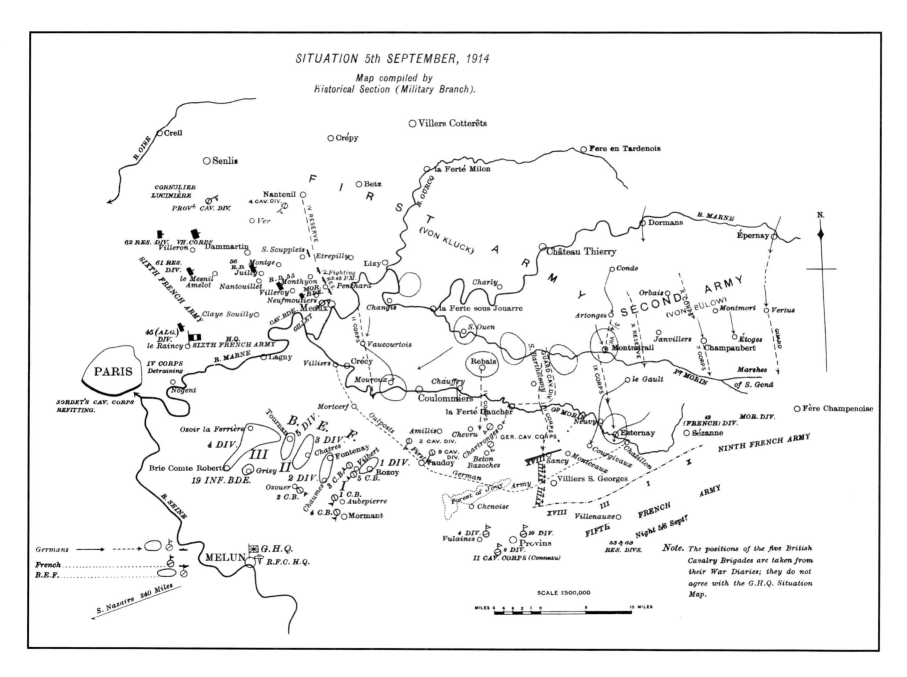

SITUATION 5th SEPTEMBER, 1914

Map compiled by
Historical Section (Military Branch).

Note. The positions of the five British Cavalry Brigades are taken from their War Diaries; they do not agree with the G.H.Q. Situation Map.

SCALE 1:500,000

MILES 5 4 3 2 1 0   5   10 MILES

THE BATTLE OF THE MARNE

By 4th September the German High Command had realised that they had failed to obtain an outright victory and that a threat to the right flank of the German Army had developed. This was to be countered by the First and Second German Armies facing the eastern front of Paris and repulsing any offensive from that direction. Meanwhile, the Third, Fourth and Fifth German Armies were to continue to advance. Further progress towards the Seine was envisaged, with the investment of Paris to follow.

At 3 a.m. on 5th September Général Joffre's intention to go over to the offensive was notified to British GHQ. Later that day Joffre and Général Maunoury visited Sir John French and plans were made to attack all along the line next day.

On 6th September the BEF moved forward and made contact with the enemy. Some fighting occurred and at 11 p.m. the bulk of II and III Corps had advanced to about a mile beyond the Grand Morin. On 7th September aerial reconnaissance confirmed that the enemy was withdrawing northwards and the advance continued behind a cavalry screen, with some prisoners being taken. The French Fifth and Sixth Armies had made satisfactory progress. At 5.20 p.m. Général Joffre gave orders based on the possible envelopment of the German right wing.

On 8th September the advance was resumed. The cavalry moved off at 4 a.m., ahead of the British troops and aiming for the Petit Morin. Heavy artillery fire and enemy counter-attacks brought the cavalry to a temporary halt, but aerial reconnaissance reported large numbers of Germans moving northwards across the Marne bridge at La Ferté-sous-Jouarre. It was found later that the north bank of the Marne at this point was being held in strength by the enemy with artillery and numerous machine-guns. The Petit Morin was crossed, though not without resistance from German

guns, and by dusk the infantry of II Corps had reached a point less than a mile from the Marne. By nightfall that part of La Ferté-sous-Jouarre which lay on the south bank of the Marne was in British hands. The bridges had been blown by the retreating enemy.

By 7.30 a.m. on 9th September troops of the 1st Division of I Corps were over the Marne. Less than an hour later the 2nd Division was also on the north bank. In the II Corps sector two bridges were found intact which enabled the 3rd and 5th Divisions to cross without difficulty. Afterwards, however, the latter ran into trouble from German guns which required an infantry attack to be put in to silence them. III Corps also ran into determined enemy opposition which held them up.

Without doubt it was the advance of the BEF which caused the Germans to give up so much ground; although had it been possible for the hold-ups to have been overcome more quickly, even better results would have been achieved on the 9th.

Not only had a large gap been created between the German First and Second Armies, but von Kluck's left wing had now become very vulnerable to attack by the British.

Small bridge over the Petit Morin River across which British troops moved forward after the retreat ended and prior to the Battle of the Marne. The Germans were driven from the high ground beyond, from which they had directed artillery and machine-gun fire at the advancing British forces.

Battle of the Marne: La Ferté-sous-Jouarre burning, right. [IWM]

Memorial to Royal Engineers of the 4th Division on the south bank of the River Marne. The bridge seen here has since been demolished and replaced by a modern construction. A similar memorial is on the opposite bank, the pair marking the location of the pontoon bridge that was put in place here at La Ferté.

1st Cameronians crossing the Marne over a pontoon bridge, La Ferté-sous-Jouarre (the original bridge having been blown by the Germans). [IWM]

The historic River Marne at La Ferté-sous-Jouarre in the mid-1980s. A scene of tranquility where once the calm water was lashed by bursting shells.

Général Maunoury's Sixth Army had failed to gain much ground on the Ourcq, and had even been pushed back in the centre following enemy reinforcement in that sector by troops withdrawn by von Kluck from the south. It became evident, therefore, that a faster advance by the British troops would not only give assistance to the French but would also make things extremely difficult for the Germans. It has to be said, though, that the terrain (especially in the valley of the Petit Morin) was ideal for the sort of rearguard actions undertaken by the Germans, who made very good use of the hilly and wooded ground in the siting of their artillery and machine-guns.

Despite 9th September having been in some respects disappointing for the British, RFC reports confirmed that long columns of German troops were moving north-eastwards. With similar enemy movements apparent all along the wide front as far as Verdun, it was clear that what was to become known as the Battle of the Marne had been one of the decisive battles of the war. With it died the hopes of the Germans for the outright victory they had expected. The need for von Kluck's First Army to change the direction of its front in order to counter the flank attack by Maunoury's Sixth Army (and including troops rushed to the front in taxis commandeered by Général Gallieni), the opening up of a gap of some fifteen to twenty miles between the German First and Second Armies, and the imposition of the BEF into that gap (albeit slower than was required by the French), forced the Germans to change their tactics. A failure to retreat would have caused a disaster; they were left with no alternative other than to abandon the battlefield. Von Kluck had believed that the BEF was too weak to be in a position to cause any real damage (he was sure that it could be held on the Marne without difficulty) and had been proved wrong. Von Bulow, too, was convinced that a retirement of his Second Army and von Kluck's First Army was absolutely necessary, and in this he was supported by an emissary from the Supreme Command (Lieutenant-Colonel Hentsch)

who had been sent, with full powers, to co-ordinate the retreat if such a move was found to be necessary. Von Kluck did not readily accept the need for a withdrawal, but, as he was then placed under von Bulow's command (as he had been for the wheeling movement through Belgium), he had little option in the matter. Ironically, on 7th September the High Command had made arrangements for the Kaiser to visit his victorious armies on the 8th, and that plan also had to be abandoned.

On 10th September, in unfavourable weather, in accordance with instructions issued by Sir John French the evening before, the BEF began its pursuit of the partly demoralised — but by no means broken — German forces. It was a pursuit that was to end on the heights overlooking the River Aisne a few days later.

La Ferté-sous-Jouarre. The British Memorial to the Missing who fell in the battles of Mons, Le Cateau, the Marne and the Aisne in 1914. The names of 3,888 men are inscribed on the memorial, which was unveiled in 1928.

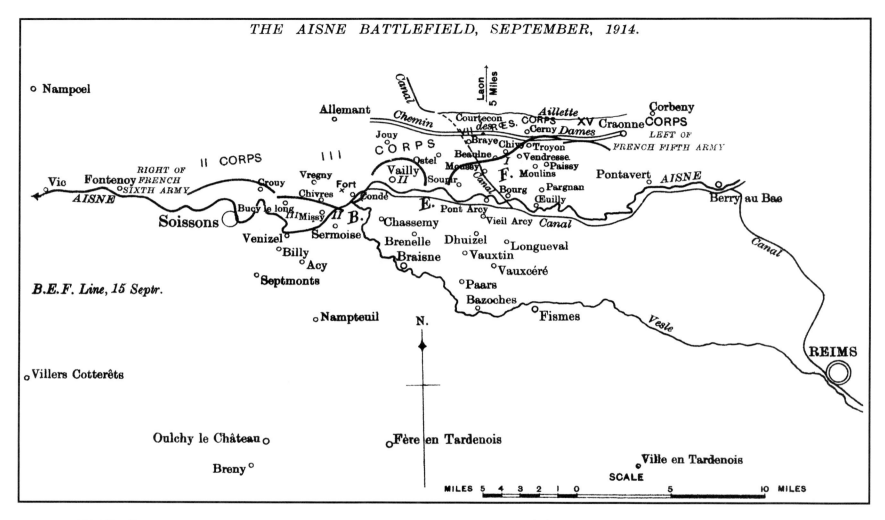

THE BATTLE OF THE AISNE

As the BEF closed up to the Aisne on 11th and 12th September, heavy rain and low clouds made aerial reconnaissance very difficult. The rain also turned the roads into seas of mud, which made things very unpleasant for the troops and horses. The River Vesle was crossed, with Braisne being captured by the 1st Cavalry Brigade, and north-east of Chassemy the 4th Hussars, with two guns, were sent forward with the objective of seizing the bridge at Vailly. It was, however, seen to have been blown up by the Germans and another — undamaged — bridge at Condé was found to be held by a strong enemy force. I and II Corps were still two miles from the Aisne as darkness fell and they halted for the night, but III Corps, on the left, had got well forward and had ascertained that the bridge at Venizel, although damaged, was still usable by infantry and cavalry. As the British approached, the Germans endeavoured to destroy the bridge, but only one of the four charges exploded. After dark, almost under the noses of the Germans on the north bank, the remaining charges were removed by a British officer of the Inniskilling Fusiliers.

The fifteen- to twenty-mile gap that existed between the German First and Second Armies (with only cavalry in between) greatly worried von Bulow, who realised the danger of the German line being pierced at that point. The immediate situation called for a continuance of the withdrawal if that gap could not be filled, but as the retreat from the Marne had already caused some demoralisation among the exhausted German troops, the effect of a further retirement could only be very damaging and might even lead to a major disaster. Fortunately for the Germans (and unfortunately for the Allies) their VII Reserve Corps had been released from its investment of Maubeuge owing to the recent capitulation of that fortress and on 13th September, by a series of forced marches, it arrived on the Aisne front just a couple of hours before the British I Corps was in a position to exploit what could have been an excellent opportunity for a breakthrough on the Chemin des Dames. Next day the left of the French Fifth Army, which was also advancing on the right of the British, was similarly held by the newly-inserted German XV Corps. Thus the immediate danger to the enemy passed and a German stand on the Aisne became a certainty. That this would usher in four years of trench warfare was something that neither side could know when on the 12th Sir John French issued orders which set the three British corps objectives five miles beyond the river: five miles that would prove unattainable.

At 11 p.m. on the 12th, on the left flank, in single file, the 11th Infantry Brigade of 4th Division began to cross the Aisne via the damaged Venizel bridge, the Germans on the north bank having evacuated their trenches. By 3 a.m. the move had been completed. The brigade was thus the first British formation to have crossed the river. Had other units acted with similar alacrity the story of the battle of the Aisne — and even the course of the war — might well have been very different.

Bridge over the Aisne, where the 2nd Division, of I Corps, crossed in 1914. [IWM]

In 1914 the bridge here over the Aisne below Missy was mostly destroyed by the Germans and was under severe artillery fire from the nearby heights. Missy was the most dangerous of all the river crossings. The 1st Royal West Kents crossed here by means of a small boat and makeshift rafts.

It was still unpleasantly wet in the early hours of the 13th when elements of the Cavalry Division were pushed forward to the Aisne on the right flank. They came under heavy fire at Bourg and waited until guns of the RFA came up to give them artillery support. Even then it was necessary to await the arrival of the 1st Division before a crossing could be effected by an aqueduct which had been only slightly damaged. To the left of Bourg the bridge at Chavonne had been destroyed. The Pont Arcy bridge was only partially damaged and usable by men on foot. The 5th Infantry Brigade crossed without much difficulty, against only light enemy opposition.

On the II Corps front, the 3rd Division moved towards the bridges at Vailly, and four miles to the left the 5th Division approached the Missy bridge. Between these two points the bridge at Condé was undamaged but was too vulnerable to machine-gun fire to risk using it. At Vailly a light railway bridge had been completely destroyed but the road bridge, although badly damaged, was still passable over a narrow plank footway inadvertently left by the Germans. The Missy bridge had actually been captured at 1 a.m. by 4th Division cyclists; these had been driven back by numerous Germans, who in turn were outflanked by two companies of the West Kents some hours later. North of Missy three German batteries in a commanding position on the Chivres Spur caused considerable trouble.

By 11 a.m. most of the 12th Infantry Brigade were across the Aisne at Venizel — the damaged bridge having been made safer — and moved on towards Bucy-le-Long under enemy gunfire. The 11th Infantry Brigade were already in position on the heights above Bucy-le-Long after the successful crossing earlier that morning.

By noon on 13th September the Aisne had been forced on both flanks of the British Army, and on the right of I Corps the French were also across. By 1 p.m. the 2nd Infantry Brigade were on high ground above Bourg, but the Royal Flying Corps reported that German troops were moving towards that area. By 6 p.m. the whole of the 1st Division was on the north bank of the Aisne. At Missy the West Kents used a small boat and rafts to cross after dark, having been unable to make progress earlier owing to enemy fire. A German patrol that came down to the river bank was wiped out, and by just after midnight the whole battalion was across. The 2nd Scottish Borderers followed.

An attempted advance on the enemy's Chivres position by the Lancashire Fusiliers and the 1st Rifle Brigade was driven back with heavy losses, and activity in that area quietened down. The Lancashire Fusiliers were relieved by the Manchesters having lost more than 170 officers and men.

Général Joffre still believed on 13th September that the enemy was continuing to retreat without offering serious resistance on the Aisne and issued a Special Instruction to that effect, coupled with an order for vigorous continuance of the pursuit. Events, however, were to prove that this was an optimistic and incorrect assessment. Sir John French, too, had similar thoughts based on information to hand and was prepared to attack all along his front on the 14th. Sir Douglas Haig, with the object of carrying out those orders, made the Chemin des Dames ridge — including Cerny — his first objective. As it happened, the last-minute arrival of the German VII Reserve Corps (with its 14th Division being directed to Cerny) was to foil his plans. By the afternoon the crisis had passed for the Germans: the gap had been closed and a mainly continuous line now existed in front of the British.

14th September turned out to be a day of confused fighting (some of it hand-to-hand) in continuing poor weather. Attack was followed by counter-attack, with the Germans receiving more and more reinforcements, including heavy guns, and as the day progressed it became evident that the enemy had no intention of relinquishing his well-sited positions on the high ground. In fact von Bulow even hoped to drive the Allies back across the Aisne and consolidate beyond the south bank of the river.

Missy-sur-Aisne. 1919. [IWM]

On the northern bank of the Aisne, with the tower of Missy Church on the left. The hill to its right is the Chivres Spur, on which the Germans were well entrenched and from which heavy fire was directed at men of the 5th Division. With the Germans was Hauptmann Bloem of the 12th Brandenburg Grenadiers, whose unit had been badly cut up at Mons by the West Kents. He was severely wounded during the fighting at Missy. Hauptmann Bloem was the author of the book 'The Advance From Mons', which gave the German version of the British retreat.

A spruce Missy Church in modern times. To the right is the main street, where very heavy artillery and small-arms fire caused many British casualties shortly after a German aeroplane had flown over it.

The quiet and peaceful River Aisne in the mid 1980s — a very different scene to that which once prevailed here.

Fierce fighting took place on the British right flank in the region of Cerney and the crossroads on the crest of the Chemin des Dames ridge. A sugar factory which was held by the Germans was attacked by the 2nd King's Royal Rifle Corps and 2nd Sussex and, with the added support of the Loyal North Lancashires, was successfully captured. Several hundred Germans in the nearby trenches surrendered to the Sussex but were then fired upon by their own men in the rear. Something similar happened opposite the KRRC, except that it was the German artillery which opened up on their comrades, who, caught between the British fire and that of the guns, were wiped out. An attempt by the Germans to remove the two batteries involved resulted in every man and horse being killed, with the twelve enemy guns then standing silent and unmanned. (Later they were recovered during a German counter-attack.)

Between 8 and 9 a.m. the fighting and the shelling increased in intensity and the 1st Coldstreams were hard hit near Cerny. After penetrating the enemy lines some of the British infantry actually looked down into the valley of the River Ailette. A German onslaught drove the British out of the sugar factory. On the left the enemy trenches were rushed and captured by the 1st Black Watch and 1st Guards. A party of fifty Camerons who were holding out on the ridge were overwhelmed by sheer weight of numbers; then two companies of the 1st Gloucestershires came up and drove the Germans back. Back and forth the battle swayed, until at about 3 p.m. things quietened down on the 1st Division's front. On its left, in the 2nd Division's sector, the Germans kept up a fierce rifle, machine-gun and artillery fire against the Royal Berkshires and KRRC, the 2nd Worcestershires and the Highland Light Infantry. Other British units also came under heavy fire but inflicted heavy loss on the Germans, who counter-attacked in force.

The situation in the centre of the British line was not very satisfactory, for there was a gap of almost two miles between I and II Corps. Had the Germans been aware of it,

the opportunity was there for an advance in force which might have cut the British Army in two. Fortunately that did not happen — and if they were aware of it, possibly they did not take advantage of the situation owing to the heavy losses they had suffered. Whatever the reason, things improved to the extent that the 5th Cavalry Brigade was ordered back, as were some artillery units.

The present bridge at Vailly, with the town beyond. In September 1914 the Germans left little of that one standing and the only means of crossing was by a few unstable wooden planks over a gap; and as the Germans had the area under observation, they kept up a constant harrassing fire. This was the 3rd Division of II Corps' sector. The French renamed the rebuilt bridge 'Pont des Anglais'.

Another important crossing place, at Bourg, where the 1st Division got over the river.

On the 5th Division's front, over to the left of the line, the wrecked Missy bridge, and heavy artillery fire directed at it, impeded progress. Attempts by the West Kents and Scottish Borderers to advance following their crossing during the hours of darkness brought down a hail of fire from the Germans entrenched on the Chivres Spur above Missy. As daylight arrived it became clear that this major topographical feature from which the Germans enjoyed excellent observation would have to be captured before further progress could be made. Orders were issued for it to be attacked from the east and south-east.

As the 14th Brigade moved forward from St Marguerite they were met with heavy enfilade fire from the spur. In spite of this the 2nd Manchesters managed to get within a few hundred yards of the German trenches before having to go to ground. By noon the 1st East Surreys had reached the northern edge of Missy village and made contact with the West Kents on their right. Fierce enemy fire stopped any further effort from the western side of the spur, but a fresh attack was launched from the south by ten companies of Norfolks, Bedfords and East Surreys. This did well at first, some of the troops getting within seventy yards of the German trenches before they too were forced to go to ground. Later they were ordered to fall back some distance.

Because of the 5th Division's slow progress, the 4th Division, on its left, was able to do very little, and was involved only in limited fighting.

As daylight faded on the 14th the overall results of the British operation can be summed up as somewhat disappointing — the envisaged advance beyond the Aisne heights having been stopped in its tracks. Only on the right flank had limited success been achieved, where I Corps had its right flank on the Chemin des Dames, four miles from the Aisne. The French, on the left of the British, were across the Aisne at Soissons having occupied Rheims. They too had met with growing resistance from a well-entrenched enemy and were unable to make decisive progress.

Crossroads at Cerny. Left and right lead to the Chemin des Dames. In the centre is a small chapel commemorating the French actions in this area. British troops were involved in bitter fighting here in September 1914 and a memorial to the Loyal North Lancashire Regiment is close to the crossroads. Also nearby is a large French military cemetery with an extensive German cemetery next to it. Along to the right is the famous Caverne du Dragon, a former German command post and now a museum.

A most moving painting in the memorial chapel which tells its own story.

That same evening von Moltke was relieved of his command, to be replaced as Chief of the General Staff by Lieutenant-General von Falkenhayn.

15th September was a day of vigorous German attacks which were all repulsed successfully at heavy cost to the enemy. A point had been reached at which Général Joffre accepted that pursuit was now no longer feasible: 'methodical attack and consolidation' were to take its place. A fresh attack was made on the Chivres Spur but this too was checked by artillery and small-arms fire, the Germans having erected new defences in accordance with von Kluck's orders to continue entrenching and to 'hold all positions at all costs'. Missy was heavily bombarded by the enemy and it became evident that the German positions on the Chivres Spur were too strong for that promontory to be captured. From these operations and those on the flanking French sectors it looked to many observers as if an impasse had arisen on the Aisne front, with little likelihood of it now being broken.

With trench warfare having now started, the thoughts of the generals on both sides turned to the possibilities of a wider enveloping movement. General Falkenhayn also had his sights set on the north-western coast of France, the capture of which would enable the Germans to control the English Channel. Meanwhile, as the weeks went by, the fighting on the Aisne sector consisted mostly of artillery duels in which the advantage lay with the Germans both in observation and calibre of guns. The weather was inclement, the trenches deep in mud, the ground waterlogged; yet, in spite of the miserable conditions, the British troops' morale remained remarkably high. The Germans launched several infantry attacks; but apart from localised advances, which brought the trenches closer, they were held all along the line.

On 28th September all British offensive action ceased on the Aisne sector as preparations began for a move to the north, in what came to be called a 'race to the sea'.

Sir John French said later that British losses on the Aisne were 561 officers and 12,980 men.

A striking panorama from the Chemin des Dames above Vendresse and looking down at the valley of the River Ailette. Fierce fighting took place in this area in 1914 and during the French offensive of April–May 1917, and British troops again saw action here in 1918 when being 'rested' after the German Spring Offensive.

EXTRACTS FROM THE DIARY OF CAPTAIN JAMES BRINDLEY, DSO, MC, 1st BATTALION EAST YORKSHIRE REGIMENT

7th September, 1914: Left Cambridge; arrived Southampton 3 a.m.

8th September: Left Southampton at 4.30 a.m. on Cawdor Castle for St Nazaire, France. Good voyage, escorted across by French cruisers.

10th September: Arrived at St Nazaire, entrained at 10.30 p.m.; arrived at Coulommiers at 5 a.m.

12th September (east of Paris): Passed French wounded in train; people good to troops. To Doue to billets; raining hard; cheerful in farmhouse — or remains of one damaged and looted by the Germans; residents pleased with East Yorks Regt.; Cpl. Barnard R.E. and sixteen Germans buried.

13th September (Sunday): Guns booming in the distance until late in the evening.

15th September: The whole division on the march; arrived at Château-Thierry at 12 midnight (distance of 24 miles); wet night and up all night; large town depleted of occupants, buildings shelled and looted but fruit in abundance; Marne River, splendid.

16th September: Marched to Hartennes, road crammed with transport, people all pleased to see troops; passed through Breny, numerous British wounded at station; guns booming.

17th September: Raining hard; moved to Chacrise, road mass of wagons, guns booming all day in direction of Soissons.

18th September: Marched to Braine at 2.30 p.m., thence to Dhuizel, Longueval, Villiers; rum to be bottled.

19th September: Arrived Villiers very wet but cheerful; very heavy artillery fire; trenches dug; German artillery positions could be located by the flashes of about 100 guns; French troops on both of

Captain J. Brindley, DSO, MC, enlisted in the East Yorkshire Regiment as a regular soldier at the age of 17 years 8 months and fought in the Boer War, being promoted Sergeant for gallantry in the field. He became Company Sergeant-Major in 1913 and Regimental Quartermaster-Sergeant in May 1914. At the age of 33 he went to France and was commissioned in October 1914. He was promoted to acting Captain in August 1916, substantive rank being granted in December 1916. In November 1914 he was actually reported dead in the 'Daily Express'. He was wounded at Hooge (Ypres Salient) in August 1915, twice during the Somme battles in August and September 1916, and then severely when with his men he captured the notorious Gird Trench, north of Flers. Invalided home he became Adjutant in the East Yorkshires and in 1919 had the honour of carrying the Colour in the Paris and London Victory Marches. He won his MC in 1915 and was awarded the DSO in 1917. He died in 1953. [Photo: David Brindley]

our flanks; raining hard. The Germans were in a fine position and were shelling, with much accuracy, all day long. We relieved the 1st Division who had occupied the trenches for six nights and days; I took rations up at dusk. The Germans repeatedly attacked us during the night but were repulsed with heavy losses on our brigade front.

20th September: The enemy, north of Vendresse and on a frontage of about 15 miles, attacked us with great force at dawn. The noise of musketry fire was terrific and shells were flying about in all directions. The Germans came right up to our trenches and things looked serious but they were charged by the regiments on our left and right; the 2nd D.L.I. and the E. Yorks left their trenches and lost a good many men. Col. Benson, Major Campion and Major Maxwell, also Lieutenants Englefield and Mellor, were wounded and Capt. Edwards died in this action. Fifty men were casualties. The 1st West Yorks also had numerous casualties. German artillery fire was fierce all day long and the enemy made several charges but were repulsed with heavy losses; very many dead and wounded lay between the lines, which were about 500 yards apart; the wounded had to be left to die where they fell and one man who had a leg off cried out but had to be left as he drew fire when attempts were made to help him. At about 10 a.m. the rattle of rifle-fire slackened off; 20 men were buried in the small churchyard, their wounds being almost too terrible to describe; the weather was very unsettled and although the troops were cheerful they were very displeased at being wet through; there is plenty of food and no-one can grumble about being hungry; a seven-mile journey has to be made, there and back over very rough roads, to get the rations up. The Germans attacked in force at about 12.30 p.m. along the whole line and fierce fighting occurred; they pressed forward in masses but were met by the British with the bayonet; losses were heavy, with the West Yorks having about 662 casualties, the East Yorks 182, Notts and Derby 250 and Durhams 200.

21st September: The regiment is still in the trenches and reinforcements have arrived; guns are on the go all day long; the French were attacked at 2 a.m. and although hard-pressed held out; more guns have arrived and it has been said that the Russians are in the Germans' rear; casualties of the 18th Infantry Brigade have been very heavy; the Notts and Derby Regt. were praised for their work in re-taking trenches lost by the West Yorks; constant streams of wounded pass through Villiers; French artillery fired by mistake on the Notts and Derby causing many casualties. The Germans are retiring and it is quiet on our front, hardly any gunfire. At 2 p.m. a German aeroplane hovered over our village and although fired at with rifles escaped to his lines. All routes through the valley to the trenches are ranged by the German guns; a German spy was discovered in a desolate farmhouse with a telephone line laid for directing the enemy artillery fire; he was shot at dawn; the 114th Bde. R.F.A. lost two guns and about 45 men through their positions being located; rations taken up as usual at night (very dangerous at times).

22nd September: Trenches still occupied, with men in cheerful moods. Two battalions of Turco troops, all coloured and commanded by French officers, passed by as reinforcements for the French lines;

they are tall and lanky and carry a pretty bulky load but are not strong-looking and seem very dejected; however, they may do well and prove to be of great help to the French. The German guns played havoc with the 18th Infantry Bde. in the trenches, and the road leading up to the positions was shelled time after time; one shell dropped into a farmhouse close by and killed an old man and a woman; the dead between the lines are beginning to smell, there must be thousands; the bodies of Capt. Edwards and Lieut. Mellor are still in front of the trenches but cannot be recovered; Pte. Bruin slightly wounded by shrapnel fire; German aeroplanes give range for their artillery by throwing out a smoke-ball and men have to take cover from accurate fire.

23rd September: Heavy fire at 5 a.m. with shells dropping all round positions; quite an artillery duel all morning, with aeroplanes of both sides hovering around positions; they were fired at without effect; numerous wounded passed by in motor ambulances, some of them bad cases caused by shrapnel; the battalion took over trenches occupied by the Notts and Derbys, their casualties having been very heavy. A hayrick was set on fire by German shells and Lieut. Bottomley with ten men went to extinguish it; sadly this officer was killed and all the others of the party were wounded; casualties for the day — one officer and twenty men; the long sought-for heavy guns arrived during the night, eight passing on their way to Vendresse and Troyon, and their fire power should make a great difference; handed in two wagon loads of arms and equipment of killed and wounded to ordnance stores; aeroplanes circling overhead fired at by guns.

24th September: Villiers. A hot day; heavy guns in action, German artillery very quiet; aeroplanes very active and although fired at apparently escaped damage; washing day — good opportunity, splendid result; checked all casualties, also officers' kit, inventory of same handed to ordnance stores; wagon load of rifles and equipment from dead and wounded of battle fought at Troyon a few days earlier and collected from the battlefield also handed in; unburied dead beginning to smell badly; at about 8 p.m. the French attacked the German lines with great vigour on our right; magnificent sight, with shells bursting in the air and on the trenches, lighting up the whole ground; the sound of musketry fire and artillery fire was deafening; the French troops advanced on the enemy positions and fire from both sides was murderous; the English were ready to support them and B Coy. was detailed for this purpose; for about an hour the attack carried on with vigour; German aeroplanes kept hovering around the positions all day dropping fire-bombs to indicate targets for their artillery; a long trail of smoke indicated English positions and shortly afterwards shells would come whistling over as they found the range; guns fired at the aircraft with no effect; during the night the French bombarded the German positions with about 150 guns and it presented a fine spectacle, with lights of all descriptions being seen; the result is not yet known but it appears to have been a success for the French; the East Yorks are in entrenchments which are something of a death trap; 30 Notts and Derbys have been buried just below the trenches.

25th September: Aroused by cannonade as usual; aeroplanes are numerous, with plenty of fire directed at them; gunfire not so heavy during the morning but several German shots dropped just outside Villiers; the battalions which have been in the trenches were relieved, East Yorks to Moulins, D.L.I. and West Yorks to Pargnan, Notts and Derbys to ?; during the day Moulins was shelled by the Germans and two chidren were killed in a house; the women were terrified and hid themselves away; snipers were numerous, one being captured; the Welsh regiment is in the trenches at Vendresse where a great attack was made by the enemy, with the British trenches being captured but then re-taken; German casualties were considerable; Moulins much shelled; E. Yorks left for trenches above the town.

26th September: The regiment moved to Vendresse after being heavily shelled at Moulins; Sgt. Durose and several cooks were wounded, Pte. Hartley was killed; much damage was caused by enemy 90lb. shells which came over all day; they made great holes in the ground and threw up mountains of earth, also making a terrible noise; 500 Germans are reported to have been annihilated by our guns; several wounded Germans were brought in from the trenches, two of them being very fat and wounded in the head; a sniper was also brought in under escort; several wounded of the Welsh Regt. came in on stretchers; Germans appear to be retiring; troops on the move.

27th September (Sunday): Very little firing from the Germans although our own howitzers kept up a heavy fire, the shells whistling loudly through the air; no reply came from the enemy so they must have moved; at 2 p.m. German 'Coal Boxes' came over, cutting up the road and making holes six feet deep and nine feet in diameter; the Camerons had their C.O., the Adjutant and 30 men buried alive when a shell dropped on a cave in which they were sheltering, the whole lot being suffocated; Moulins was shelled again, with much damage being caused; the Germans again attacked the British trenches above Vendresse in force but were once more repulsed with great slaughter, machine-gun and rifle fire being very vigorous; six horses were killed in an artillery battery and a limber badly damaged; the E. Yorks went down into cellars for safety.

28th September: The regiment is in the trenches again and under heavy German artillery fire (Coal Boxes); one shell struck a water cart and blew it right over another one nearby; a dead German who had been shot and bayoneted was found by me with others in the vicinity; rifle-fire was very heavy in the direction of the trenches as we passed along the road with supplies; the Black Watch were by the Vendresse road in support; the Sussex Regt. in the trenches suffered badly; oil for rifles very scarce, with the weapons being in poor condition, but managed to get twelve gallons; letter came from Nan; one of our men from ammunition column was shot dead by a sentry of the 11th Hussars after being challenged four times; collected rifles and equipment from battlefield at Vendresse.

29th September: Great battle during night of Monday–Tuesday with terrible rifle-fire; casualties not yet known; a few occupants of the town have returned although firing from guns still continues; roads cut up by shellfire; reinforcements arrived on Sunday; handed in to Ordnance a great number of rifles and bayonets of killed and wounded, many of them being covered in blood; the Royal Sussex suffered in the trenches; wounded were brought into Villiers with awful injuries; shells busting near supply stores and along Longueval–Villiers road; 13 men killed at Longueval by one shell (9th Lancers); German aeroplane hovering over Villiers shelled by British guns and then chased by one of our aircraft but he disappeared into the clouds; shells dropping on the road from Longueval; the East Yorks had four killed and eight wounded at Vendresse by the last shot of the evening.

The King commands me to assure you

of the true sympathy of His Majesty and

The Queen in your sorrow.

He whose loss you mourn died in the

noblest of causes.   His Country will be

ever grateful to him for the sacrifice he has

made for Freedom and Justice.

Milner

Secretary of State for War.

30th September: The battalions are still at Vendresse, on a slope above the town; wounded are in hospital at Villiers; saw Tom Saunders R.E. and Sgt. Shea, East Yorks; German spies dressed as Frenchmen reported to be driving around British positions in motor car with red body and green top; description circulated; Lyons saw eight horses and a man killed by a shell at Bourg; the man was reading a letter from his wife when he was struck on the head; received a letter from Nan, also one from the base; wrote back; aeroplanes of both sides hovering around positions and being fired at; supply depots at Villiers shelled with Coal Boxes and shrapnel, the supplies then being removed; Zouaves digging trenches were shelled without damage; no casualties in the regiment today in spite of being shelled occasionally; at dusk the German artillery fired very heavily on the road on which the supplies had to come; we just missed it otherwise we most certainly would have lost our wagons.

1st October: Villiers–Vendresse–Vauxtin. Very quiet, the battalion still at Vendresse; rumour that the Germans have retired although their guns still firing from time to time. The battalion is relieved by the 3rd Division, with the 6th Division concentrating in the vicinity of Braine, the 18th Brigade being at Vauxtin, a small and dirty village. The women there did sentry duty over their barns to prevent our troops taking straw to sleep on; one indignant woman was shouting at the top of her voice for a long time complaining about troops taking straw; the men looked awfully tired and fed up when they marched into Vauxtin from Vendresse — in fact the whole brigade looked worn out, tired and dirty and needing a rest; being away from the trenches and having a night's rest will do wonders. We arrived here very late and it was not until about 1 a.m. that we settled down.

2nd October: The battalion was much refreshed after the night's rest although it was very cold sleeping out. There was not much water, which was hard to find, with the well in a bad state and the water not fit to drink; went to Villiers for supplies but the horses were absolutely done in; started for Braine-Jury taking all night; very cold and misty. The brigade moved from Vauxtin to Jury; night moves seem to be general. Reported Col. Benson and Capt. Maxwell died and buried at St Nazaire; it is reported that 80,000 Germans have surrendered; the women who have stayed on in towns are very brave, with much pluck and endurance; shells often come into towns, some being reduced to ruins; crops of all descriptions are being ruined, some by not being gathered, others through being trampled by troops.

3rd October: Arrived at Jury about 2 a.m.; heavy guns in position firing all day; reported 18,000 German casualties around our positions at Vendresse and Villiers; 6th Division concentrating; hopes for move in few days; supplies come from Searches two miles south; trenches for miles around but also beautiful country; battalions at rest in very dirty billets.

6th October: Marched from Jury to St Reiny, transport in rear; all marches being carried out by night; arrived about 1.30 a.m.; none of the houses appear to have been damaged; sleep soundly; talk of move to Belgium.

29th October 1914. Following its move north from the Aisne sector the battalion is at Le Armee, south of Armentieres. 'C' Company is billeted in a farm house — very comfortable! During the night of 28th-29th the battalion was attacked in the trenches by the Germans who were slaughtered as they advanced with 300-400 being left dead on the battlefield and around the British trenches. Twelve of the enemy surrendered or were taken prisoner, with these men afterwards looking quite pleased at being taken prisoner. The battalion was tired out by the fighting and deserved a good rest; it certainly earned the praise which followed from the General. Our casualties included five officers and 114 other ranks killed or wounded. However, the Germans have been taught a lesson and do not appear to be anxious to repeat the experience.

30th October: Battalion in the same billets; ordered to move in Reserve to 12th Brigade. Marched to Armentieres and slept in the swimming baths until 4 a.m. Moved to end of town towards Chapelle Armentieres and there awaited an attack which, when it came in, was very feeble. Went into billets in Armentieres. Company located in Brasserie and Brewery, others situated along the main street; very

Another of the Aisne bridges. The one that stood here at Pont Arcy (west of Bourg) in 1914 was only partly demolished and so could be used by men on foot, especially as it was only feebly defended. The greater part of the 5th Infantry Brigade were able to cross here practically unopposed.

Vendresse Military Cemetery (Aisne), twelve miles south of Laon and on the road to Cerny-en-Laonnis. The Chemin des Dames, a coach road constructed during the reign of Louis XV to make travelling easier for his daughters, is on the crest above. The cemetery, which was created after the Armistice, records 657 UK burials and 49 special memorials. There were numerous caves in this area which were used for sheltering British troops. Severe fighting also took place here in 1918.

comfortable. Shelling going on all day around town and at night — quite used to it. Plenty of people in the town; they don't appear to be afraid at all of the shellfire and take it as a matter of course, all in the day's routine.

31st October: Battalion in billets in the town. Stood to at 4.45 a.m.: too early, very dark. No attack but shellfire searching for batteries. Detailed for digging trenches with civilians at Chapelle Armentieres. The civilians, who had not been paid for earlier work, did not turn up; work cancelled. Billets very nice, landlady good. Earlier the Germans had been in Armentieres and in one house they demanded champagne but apparently got short shrift from the lady of the house.

1st November (Sunday): Battalion still in billets; stood to at 4.45 a.m. in supporting role. Detailed again for trench digging. Worked all day from 6 a.m. to 9.30 p.m. digging long line of trenches with the help of about fifty Frenchmen with an interpreter. Sniped at by some Germans; the Frenchmen took cover for a time before they would work. Detailed for a Board of Inquiry; Sgt Lacey, who shot off his finger. First Board and first job as 2nd Lieutenant; very pleased with oneself. People all in black going to church service.

2nd November: Armentières. Stood to at 4.45 a.m. An attack took place, but of a weak nature, on the 12th Brigade. Shelling commenced at 4.30 a.m. and continued for an hour; reinforcements not required. A shell fell in the town and killed five people. East Lancs lost Captain Clare and Lieut. Mathews, both shot through the head by a sniper. Walked round the town, shops had been shelled in the market square.

3rd November: Stand to at 4.45 a.m.; no alarm. At about 10.30 a.m. the German artillery commenced to shell the town; the first one struck our billets at the Brasserie, the second burst in front of our house, killing four horses and five men. I picked up Cpl. Roseblade but could not do any good. An engineer, who was riding a horse and leading another, was killed. The horse caught the full explosion of the shell and only its head and one shoulder were together, with one leg hanging from it; it was a most awful sight. People in town were wounded including a girl of seven and a boy of six — pitiful to see. The old man in our billet was badly wounded in the arm and we have not seen either him or his wife since. The battalion had promptly to vacate the buildings, with shells following us into the centre of the town. People were flying in all directions, many crying bitterly. Most left the town, abandoning their homes and belongings. We had many narrow escapes and after forming up in the centre of the town marched off to the trenches to relieve the West Yorks. There at about 9 p.m.

Left: Vailly British Military Cemetery (Vailly-sur-Aisne) lies ten miles east of Soissons and west of Vailly village. It was created after the Armistice from isolated graves and small cemeteries in the vicinity and records 678 United Kingdom burials, 1 Canadian, 1 French and 1 German. Here too is buried Captain Theodore Wright, VC, of Mons fame.

THE MOVE NORTH

At the end of September, and with stalemate on the Aisne, Général Joffre agreed to a proposal from Sir John French for the BEF to be transferred to the north — that is, the left of the line. Such a move meant shorter lines of communication for the BEF, by its being nearer the coast, and that it could be reinforced more swiftly.

Mainly because of a lack of sufficient troops, and the need to invest Antwerp, to which the bulk of the Belgian Army had retired in August, the Germans had omitted to capture Ostend, Calais and Boulogne during the early days of their successful advance, and they now set about remedying that. The preliminary bombardment of Antwerp opened on 28th September, while north of the Oise the German and French armies were already fighting to outflank one another in a series of such attempts that developed into a so-called 'race to the sea'. Thus Antwerp assumed a fresh significance for the Allies — British reinforcements for the Belgians including the despatch of a naval division — and, for the British, the German threat to the Channel ports heightened the importance of defending them and preventing the enemy from gaining control of the coastline and the shipping lanes.

The withdrawal of British troops from the Aisne sector began in utmost secrecy on the night of 1st/2nd October. By moving only at night and also using other means of concealment the evacuation was successfully completed by mid-October, and the Germans remained unaware of the changing situation until it was too late to interfere with its implementation. II Corps detrained at Abbeville on 8th and 9th of Otober, III Corps concentrated at St Omer and Hazebrouck several days later, and on the 19th I Corps also detrained at Hazebrouck and then moved to the north of Ypres, on the left of IV Corps, which it incorporated on the 27th, this force having landed at Ostend and covered the Belgian and British withdrawal down the coast from Antwerp. GHQ moved to Abbeville on the 8th and thence to St Omer.

On 10th October General Sir John French attended a conference at the headquarters in Doullens of the commander of the French northern group of armies, Général Foch, at which it was agreed that the British and French troops in the north should make a combined advance eastwards, with the intention of turning the enemy's northern flank. However, any attempts at an eastward movement were foiled by the Germans who, following the fall of Antwerp, were able to put into the field four newly-organised corps with which they, in turn, hoped to turn the Allies' flank. Lille was occupied by the Germans on the night of 11th/12th October and also on the 11th the enemy attacked all along the French line from Arras to Vermelles (near Loos). These attacks were successfully repulsed except at Auchy (north of Loos), which fell to the enemy, as did Fosse (Pit) 8, which became notorious during the Battle of Loos in September 1915.

The town of Bailleul, across the fields from near Meteren. This area was the scene of much cavalry activity in October 1914 and was captured by the British 4th Division after the withdrawal of the German IV Cavalry Corps. Although well behind the British lines for most of the war, the town fell to the enemy during the German Lys Offensive of April 1918.

German cavalry also captured La Bassée, which was to remain in enemy hands for four years.

To the British the actions of this period became known as the Battle of La Bassée (10th October–2nd November) and the Battle of Armentières (13th October–2nd November). Fierce fighting occurred at Givenchy, north of the La Bassée Canal, with the village being lost but then recaptured, and at Cuinchy, which subsequently became notorious for the intensive mining activity carried out at the brickstacks just east of the village. It was here that the line remained virtually static for the whole of the war. A footing was gained on the Aubers Ridge and at Fromelles but both places were subsequently lost to the advancing enemy. Meanwhile the Battle of Messines also began.

On 20th October Sir John French abandoned the attempt to turn the German flank in this sector and gave orders for the line to be held against the continuing German

Above: The village of Meteren, west of Bailleul. It was during the fight for this village in October 1914 that a certain young subaltern was badly wounded by a sniper. Had his life been snuffed out, as it nearly was, there would have been no Field Marshal Viscount Montgomery of Alamein.

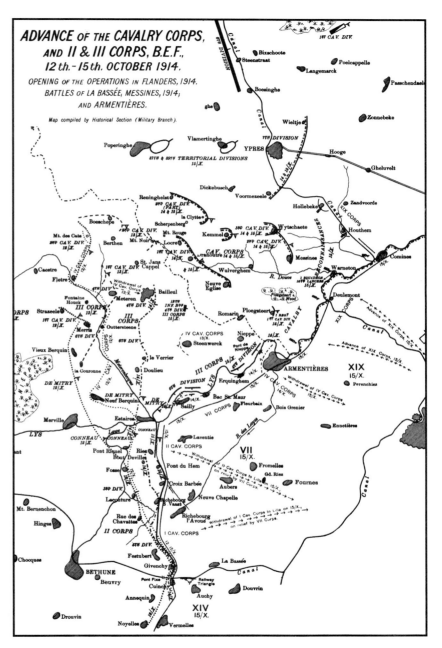

ADVANCE OF THE CAVALRY CORPS, AND II & III CORPS, B.E.F., 12th.–15th. OCTOBER 1914.

OPENING OF THE OPERATIONS IN FLANDERS, 1914. BATTLES OF LA BASSÉE, MESSINES, 1914, AND ARMENTIÈRES.

Map compiled by Historical Section (Military Branch).

attacks while further efforts at outflanking the enemy were made by I Corps, then arriving to the north of Ypres. This plan was also destined to fail as more and more German troops were sent to that part of the front (including some from the Aisne sector) and the tide of battle moved closer to the historic Flemish town which was to become immortalised by nearly four years of siege warfare.

Before the attempt was abandoned here, the British met with success in driving German cavalry from Bailleul and the nearby hills of Mont de Cats and Kemmel, and in capturing Meteren, where the enemy first gave the appearance of making a stand in well-sited positions (the church tower giving excellent observation over the surrounding countryside). Estaires was secured by the French on the 15th — the

Indian troops on the outskirts of Wytschaete at the end of October 1914. These men of the 129th (Duke of Connaught's Own) Baluchis (Lahore Division) are manning a temporary parapet before a permanent trench system came into being and trees and houses disappeared into a sea of desolation. The Indian Corps served on the Western Front for the first year of the war but they were unsuited for the cold, damp conditions of France and Flanders. In November 1915, except for some Indian cavalry units that remained in France, they were transferred to the warmer climate of Mesopotamia. [IWM]

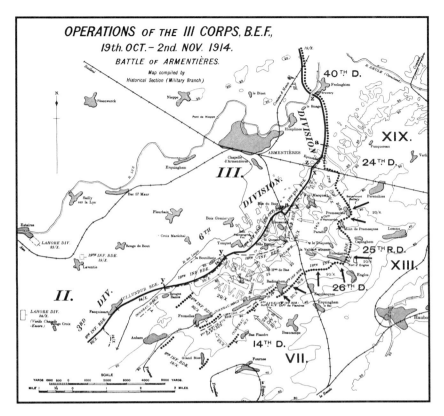

OPERATIONS OF THE III CORPS, B.E.F.,
19th. OCT. – 2nd. NOV. 1914.
BATTLE OF ARMENTIÈRES.
Map compiled by
Historical Section (Military Branch)

same day that Ostend, in the north, was occupied by the Germans — and on the 17th Armentières, which had been in the possession of the enemy, was taken by 4th Division (10th Brigade, III Corps), the Germans having left the town in some haste. The Germans dug in on a low ridge about four miles east of Armentières, and it was here that the line stabilised in this sector. By then a complete defence line (albeit a thin one) consisting of alternate infantry and cavalry units — and including French and Belgian forces — had been established from south of Béthune to the sea.

British casualties between 9th and 18th October were just over 4,500, but these were to be greatly exceeded in the near future by what became known as the First Battle of Ypres. It was on that major confrontation that the curtain was about to rise.

Opposite page, above right: This photograph of a group of young soldiers is on the reverse side of a postcard written by Private S. T. H. Ross to his mother. Private Ross (seated left) was in the London Scottish and took part in the fierce fighting on the Messines Ridge in October 1914. His exploits are described in the author's book 'Flanders Then and Now'.

Right: The Hôtel de Ville in the town of Armentières — a name made famous by the song about the mademoiselle from there. The Germans entered the town in 1914 but withdrew at the approach of the British 4th Division of III Corps. Armentières remained in British hands until the Battle of the Lys in April 1918, after which the front lines were some miles west of the town until it was finally recaptured in October 1918.

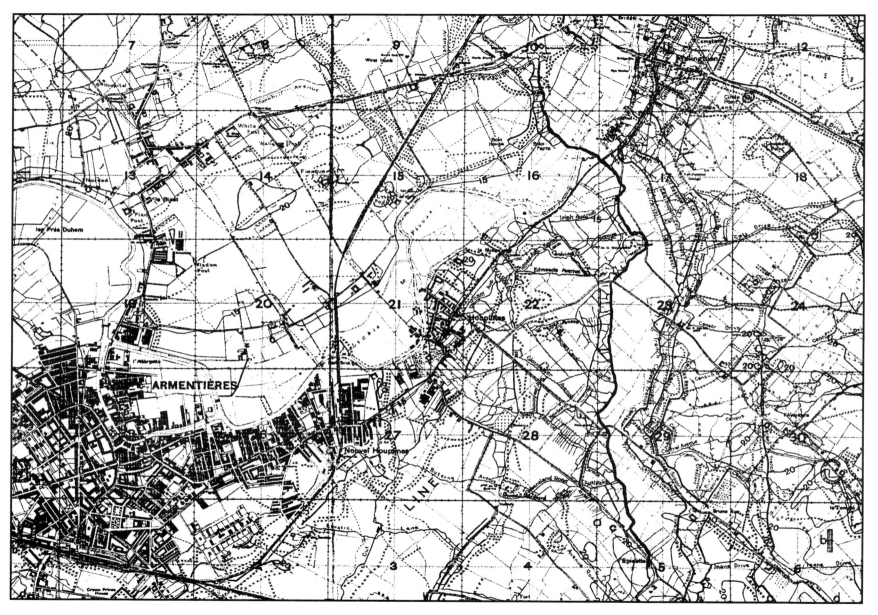

Extract from Trench Map sheet 36 NW, Edition 9A of the Armentières area in which the 1st Cameronians were based in 1914.

Looking out on No Man's Land near Armentières, from positions held by the 1st Cameronians. As static warfare set in, the light barbed wire defences would become more dense; the houses would be pounded to rubble. [IWM]

1st Cameronians, Houplines sector, 18th November 1914. A cup of tea to look forward to, outside 'D' Company's Mess on a frosty morning. [IWM]

40 W.O. 2662.

8.A.

Specimen of Battalion
TRENCH STANDING ORDERS.

1. Trenches are usually divided up into a certain number of Bays ; the number of men to defend these Bays depends on the length of trench allotted to each Company. Each Section is detailed to guard a certain number of Bays.

2. N.C.Os. and men must always wear their equipment by day and night ; a man found not complying with this order commits a " crime."

3. Every Company will stand to Arms daily half an hour before dawn, and half an hour before dusk and will remain so till dismissed by O.C. Company.

4. The enemy's trenches are so close that it is very important for the men to have their rifle sights always at " normal," so that there will be no necessity to alter the sights in case of alarm.

5. By night all bayonets are to be fixed, and 50% of the men on duty in the trenches are to be sitting on the firing platform with their rifles by their sides.

6. In case of an attack, especially at night, it should be impressed on the men that they should fire low ; for one bullet that goes too low, at least 90 go too high. A bullet that goes too high is wasted, whereas a bullet that goes too low is a Ricochet, and is often more dangerous than any other kind of bullet.

7. Section Commanders are responsible that the men under their Command have sufficient standing room for the purpose of firing over the parapet. It is very important to ensure that the men have a clear field of fire, and are able not only to see the enemy's trenches but also the ground in the immediate vicinity of their own trench. It is of the greatest importance to arrange that the men can fire comfortably from the parapet and that they can get the but comfortably into the hollow of the shoulder when the ri. is resting on the parapet.

(B 14090) Wt. w. 9643—3475 12M 9/15 H & S P.15/612.

2

8. When making new trenches it should be impressed on the men that the parapet must be at least 5 ft. thick at the top in order to be bullet-proof.

9. If any part of the parapet requires repairing or altering, the matter should be reported at once by the Section Commander to his Platoon Sergeant, who will in turn report the matter to superior authority.

10. The general work of repairing the trenches, fatigues, etc., will be carried out either by day or by night according to Company arrangements. Certain hours will be allotted for these tasks, and no man in the Company is to be employed in any kind of work out of these hours, unless permission is obtained from O.C. Company.

11. No man should ever leave his post in the trenches either by day or by night, without the permission of the N.C.O. in charge of that post.

12. As a general rule, by night there should be at least one sentry post to each ten yards of parapet.

13. By night, double sentries should always be posted if possible, and no sentry should be kept on duty for a longer period than 1 hour at a time. It should be so arranged that when one of the sentries is doing his last $\frac{1}{2}$-hour on sentry, his comrade will be doing his first $\frac{1}{2}$-hour on duty.

14. Sentries by night should always have their rifles resting on the parapet ready to fire at moment's notice.

15. As few sentries as possible should be posted by day, so as to give as much rest as possible to the remainder of the men.

16. By day any existing loop-holes may be used by a sentry for observation purposes, but this is strictly prohibited at night, when the sentry must look over the parapet.

17. If a sentry is continually fired at, the Section Commander will take steps to post him in another position but not far away from the original position.

18. By night, arrangements must be made in each Platoon for a N.C.O.* to be continually on duty for the purpose of visiting the sentries, etc., etc. He will report to his Company Officer at odd hours and to his Platoon Officer at even hours.

19. Cases have occurred of men going to sleep on Sentry duty. This is the most serious crime a soldier can commit on Active service. The G.O.C. has clearly stated that in

* An acting N.C.O. will not be employed on this duty.

future, if any man has been convicted by Court-Martial for this offence and sentenced to be shot, he will confirm the sentence. There is no excuse for a man going to sleep on Sentry duty ; if he is feeling too ill to perform this duty he should report the fact to the N.C.O. on duty of his Platoon, who will in his turn report the matter to superior authority.

20. If an armed party of the enemy approaches the trench under a flag of truce, they should be ordered to halt at a distance and lay down their arms, and the matter should be reported at once to the O.C. Company. If the party fails to halt when ordered to do so, or does not convey a flag of truce, they should immediately be fired upon. An unarmed party should be halted the same way at a distance, and the matter be reported to the O.C. Company.

21. By night it is not necessary to challenge anyone in advance of the trenches, but fire should be opened at once. If, however, the Company is sending out listening, working or covering parties these orders should be modified, and special instructions issued to meet the case.

22. Men will be specially picked from the Company for listening patrols and as sharp-shooters. These men will be given special privileges and their work is such that they will be afforded greater opportunities of being mentioned in despatches.

23. It is the duty of Officers and N.C.Os. to check men talking loudly during the night, as this practice makes it impossible for the sentries to hear any movement in front of the trenches. The Germans take advantage of this talking by the British soldier during the night to send listening patrols quite near to our trenches, and even build trenches on clear moonlight nights close to our lines without our knowledge.

24. All working parties must wear their equipment and carry their rifles, but when actually working they can lay these on the ground close to them.

25. All picks and shovels after use will be returned to the Company Store.

26. Ration parties and parties carrying materials for repairs, etc., etc., need not wear their equipment or carry rifles, but should be accompanied by a fully armed N.C.O. as an escort.

4

27. Not more than twenty men are to be away from the Company at the same time. 1 N.C.O. and 4 men per Platoon.

28. Every soldier must remember it is of the utmost importance to keep his rifle clean and in working order whilst in the trenches. His very life may depend upon this, as he is liable to be rushed at any moment, either by day or by night. The dirty rifle means probably a jammed one after the first round.

29. The first duty of a soldier, therefore, is to clean his rifle every morning as soon as there is sufficient light to enable him to do so; an hour will be appointed by O.C. Company for this purpose. The Platoon Serjeant will be responsible that Section Commanders superintend this work, and inspect the rifles of their Section. Any man who is found with a dirty rifle will be made a prisoner.

30. All rifles by day to be in racks, except those used by the sentries, and arrangements should be made by Section Commanders to improvise racks if they are not provided.

31. Great care is to. be exercised to keep the trenches clean and in a sanitary condition. Platoon Commanders will be responsible for the latrines in their Section of the trenches. Any man fouling the trenches will be severely dealt with. No water is to be taken for drinking or cooking purposes except from the water-cart or tanks provided for this purpose. Disregard of this Regulation will probably cause an outbreak of Typhoid or Dysentery amongst the men of the Company.

32. Stretcher-bearers will be stationed at a place appointed by the C.O. If a man is wounded information should be sent at once to these stretcher-bearers, whose duty it is to carry wounded to the aid post or dressing station.

Men should not be taken from the firing line for this purpose.

33. No soldier is to be buried nearer than 300 yards from the trenches.

34. In each Platoon a N.C.O. will be detailed for duty by day. This N.C.O. will do no night duty but will get a full night's rest. His duties are to post the day sentries and to see that they are alert and carrying out their duties correctly. He will be generally responsible for the cleanliness of his lines and will frequently visit the latrines. It is part of his

duties to see that any loose ammunition lying about is collected.

35. The Platoon Serjeant will always send, if possible, a N.C.O.* to draw the rations, and this N.C.O. will be responsible for their safe delivery. This especially applies to the issue of coke. The C.S.M. will, prior to his day of relief from the trenches, always collect the articles of trench equipment supplied for his Company and make out a list of the same. These articles will be handed over to the Company Serjeant-Major of the relieving Company.

36. The system of passing down messages by word of mouth, man to man, must not be used. If an Officer or N.C.O. has anything important to report, he should do so in writing. If there is no time to do this, a special messenger should be entrusted with a verbal message which should afterwards be confirmed in writing.

37. Special instructions have been issued as to precautions against Gas. These are to be strictly followed.

---

* An acting N.C.O. will not be employed on this duty.

PARLIAMENTARY RECRUITING COMMITTEE.

12, DOWNING STREET, LONDON, S.W.

December, 1914.

Dear Sir or Madam,

We desire to draw your attention to the enclosed form, in which you are asked to state the names of those of your household who are willing to enlist for the War. By filling in and posting the Householder's Return without delay, you will render material assistance to the War Office. The names returned will be entered in a Register, and the nearest Recruiting Officer will arrange to attest those registered as their services are required.

There has been a generous response to the appeal for men for the new Armies, but the number of recruits, though large, does not nearly meet the Nation's need. In order to maintain and reinforce our troops abroad and to complete the new Armies which we hope within a few months to throw into the field, we need all the best the Nation can give us of its youth and strength.

If we are to repair as far as may be humanly possible the innumerable wrongs inflicted on our Allies, if we are to avoid for ourselves the ills which they have suffered, if we are to maintain for our children all that we hold dear – honour, freedom, our very life as a Nation – we must fight with the courage and endurance which won for us the struggles of the past.

Every man, therefore, who is eligible will ask his own conscience whether, in this emergency, it is not his duty to hold himself ready to enlist in the forces of the Crown.

The difficulties and dangers which confront us have never been so great; we await the issue with confidence, relying on the spirit and self-sacrifice of our fellow-countrymen to prevail.

We are,

Your obedient Servants,

W. H. Asquith

A. Bonar Law

Arthur Henderson

Presidents

78

FURTHER EXTRACTS FROM THE DIARY OF
CAPTAIN JAMES BRINDLEY, DSO, MC,
1st BATTALION EAST YORKSHIRE REGIMENT

4th November: Rue du Bois. In the trenches; snipers going it all night. Not much sleep; took it in turns with Major Bogle keeping watch. Early in the morning a few shells dropped and later, on our right, there was a regular barrage for about an hour. North Staffords in trenches; about four 'coal boxes' on our left and a few shrapnel. Our trenches strongly improved, unsanitary; no water, no tea, very thirsty. Rain at 4 p.m.; digging in; our shells flying over trenches shelling a house containing snipers — snipers stopped firing. A regular fusillade of gun-fire on our right for a long time during the night. A few snipers still firing at the trenches. Raining until about midnight; very muddy, we are like a lot of mudlarks in the trenches. Received letter from Maudie Brindley and one from Mabel, both answered that night. Very dreary night, dull and wet.

5th November (in the trenches): Waiting patiently for an attack which did not come; wet and cold. At about 9 a.m. a regular German bombardment commenced with shells of all sizes flying through the air; they fell on our left and right and over our trenches (coal boxes and shrapnel being much in evidence). The day turned out fine but cold until the afternoon, when the sun came out. The guns began again at 3.45 p.m. and shells dropped on the trenches on our left; a nearby hayrick was set on fire. It was amusing to watch all the shells flying around; they burst just on our trenches but happily there were no casualties. Slept soundly from 10 p.m. until 1.30 a.m.; felt stiff in the joints and with numbed limbs when I woke up. Some cabbage stalks were mistaken for the enemy digging in the mist. No fire was directed at them but it shows how one can imagine things and also how advisable it is to look at the ground in daylight if possible.

6th November (in the trenches): Cold and damp as usual; stiff in joints; dirty and covered in mud but feel happy. Men all ready to receive any of the enemy who would like to come on. Ammunition cleaned and put ready on a board just by the right elbow; rifles cleaned, bolts oiled; head cover and box loopholes supplied. Foggy morning; at about 9 a.m. enemy commenced the usual morning shelling with shrapnel on our trenches; no damage but with first lot a splinter hit a man on the hand. On our left the artillery are at it; sounds like the French guns. Communication trenches being dug back and latrine places being made. In our trench are Major Bogle and myself, Dr Milliage, Corpl. Huitt, Ptes Donarchy and Lyddy. We dig to get warm; no wash for four days; living in hope of hearing good news. Most think it will all be over by Christmas; let us hope so for every one of us has had quite enough of this murderous war. At about 4 p.m. shelling commenced again; one trench was blown in and Pte Laxton was buried but dug out. A few very dangerous hits on trench; Major Loma was in trench when shots fell.

7th November (Saturday): Very cold night and very misty. Not much sleep, too cramped and cold. Moved up and down the trenches to keep warm; charcoal issued for cooking purposes. With the men not being able to get a hot drink day after day it begins to tell on the stomach. As the fog lifted the German shells began to drop as if to say 'good morning'. They whistle over and fall very near; Pte Bond is wounded in the foot by a splinter. The shells burst with a big roar and spread so. Snipers as usual send their morning salute. The guns all round are barking and flinging shells all over the area. We make a good trench dugout to sleep in; perhaps it will be more comfortable — not so cramped and cold. The dew is very thick and one is quite wet through by morning. Still no wash, good beard. Troops are more cheerful; good news from Russia. Wrote letters to Nan and P, David, Maudie, Mabel, Hamer. At about 7.30 a.m. an attack took place on our right and then developed on our left (N. Staffords); the enemy had one machine-gun. The whole line took up the fire as one man, then the artillery fire commenced on both sides. Shells came whistling down on our trenches, exploding with bright flashes and a loud roar. Very cold during the night; cannot feel feet but dangerous to show oneself above ground as the enemy is alert for any movement.

8th November (Sunday): Very cold in the morning, same old fog and mist; sun came out at 9.30 a.m.; morning salute, shell-fire, no damage. Change of socks; first change for a month. Becoming very tiring in the trenches as one cannot possibly move out except at night, when it is all muddy from the heavy dew. Battle raging on our left with heavy artillery fire and, in the evening, musketry; attack evidently took place.

9th November: Last night one could not help thinking of earlier youthful days, going to Free Trade Hall as a young man on a Sunday; pleasant recollections. People praying all over the world for peace; who is to get the victory? Received letter from Nan which was cheering especially when read under difficulties. Very cold indeed; we got a blanket, thank goodness. Artillery still at it. What would we give for a wash and change and a nice warm bed (a luxury). Digging is our pastime whilst waiting for shells and the evening to come. My feet were numbed when I woke from a sleep in the small dugout; very stiff in joints. Comforts of life one has to forget but not the pleasant thoughts of knowing that someone feels for you at home in England and whom we are all fighting for. A scare came down the line of trenches about 1.30 a.m. that six Germans were creeping up to our lines; with investigation they turned out to be REs working on wire. Pig shot — result pork chops for tea. Snipers very active, some shots fell on our trench; very close. Wrote home.

10th November: Trench digging and communication trenches improved considerably. Shells commenced to come over at about 11 a.m. in answer to our batteries. On our left the roar of guns continues with awful noise; there must be about 100 guns engaged from the sound of the cannonade. The snipers send several shots in our trench having apparently discovered our exact position; we have to be very careful. As I write this a shot just struck the trench immediately above me — very close! No wash or shave for nine days; beard growing pretty well. Troops in good spirits; comforts are being sent in plenty and they are most welcome. Shells are hitting our trenches and we expect to get a heavy shelling soon as they seem gradually to be finding the range. On our left the artillery are banging at each other; big guns are at it and the fire of these must be awful. Shrapnel flies about all over the place here. We dig ourselves in; the only thing is that we may be buried alive by the explosions of the 'Coal boxes'.

11th November: On duty until 2 a.m.; woke the Major at 2.30 a.m. Went from one trench to another to see that everyone is on the alert; some sentries imagined they could see the Germans cutting the wire and pulling up the posts but it was not so. A few shells fell on the trenches in the morning. A rumour brought by the cook was that 6000 Germans had been killed or captured on our left; hope it is true. Very cold, digging to keep oneself warm. At about 4 p.m. a regular bombardment on our trench took place for about ten minutes; the range was accurate and they practically smothered some of our men. Major Bogle was wounded in my dugout which I had occupied just before. We were sorry to lose him; the Company feels it and I feel that I had lost a very dear friend. At about 6.30 p.m. rain came down in torrents and then some snipers — about thirty I should think — commenced rapid fire which drew our fire. Then the artillery started on our left; the fire was awful, crashing and banging for about half an hour; glad when it ceased.

12th November: During the night the rain had no pity; the men and myself are like muddy navvies, up to our necks in mud and wet through. Awfully miserable as there are no means of drying clothes and the trenches are ankle deep in mud. Still the shells come over and the snipers are engaged on our front. Report received that the Russians are in all the German territory in the east; very good news. The troops cook their food in charcoal which burns all night in bully beef tins with holes bored in them. The only trouble is that they are inclined to make a lot of smoke which draws enemy artillery fire. Shaking out ourselves from wet and mud with sun above for a time which did wonders; got nearly dry. Snipers had a go at our wet clothes which were on the sides of the trenches.

Author's note: The remainder of November 1914 continued more or less on the same lines, with the battalion continuing to suffer in waterlogged trenches and under constant artillery and sniper fire, with little cover from either the elements or from enemy activity. During part of that time the First Battle of Ypres had been raging further north, which resulted in the near annihilation of the old British Regular Army. The way to the Channel ports, however, remained barred to the enemy. November turned into December and any thoughts of the war ending by Christmas promptly dissolved.

23rd December: In billets near Armentières. Billets are in a bad state. Snowing and very cold.

24th December (Christmas Eve): We sit round a fire in the Engine room of our billets and talk of old times. A good many officers came to visit us. We have plenty of luxuries.

25th December (Christmas Day): Church and Holy Communion. Walk to Erquinghem; a good frosty morning; people jolly, everyone seems happy; no firing heard at all. Troops in trenches making friends with the Germans; several football matches took place between our men and the Germans. A little firing occurred at night time.

26th December (Saturday): To the trenches, Houplines. Marched from Erquinghem to the trenches at Houplines, relieving the Camerons. Snowing and very cold and we went in pitch darkness. Just getting nicely settled down when the stream in front of our trenches burst and we were knee deep very soon. Capt. Maconochy and myself were left without dugouts and were wet through. It was freezing hard and very uncomfortable; was pleased when daylight came. All our belongings were sodden but we made the best of it and all very cheerful. Mud and water in the trenches and raining. Cold — one could not get warm. Dug a trench in rear passing through a dozen graves of our men killed and buried earlier. About forty Germans are buried just in front. Snipers very busy but we kept them down a bit; they were cleverly concealed. Trenches only 200 yards away from Germans (further at some points).

27th December (Sunday): Trenches. After a cold and rainy night went round the trenches at 3 a.m. through mud and water; got wet through. Pitch dark; hailstones were falling heavily; impossible to keep dry; awfully cold. Trench dug in rear getting full of water. The Germans are seen carrying timber to build up their trenches which are just as bad as ours. Our artillery dropped several shells right on top of their trenches; they also dropped two shells near our own trenches — one twenty yards in front and one the same distance in rear — very dangerous! I was quite close and saw them drop. Our trenches are very bad and getting worse with mud; still wet.

28th December: Still raining; all are suffering from colds. No coke issued to make fires; very bad. The water is now about waist deep in parts; by-pass trenches are being dug round the main trench. My feet have been wet for two days and nights and all clothing, blankets etc. are wet through; still raining. The snipers are not too energetic today — too cold for them? Probably getting over Christmas fare. Shall probably be relieved tomorrow. My legs are getting numbed with cold and sometimes cannot feel them. Dugouts are falling in all along the trenches; all have to be built up again. Enemy snipers are active; some shots very close but no damage done.

29th and 30th December: Trenches are very bad but are improved by aid of footboards and fascines; also planks. Three pumps are working at baling out water which is very deep in places. At this point the German trenches are about 400-500 yards away. On New Year's Eve a temporary truce was made between the Germans and some British troops, in some places the dead, which had been left for some time, being buried with both sides showing respect. After the truce had expired, the firing commenced as usual, just to show no friendliness really existed in warfare.

Thus the war continues — and vigorously too!

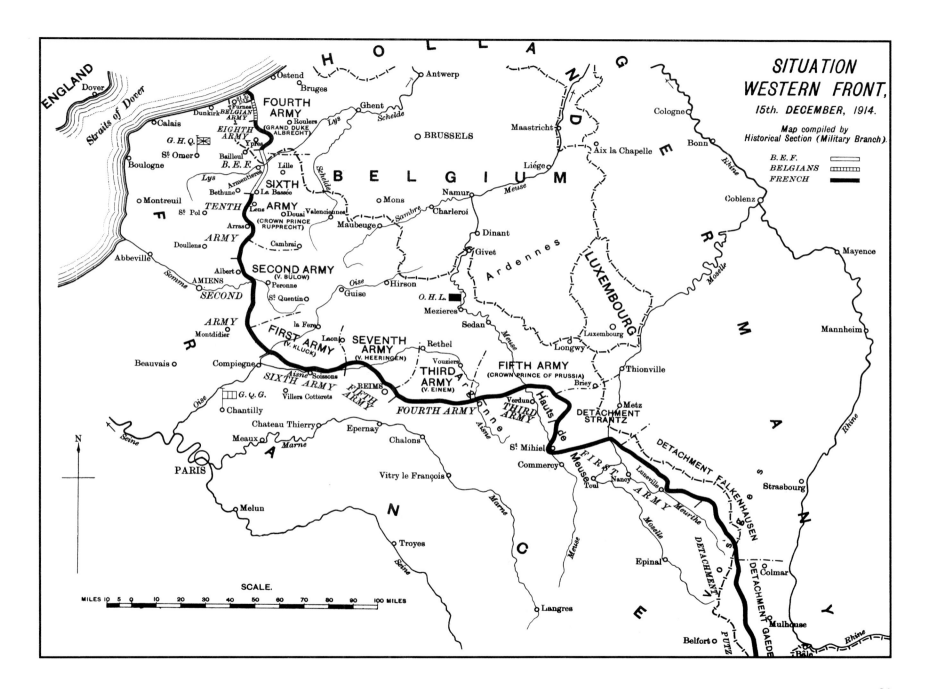

SITUATION
WESTERN FRONT,
15th. DECEMBER, 1914.

Map compiled by
Historical Section (Military Branch).

B.E.F.
BELGIANS
FRENCH

ENGLAND

Dover

Straits of Dover

HOLLAND

Ostend
Bruges
Antwerp

Cologne
Bonn

GERMANY

Maastricht

Aix la Chapelle

Liége

Coblenz

Mayence

Mannheim

Strasbourg

Colmar

Mulhouse

Bâle

Rhine

Calais
Dunkirk
Furnes
BELGIAN ARMY
FOURTH ARMY
(GRAND DUKE ALBRECHT)
Roulers
Ghent
Lys
Schelde
BRUSSELS

EIGHTH ARMY
Ypres
G.H.Q.
St Omer
Bailleul
B.E.F.
Lille
SIXTH
Boulogne
Lys
Armentieres
Bethune
La Bassée
ARMY
Mons
Namur
Meuse

Montreuil
St Pol
TENTH
Lens
Douai
Valenciennes
ARMY
(CROWN PRINCE RUPPRECHT)
Maubeuge
Charleroi
Sambre
Dinant

Arras
ARMY
Cambrai
Doullens
SECOND ARMY
(V. BÜLOW)
Abbeville
Albert
AMIENS
Peronne
St Quentin
Oise
Guise
Hirson
Givet
Ardennes
LUXEMBOURG

Somme
SECOND
la Fere
O.H.L.
Mezieres
Luxembourg
Longwy
Thionville
Moselle

ARMY
Montdidier
FIRST ARMY
(V. KLUCK)
Laon
SEVENTH ARMY
(V. HEERINGEN)
Rethel
Vouziers
Sedan
Meuse

Beauvais
Compiegne
Aisne
Soissons
THIRD ARMY
(V. EINEM)
FIFTH ARMY
(CROWN PRINCE OF PRUSSIA)
Briey
Metz
DETACHMENT STRANTZ

SIXTH ARMY
G.Q.G.
Chantilly
REIMS
Villers Cotterets
FIFTH ARMY
FOURTH ARMY
Verdun
Hauts de Meuse
THIRD ARMY
St Mihiel
DETACHMENT FALKENHAUSEN

Chateau Thierry
Epernay
Chalons
Aisne
Commercy
FIRST ARMY
Laneville
Nancy
Meurthe

Meaux
Marne
Toul
Moselle

PARIS
Vitry le François
Marne

Melun

N
Seine

FRANCE

Troyes
Meuse
Epinal
DETACHMENT GAEDE

Langres
Belfort
PUTZ
DETACHMENT
Rhine

SCALE.

MILES 10 5 0   10   20   30   40   50   60   70   80   90   100 MILES

81

Christmas Bells

1914

By AUSTIN DOBSON

WHAT do your clear bells ring to me
In this glad hour of jubilee ?
Not joy, not joy. I hear instead:
      So many dead ! so many dead !

So many who but yesterday
Went out, great-hearted, to the fray,
Giving up all that they could give
To fight, forsooth, for "right to live".

Life was before them. larger scope,
Space for the Future's quenchless hope —
Now they are stark and cold afar,
Pawns in the ruthless Game of War.

Glory and Power, Honour, Ease,
What are all those, to-day, to these ?
What their laudation, now they lie
  Piled in the trenches, three feet high ?

This surely, that, to duty's call,
They answered nobly, each and all;
This also, that their blood is seed
For bonds unloosed, for peoples freed !

    *   *   *

Not less your peal of bells to me
Rings mourning more than jubilee :
Listen ~ and with uncovered head ~
      So many dead ! so many dead !

HAROLD NELSON

Cards and original cigarettes in one of the Christmas 1914 gift tins distributed to troops by Princess Mary and retained by WWI veteran, the late 'Josh' Grover (see page 235).

Ground south of Messines and near Ploegsteert where fraternising between British and German soldiers took place on Christmas Day 1914. The Messines Ridge is in the far distance — the dome of Messines Church on the right. Ploegsteert Wood is to the rear of where this picture was taken. Fraternising also took place in other parts of the line further south. It was severely frowned upon by the authorities of both sides, and orders were issued forbidding any future such contact with the enemy.

1915

Corporal Robertson wades along a flooded trench, 5th January 1915. [IWM]

Men of 'A' Company in the trenches, January 1915. Note the rum jar on the right, its contents doubtless put to good use. The longer the war continued, the deeper and more complicated the trench systems would become, while in wet areas they had to be built up above ground with sandbags. [IWM]

1st Cameronians: Captain Lee gets on with his writing. [IWM]

2nd Cameronians: The Orchard, La Cordonnerie Farm, Rue du Bois, 5th January 1915. [IWM]

Breastwork and mud, Rue du Bois, February 1915. [IWM]

Five of 'A' Company with not much to smile about. [IWM]

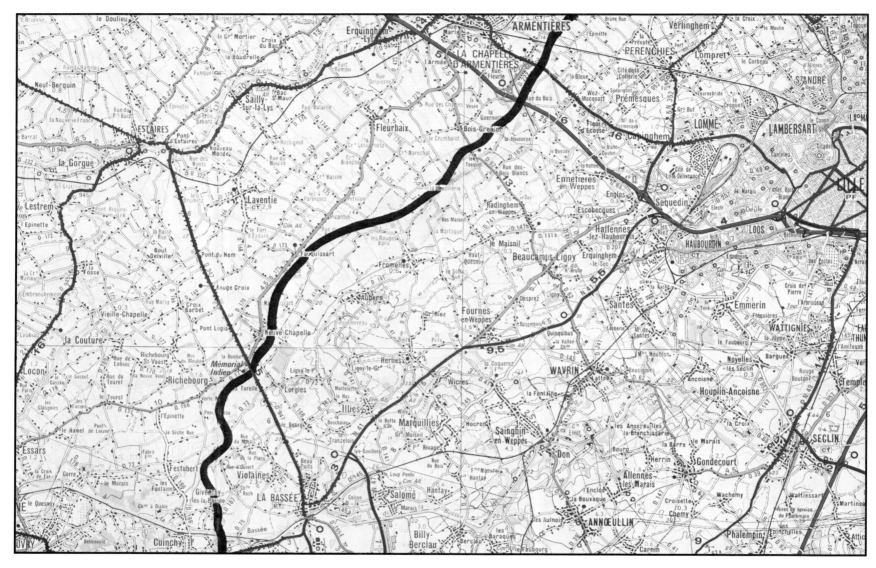

Modern map on which has been transposed the approximate position of the British front line in mid-1915 from south-east of Armentières to south-west of La Bassée. Most of the terrain in this sector is flat and waterlogged in winter — a factor which caused many problems for the troops, as can be seen from the photographs of the Cameronians on the preceeding pages. Institut Geographique, France, Carte Touristique No. 2 Lille–Dunkirk. 1:1000000 1cm represents 1km. [See acknowledgements]

View from a former German observation post on Fromelles Church looking towards ground over which the Australians attacked. [IWM]

The village of Fromelles from the opposite direction to the photograph taken from the observation post. This village was attacked in May 1915 without success when an attempt was made to capture Aubers Ridge. It was also the scene of fierce fighting in July 1916 when it was assaulted by Australian and British troops in a diversionary attack aimed at easing the pressure during the Somme battles. That too was unsuccessful and losses were high, particularly those of the Australians, who never forgave the British Staff for what was considered to be an ill-conceived and badly planned battle.

Aubers Ridge from the Armentières road — the church tower on the skyline. Although only a comparatively small hill, the ridge stood out from the surrounding flat countryside and gave excellent observation to the Germans for many miles around. Aubers was a First Army objective in May 1915, but the attack failed with heavy losses and it remained in German hands until it finally fell to British troops in 1918.

VC Corner Military Cemetery, about two miles north-west of Fromelles, created after the Armistice with 410 graves of men who fell in the abortive attack of July 1916 and whose remains were subsequently found on the battlefield. On the rear wall are the names of 1,298 Australians who fell and whose graves are not known. VC corner was the name given to the crossing of the Rue Delvas and the Rue du Bois. Two VCs were won in this sector during the 1915 Aubers Ridge attack.

Suicide Corner, on the Armentières–Neuve Chapelle Road. The row of buildings were used by the RHA and RFA for observation to help the guns cut the German wire. [IWM]

An 18-pounder field gun in a concealed position. [IWM]

Minus shell-holes, plus roof.

A spot well-known to British troops in 1915, near Neuve Chapelle.

The grave of twenty-four men of the 2nd Battalion, East Lancashire Regiment, who were killed by one shell on 14th March 1915, during a rifle inspection at the Rouge Croix crossroads on the La Bassée road. [IWM]

The graves of many thousands of men of the British Empire are to be found in the area around the Rouge Croix crossroads today and the Commonwealth War Graves Commission's signposts point to just some of them via the road on the right.

Obliteration has long since given way to cultivation at Neuve Chapelle crossroads. In the distance, the Bois du Biez. This is where 1st Royal West Kents put up a stout defence in late October 1914 before the village fell to the Germans.

THE BATTLE OF NEUVE CHAPELLE

10th–13th March 1915

Neuve Chapelle was the first real offensive by the British on the Western Front and the first of the 'battles of the trenches' after stalemate had set in several months earlier. The village had been captured by the Germans in 1914 and had been the scene of a gallant stand by the 1st Royal West Kents in the region of the crossroads to the south-west of the village, where the Indian Memorial now stands.

The battle stemmed from a suggestion by Sir John French to Général Joffre for a combined Franco-British attack, and at Chantilly on 21st January 1915 basic agreement was reached by the two military leaders on the timing and places for the offensive. The British would attack in the direction of La Bassée and Aubers Ridge (with an eye to a possible later assault towards Lille) and the French objective was the dominant Vimy Ridge further south. As things turned out, however, the British assault became entirely independent apart from limited French artillery support.

The enemy trenches at Neuve Chapelle formed a large bulge in the British sector. This favoured the Germans in a number of ways — including general observation and sniping, etc. — and capture of this salient would be of some benefit, apart from promoting the good name of the British Army by showing its offensive capabilities.

On 15th February 1915 Sir John French approved a plan submitted by General Haig, commander of the First Army, which would undertake the task, and initial instructions were issued to those who would be involved. The First Army held a thirteen-mile frontage from the La Bassée Canal to Bois Grenier and consisted of six divisions, while the Germans opposite had only two divisions, which were part of their Sixth Army. Their troops were particularly thin on the ground in the Neuve Chapelle sector (although they were rapidly reinforced later). They were in fact aware of an impending attack but were not certain when it would be delivered.

The British troops allocated for the assault were two infantry brigades (23rd and 25th) of the 8th Division of IV Corps and the Garhwal Brigade of the Meerut Division of the Indian Corps. Some 340 guns were assembled and the Royal Flying Corps carried out reconnaissance and observation duties for the artillery which, because of the flat landscape, was particularly helpful.

March 10th was chosen as the date of the attack and on March 9th the assault battalions began to move into position. Dawn on the 10th was misty, which hindered artillery observation and aerial reconnaissance, but at 7.30 a.m. the British bombardment opened up on the German trenches, which were soon covered in a pall of smoke and shell-bursts.

The deadly German Maxim. Artillery, not the machine-gun, in fact claimed the most lives, but the machine-gun took its fearsome toll — especially during attacks made over open ground. Once out in No Man's Land the advancing troops made prime targets for the German machine-gunners, who raked them with fire. Shelling caused endless casualties behind the lines as well as up at the front. The British Machine-Gun Corps was formed in October 1915. [IWM]

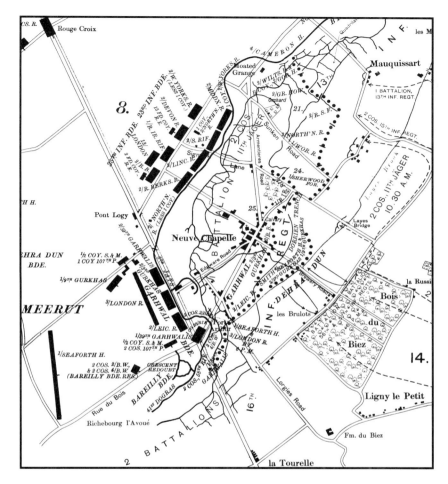

A private memorial to Second Lieutenant A. W. Crichton of the 3rd Battalion, Royal Fusiliers, who was believed to have been killed near this spot at the Battle of Neuve Chapelle. The memorial was originally closer to the nearby crossroads but was moved to its present location behind the imposing Indian Memorial because of road widening.

At 8.05 a.m., to the roar of the guns, the attacking troops went over the top and, except for an error in direction by some companies of the Garhwal Brigade, the assault went well. Leading battalions of 25th Brigade got into the village at 8.50 a.m., with the German first line having been broken at several points. Dazed survivors offered little resistance and several hundred prisoners were taken.

Further to the left things had not gone so well on the 23rd Brigade front owing to the wire not being properly cut because some medium guns had not arrived. There the 2nd Middlesex came under heavy machine-gun fire which annihilated the leading waves. The 2nd Scottish Rifles were also badly hit.

In spite of these set-backs the 23rd and 25th Brigades had reached their objectives by about 1 p.m. and the reserve brigade of 8th Division (24th Brigade) was ordered to assemble ready to move forward. Unfortunately a muddle occurred as a result of difficulties in communications and it was not until 6 p.m. that a further advance began on that front. Meanwhile success had been achieved in the Indian Corps' sector, where some of the men actually reached the Bois du Biez before being forced to withdraw to the Layes Brook. Even so, a maximum advance of 1,200 yards had been effected, and the ruined village was now in British hands.

The famous crossroads which in 1915 were 'berthed' in Port Arthur — the name given to the part of the British line which formed a salient here just south-west of Neuve Chapelle (the village church being just visible). An artillery observation post once existed just behind the estaminet on the corner.

Over the Top. Bodies of 2nd Cameronians lying on the parapet of a front line trench, Battle of Neuve Chapelle, March 10th–13th 1915, 8th Division. [IWM]

At the crossroads, the entrance to the impressive Memorial to the Indian Missing, on the walls of which over 4,800 names are inscribed. Nearby, on the La Bassée road, is a Portuguese Military Cemetery. This was the area where the Germans broke through in 1918.

Looking across the former battlefield of Neuve Chapelle towards the church from the La Bassée road. This ground was once slashed with trenches and was the scene of fierce actions in 1914, 1915 and 1918. The British front line at the end of the battle in March 1915 was on the approximate position of the tyre marks.

Photograph of a coloured lithograph after J. P. Bendle (published by George Pulman & Sons Ltd, London, 1916) of men of the 2nd Rifle Brigade and 2/39 Garhwal Rifles clearing the village of Neuve Chapelle, March 1915. [National Army Museum]

Neuve Chapelle main street in the 1980s.

The Moated Grange stood where this photograph was taken north-east of the village. The view is looking towards the Bois du Biez across ground once covered with hissing bullets and exploding shells.

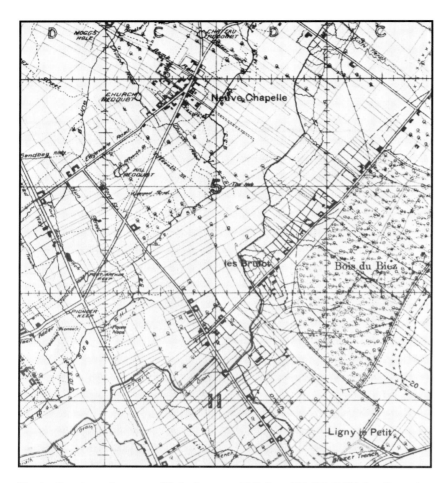

Part of a trench map, Richebourg, Edition 7B 36 S.W.3, after the capture of Neuve Chapelle, with the British front line just to the east of the village and the German trenches in front of the Bois du Biez.

Above right: Neuve Chapelle immediately after the battle, March 1915. The village was taken by the 25th Brigade, 8th Division. The crucifix remained undamaged to the end of the war. [IWM]

Below right: Crucifix in Neuve Chapelle in the late 1980s.

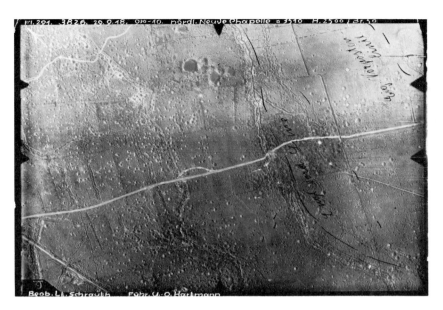

German aerial photo of the Neuve Chapelle battlefield, 1918.

Outside Charing Cross Hospital, London, where many of the wounded were taken to recuperate. [IWM]

Orders were issued for a further attack on a wide frontage following a short bombardment at 6.45 a.m. on the 11th but everywhere the troops became bogged down in the morning mist as the Germans put up a determined resistance from their — as yet unfinished — second line.

The Germans themselves then delivered a strong counter-attack with 6,000 men at 5 a.m. on the 12th under cover of the mist but they were driven back with heavy losses. The British 7th Division had now been brought into the fray, albeit belatedly and not without some confusion, but they halted the German advance at a place called the Moated Grange. The enemy was also held elsewere.

At 12.30 p.m. on that same day the British launched a fresh attack but the mist caused complete chaos and the assault ground to a halt all along the front.

At 9 p.m. the commander of the Indian Corps ordered a cessation of attacks, and at 10.40 p.m. General Haig instructed the two corps commanders to cancel further operations. Thus the battle petered out; the line was consolidated and reliefs were arranged.

British losses in the Battle of Neuve Chapelle in killed, wounded and missing amounted to 583 officers and 12,309 other ranks, and the German casualties were also about 12,000. Both sides considered that they had won a victory. The British were at least able to claim a limited breakthrough. The French too were sufficiently impressed for Joffre to send some of his corps commanders to find out more about the British success in ousting the enemy from entrenched positions.

Even the Germans had been made well aware of the new aggressive spirit of the British, although in their eyes the battle vindicated their own tactics, particularly in relation to the prompt manning of their second line of defence and the closing of a breach. It was, though, a close-run thing, at least in the early stages of the battle; and if that momentum could have been kept up, who can say what the final result might have been.

THE BATTLE OF AUBERS RIDGE

9th May 1915

The dust had hardly settled following the somewhat unsatisfactory result of the Battle of Neuve Chapelle when, on 24th March, Général Joffre enquired whether the British would be prepared to co-operate with the French in a combined offensive towards the Douai Plain and Aubers Ridge. It was similar to what had been discussed a while earlier.

With everything pointing to the Germans planning an offensive in Russia — and even reducing their forces on the Western Front for that purpose — the time appeared to be right for the proposed assault, and on 1st April Sir John French confirmed his readiness to attack in about four weeks time. It was felt that such an offensive would not only cause the pressure on the Russians to be eased but, with the German reserves already committed on the Eastern Front, could possibly even lead to the enemy being driven out of France and Belgium.

The French Tenth Army, suitably reinforced, had as its main objective the crest of Vimy Ridge between Farbus and Souchez, which would enable it to overlook the Douai Plain — with further advances in mind. Auxiliary operations were to be mounted the day before and the day after the main attack, during which the eastern spur of the Notre Dame de Lorrette Ridge was to be taken.

The British attack by the First Army was to be directed towards Aubers Ridge and La Bassée, with possibly ten divisions being employed and about 600 guns, 100 of them heavy. Some assistance from French heavy artillery was envisaged. The initial main attack was to be by I Corps and the Indian Corps on the line Festubert–Neuve Chapelle, and a secondary attack was to be mounted further north by IV Corps in the direction of Aubers–Fromelles, with both forces converging to obtain a foothold on the ridge at Aubers,

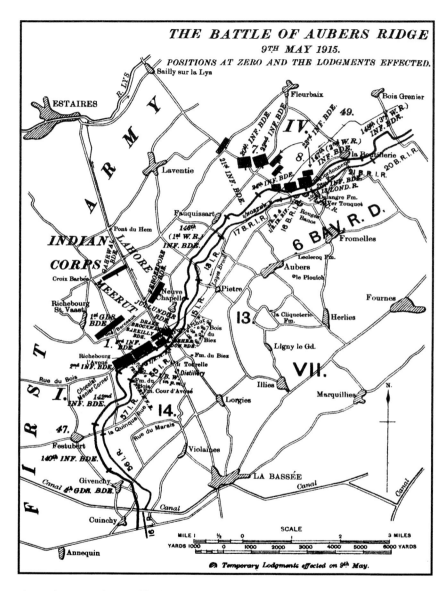

thereby cutting off those Germans within the pincer movement. If success were achieved, more distant objectives would be attacked.

A German signal station on Aubers Ridge, 1919. [IWM]

Ex-German strongpoint and observation post in Aubers village.

On 22nd April the Second Battle of Ypres began in the north, during which poison gas was introduced by the Germans, a sinister development which was to lead to great suffering on both sides as its arbitrary use increased. It continued until 25th May, with heavy casualties being incurred by both sides. However, although the front had been broken wide open — with French North African troops fleeing from this new horror weapon — the Germans failed to follow up their advantage. With the Canadians holding fast on the right flank in desperate conditions the initial advantage obtained by the enemy was lost, and the British front was stabilised further back.

In spite of the savage fighting in the Ypres Salient, preparations continued for the proposed May offensive. The French planned to attack on 7th May and the British on 8th May. Changes were made in divisional dispositions, and the Royal Flying Corps carried out defensive patrols and reconnaissance. Partly because of shortages of ammunition and heavy guns, the British arranged a short and intense bombardment similar to that of Neuve Chapelle. The French, on the other hand, opted for a bombardment of at least four days, mainly by heavy guns of which they had a good supply.

On 6th May it rained heavily, and on the 7th a dense mist covered the battle area. It was similar in the French sector and in consequence it was decided that the attacks by both armies should be simultaneous instead of on consecutive days, and would go in on 9th May. For the British the task would be far more difficult than at Neuve Chapelle, as the Germans had learned their lesson from that battle and had been devoting much time and energy to building up strong fortifications, including well-concealed machine-gun emplacements every twenty yards. They also increased their trench garrisons opposite the First Army and even covered their communication trenches in order to conceal the arrival of reinforcements. By the time of the assault the German lines had been converted into a formidable obstacle.

Aubers Ridge. The church and a sinister reminder of a past era.

Sunday, 9th May, dawned fine and clear. At 5 a.m. the early silence was broken by some 600 guns opening up the preliminary bombardment. When 5.30 a.m. arrived, it intensified. At 5.40 a.m. the infantry went over the top.

In spite of the bombardment some Germans actually showed their heads above the parapet, observing every movement. As the attackers left the cover of the trenches heavy machine-gun fire was immediately directed at them. Many men fell there and then — on the parapet and on the ladders placed in the trenches as an aid to climbing out. On the southern front the Indian Corps was hard hit, as were others, and its attacking brigades were met with a devastating fire from machine-guns and artillery. Much of the German wire was found to be uncut and most of the strongly-built six-foot-high enemy breastworks remained intact. However, in spite of the lack of adequate artillery support, and serious losses, parties of men from the various battalions pushed forward; but everywhere the intense enemy fire frustrated those gallant efforts and only a few men managed to get back to the British trenches during

Left: There are several pill-boxes in the vicinity of Aubers Ridge — remnants of the strong German defences on this once-important high ground. Ex-Captain G. B. Jameson, MC, RFA (aged 93 when this picture was taken and aged 98 in April 1991) stands in front of this battered specimen on the ridge and is holding the Kodak VPK camera which he had with him during the First World War. 'G.B.' went to France in October 1914 in the Northumberland Hussars Yeomanry and was there until January 1916, and then again (in the RFA) from July 1916 to November 1917. After that he served in Italy until April 1918 and then once more returned to France, where he remained until April 1919. He experienced much action and won his Military Cross in April 1917 as a result of a gallant exploit as a Battery Forward Observation Officer below Vimy Ridge (in the Oppy–Arleux sector) after it was captured by the Canadians, when he was instrumental in breaking up a strong German counter-attack with the accurate placing of heavy artillery fire.

daylight. The number of casualties was grievous: the 1st Division, for example, lost 85 officers and 2,135 men from the six battalions that crossed the British parapet; that is, about 60 per cent of their strength. The story was similar elsewhere.

A fresh attack was ordered for 2.40 p.m. by General Haig — which was later postponed to 4 p.m. Meanwhile, reliefs were carried out, and more losses accrued to German artillery fire. At 3.57 p.m. men of the 1st Black Watch dashed forward, their pipes playing them across No Man's Land. The Germans were taken by surprise and within minutes a number of the Highlanders reached the German parapet, where most of them were shot down. Everywhere on the southern front the story was repeated — the machine-guns taking a heavy toll of any British troops who tried to move forward. Many fell dead and others lay in No Man's Land waiting for darkness to come so that they could crawl back to the British line. The German infantrymen even exposed themselves recklessly by standing up and firing above the parapet in their eagerness to repulse the attack.

On the other sector 6,000 yards to the north, where two mines had been fired at 5.40 a.m., the assault was at first more successful — the Germans actually having been surprised in this sector — but there too things afterwards went badly. The 8th Division was aiming for Fromelles, and the 7th Division, just behind, had Aubers as one of its first objectives.

At one place an officer and about thirty men of the 2nd Northamptonshires managed to get into the German front line in spite of the heavy fire, but others were checked by the wire, which had not been properly cut. Nearby men of the 2nd Rifle Brigade and 1st Royal Irish Rifles (25th Brigade) rushed the German positions where the wire had in fact been well cut and regardless of heavy losses stormed the enemy breastworks and captured a number of prisoners. Great confusion then ensued, with some of the men retiring, and the German prisoners who were running for cover behind the British lines even being mistaken for a counter-attack. In the main the attack had come to a standstill. Those who had formed a lodgement found themselves cut off. Any movement became impossible because of the German fire from unattacked portions of the front.

General Haig nevertheless ordered the IV Corps commander, General Rawlinson, to press the attack. A renewed assault by 24th Brigade encountered violent artillery, machine-gun and rifle fire which quickly brought it to a halt. Yet another attack was ordered by Haig, which was later cancelled, and although further limited attempts were made to get forward during the night, these too ended in failure. By 3 a.m. on the 10th all the survivors were back in the British trenches and the enemy had regained his front line.

The results of the offensive of 9th May towards Aubers were a serious disappointment and General Haig ordered the IV Corps' attack to be suspended. Losses had been grave — 458 officers and 11,161 other ranks from the divisions engaged in the north and south. The failure was due, first, to the strength of the German defences, especially the concealed machine-guns; second, the acute shortage of heavy shells to batter down the strongly-built breastworks and other defence works; and third, inferior fuzes and ammunition. Another major drawback was the flatness of the terrain, which prevented proper artillery observation.

Further south, the French offensive of 9th May had met with initial success. One of the Tenth Army's corps had advanced two-and-a-half miles on a frontage of four miles after a heavy and prolonged bombardment. Fighting of a desperate ferocity, and at close quarters in the trenches, continued day and night for a week, with the commanding position of Notre Dame de Lorette being won, and Carency and Ablain St Nazaire gradually being captured house by house. Casualties, though, were extremely high, and the principal goal of Vimy Ridge had not been attained.

On 15th May Général Foch decided to continue the battle.

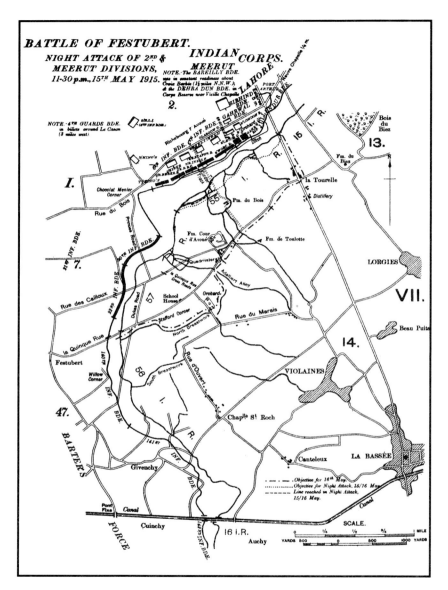

Map labels (clockwise / as shown):

BATTLE OF FESTUBERT.
NIGHT ATTACK OF 2ND & MEERUT DIVISIONS, 11·30 p.m., 15TH MAY 1915.
INDIAN CORPS.
MEERUT
NOTE:- The BAREILLY BDE. was in constant readiness about Croix Barbée (1½ miles N.N.W.); & the DEHRA DUN BDE. in Corps Reserve near Vieille Chapelle (¾ m.

NOTE:-4TH GUARDS BDE. in billets around Le Cœan (3 miles west).

LAHORE

Richebourg l' Avoué
Bois du Biez
Fm. du Biez
la Tourelle
Distillery
Fm. du Bois
Chocolat Menier Corner
Rue du Bois
LORGIES
Fm. Cour d'Avoué
Fm. de Toulotte
Quadrilateral
la Quinque Rue
School Houses
Orchard
Rue du Marais
Beau Puits
Stafford Corner
North Breastwork
VIOLAINES
Festubert
Willow Corner
South Breastwork
Chapelle St. Roch
LA BASSÉE
Canteleux
Givenchy
BARTERS
Pont Fixe
Canal
Cuinchy
16 i.R.
Auchy
FORCE

Objective for 16th May
Objective for Night Attack, 15/16 May
Line reached in Night Attack, 15/16 May.

SCALE.
¼   ½   ¾   1 MILE
YARDS 500   0   500   1000 YARDS

Right: an old British blockhouse/shelter in the main street of Festubert. For many years after the war it was used by a lady who made it her home.

THE BATTLE OF FESTUBERT

15th–25th May 1915

Considerable pressure was put on Sir John French by Général Joffre and Général Foch to continue offensive action and although Sir John was worried about the situation at Ypres, plus the overall shortage of shells and rifle ammunition (whereas the French had plenty of both), he consented to the First Army carrying out a fresh offensive. Relations between the two Allied commanders were at this time rather strained, with Joffre intimating that the British were not 'pulling their weight' and were thus upsetting his plans.

Following a request by Général Joffre, the French 58th Division, on the British right, was relieved and its positions south of the La Bassée Canal at Cuinchy were taken over by the British 1st Division. The Canadian Division, which was in reserve at Bailleul, was brought down to strengthen I Corps.

At a conference on 10th and 11th May General Haig submitted final details for the new attack — which would be in the Festubert sector — to his corps and divisional commanders. He now proposed to follow the French method of a long, slow and sustained bombardment by heavy artillery with a view to destroying the enemy's wire, machine-gun positions and other strongpoints before the infantry were committed to the battle. The date chosen for the infantry assault was 15th May.

As in the abortive offensive of 9th May, the plan was to attack at two points, except that in this case there would be a gap of only 600 yards between the two divisions concerned, i.e. the 7th Division north of Festubert and the 2nd Division below it. They were to join up by the time the first objective was reached about 1,000 yards ahead. A further bombardment was then to follow preparatory to attacking the next objective.

On 13th May the artillery bombardment began and continued all through the 14th and 15th, with three French heavy batteries giving assistance south of La Bassée Canal. The assault was postponed for 24 hours to give more time for wire cutting and at nightfall on the 15th the assaulting brigades moved up. During the 14th and 15th feints had been made to mislead the enemy by changing the pattern of the artillery fire, and other ruses.

At 11.30 p.m. on 15th May — a very dark night — the assault began, this being the first British night attack of the war. On the right of the 2nd Division the 6th Brigade met with complete success; the enemy breastworks were captured without difficulty, and the hoisting of two motor headlamps on the German parapet signalled that success. Unfortunately, the two other brigades involved were not so lucky and were raked with fire as soon as they started off, the Germans even using searchlights, apart from flares and other means of illuminating No Man's Land.

A further effort was ordered for 3.15 a.m. to coincide with a dawn attack by the 7th Division, but things went wrong owing to heavy losses, and the planned attack by the 2nd Division and the Meerut Division failed to materialise.

The 7th Division, which attacked at 3.15 a.m. on the 16th, was more successful, although severe casualties were incurred by the 2nd Queens and 1st Royal Welch Fusiliers of the 22nd Brigade who led the assault. In spite of this they stormed the German breastworks and continued to advance under heavy fire. By 7 a.m. the 22nd Brigade had completely gained its objective.

On the 20th Brigade's front, leading companies moved across No Man's Land before the bombardment ended, and in their keenness to reach the German parapet they suffered badly from the British shellfire. They still managed to take the enemy's front defences, but enfilade fire from a strongpoint named the 'Quadrilateral' caused a serious problem. The 2nd Scots Guards pressed on and reached their objective, then had to withdraw as shells from British guns came down on them. A German counter-attack began and one company of the Welch Fusiliers was virtually wiped out — just one officer and three other ranks surviving, only to be taken prisoner. By 9 a.m. the situation was that the 22nd Brigade had advanced about 600 yards; the 20th Brigade had been unable to advance beyond the enemy breastworks. The 2nd Queens lost 21 officers and 433 other ranks (out of 22 and 733 respectively); the 1st Royal Welch Fusiliers, 19 officers and 559 other ranks (out of 24 and 806). Only partial success had been achieved, and the two divisions had yet to join together.

Fresh orders were issued by the commander of I Corps (General Monro) to continue the operations, but further efforts were again unsuccessful at some points and only partially successful at others, with a withdrawal by the Welch Fusiliers and the Queens being necessary.

During the night of 16th May the Germans withdrew about three-quarters of a mile to a new line in the rear of their original front. This did not include the Quadrilateral and some other trenches. These were then subjected to a heavy bombardment from British guns, which caused a number of Germans to surrender under the white flag. They were shelled by their own artillery, and most were killed. Another 450 then ran towards the British trenches to surrender and they too were shelled by their own guns, though most of them made it and became prisoners of war.

At 8 a.m. on 17th May rain fell and continued at intervals during the day, turning the battlefield into a quagmire. At 9 a.m. a fresh attack was mounted and by 10.15 a.m. the

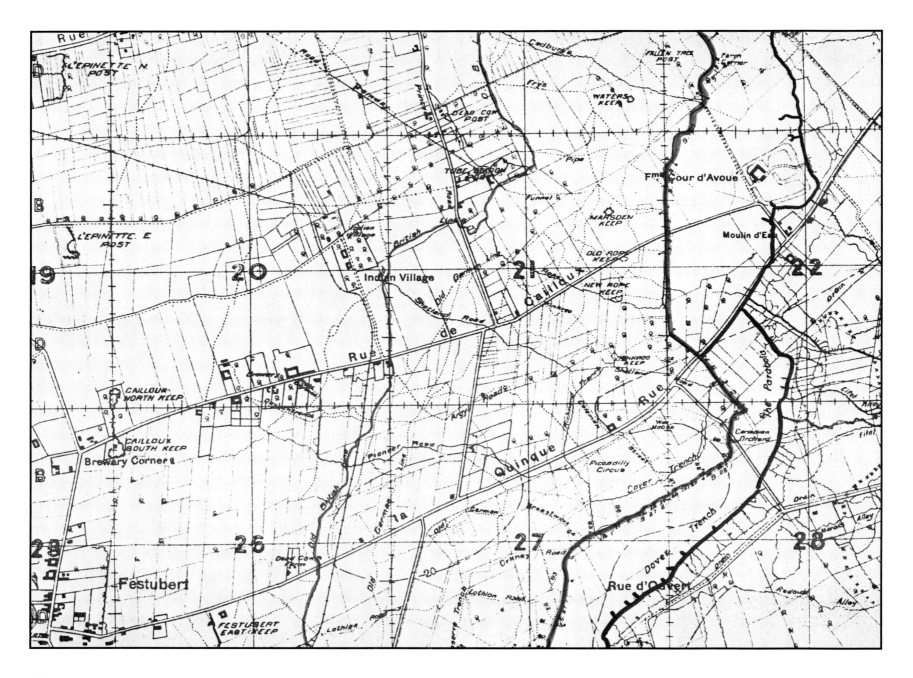

Quadrilateral was in the possession of 2nd Royal Fusiliers and 2nd Green Howards of 21st Brigade. Heavy enemy fire held up the advance north of the brigade front and frustrated further attempts to get forward from the Quadrilateral. The First Army's ultimate objective was then changed from Aubers Ridge to La Bassée and the 'Railway Triangle' south of the La Bassée Canal, all further attempts to move forward from the previous objective (La Quinque Rue, east of Festubert) having failed and the leading companies of the Guards having lost half of their men in a few minutes in advancing a mere 100 yards.

The 7th and 2nd Divisions were then withdrawn, and the 47th, 51st and Canadian Divisions took over the front. During the period 19th–22nd May the 3rd Canadian Brigade succeeded in pushing the line forward and occupied a position known as the 'Orchard', which then became 'Canadian Orchard'. The Canadian 2nd Brigade also moved forward about 150 yards. A main attack by the 47th Division and the Canadian Division took place on the night of 25th May and although this proved partially successful fierce German fire caused heavy losses amongst the attackers and brought the advance to a standstill.

On the 26th Sir John French decided to bring the battle to a close, and over the next couple of days these operations ground to a halt. Losses came to about 1,500 for the 47th Division and about 2,000 for the Canadians.

Battle of Festubert. German first line trenches with shells bursting in the distance. The ditch between the British and German lines was at some points 15 feet wide and filled with water. Festubert, May 1915. [IWM]

This area once shook to the rumble of intense artillery fire — it seems hard to imagine that this, today is the entrance to the sleepy village of Festubert, close to where the British front line once crossed the road.

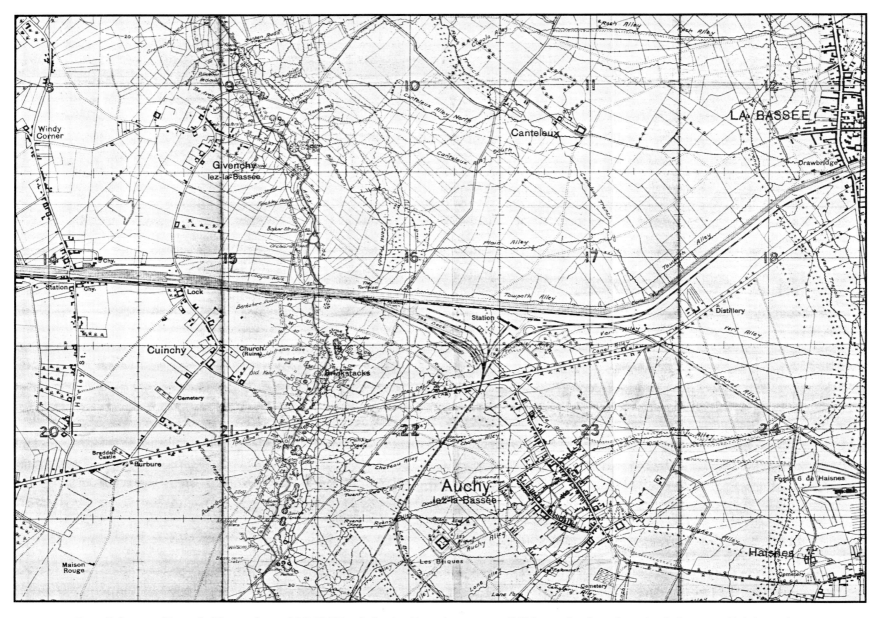

Detail from a Trench Map, sheet 36C N.W. of the La Bassée sector, Edition 7C, showing the infamous Brickstacks.

Ruined street in La Bassée, 1919. [IWM]

Street in La Bassée in the 1970s.

The railway line and the station at La Bassée. British harassing fire did the damage. October 1918. [IWM]

Women war workers with some of the shells for the hungry guns. [IWM]

Above and below: Cambrin and Cuinchy — two famous villages which were just behind the British lines in 1915. It was in this sector that the trenches remained almost static for four long years. A short distance beyond, on the Béthune–La Bassée road (seen in both pictures), were the infamous brickstacks.

The barricade at Cuinchy railway station, 27th June 1917. [IWM]

Cuinchy main street today, where it is crossed by the Béthune–La Bassée railway line.

Some of the infamous Cuinchy brickstacks. This photograph is part of a 13-section panorama taken north of Cuinchy and looking in the general direction of La Bassée, Auchy, etc. [IWM]

The former location of the Cuinchy brickstacks, and the site of intensive mining and counter-mining in 1915 between the British, who held one side of the huge stacks, and the Germans, who held the other (see aerial picture on page 109). The steep bank in the centre is the site of the Railway Triangle, held by the Germans, which gave them observation over much of the ground.

Inniskillings in a trench at Cuinchy brickfields, spring 1915, after a day of attack and counter-attack. A sniper's post was situated on the stack from which this picture was taken. [IWM]

Woburn Abbey Military Cemetery, Cuinchy, with the village church to the left. The cemetery was just behind the British lines and took its name from that given to a house to the east of it which was used as a Battalion Headquarters. 556 men are buried here, including 12 Canadians.

Cuinchy, from 'Old Boots Trench'. La Bassée, March 1916. [IWM]

Cuinchy, across quiet fields with not a trench to be seen.

La Bassée Canal, from Cuinchy Lock. [IWM]

A much changed La Bassée Canal, Cuinchy Lock, early 1980s.

Left: Aerial view of the La Bassée Canal at Cuinchy. The rows of brickstacks can be seen in the bottom left of the photograph. The British front line runs along the left group of stacks; the German along those on the right, with, in between, a series of overlapping mine craters. [IWM]

Below left: View along 'The Dock', with traces of old trenches still in existence on the left. The water tower is close to the site of the old brickstacks.

Below: Typical conditions in the La Bassée sector. [IWM]

A shell-damaged bridge over the canal, Cuinchy/Givenchy sector, June 1917. [IWM]

Modern bridge over the La Bassée Canal.

A photograph belonging to a 9-section panoramic view of east of Cambrin, looking in the direction of Auchy-lez-la Bassée. [IWM]

East of Cambrin on the opposite side of the Bethune–La Bassée road by the former location of the brickstacks. Traces of trenches could still be seen here when this picture was taken in the 1970s. In the right distance is the slag-heap of Fosse (Pit) 8, Loos, seen here before its top was flattened out. Auchy is beyond the bank on the left.

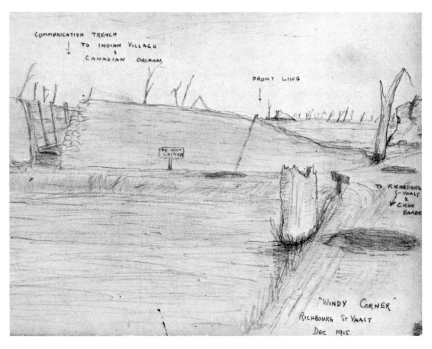

Left: A wartime drawing, by an unknown artist, of 'Windy Corner', three-quarters of a mile north of Cuinchy Station and west of Givenchy. The crossroads here were a regular target of German machine-gunners. [Picture: Richard Dunning]

Below left: Windy Corner in the early 1980s.

Below right: Guards Cemetery, close to Windy Corner, which contains 3,364 United Kingdom and 32 Canadian graves. A dressing station was once located nearby.

THE SECOND ACTION OF GIVENCHY

15th–16th June 1915

In deciding on 26th May to call a halt to the Battle of Festubert, Sir John French gave orders for offensive action to be continued where possible by First Army in support of the French attack in Artois. Because of ammunition shortages any assault was to be of a limited nature only, and on a narrow front. The location chosen was Givenchy, scene of stiff fighting in 1914, and the formations involved were the 7th and 51st Divisions of IV Corps, with the Canadians creating a defensive flank on the right. The latter also attacked a German strongpoint known as 'Stony Mountain'.

At 5.58 p.m. on 15th June, and after a 48-hour bombardment, a mine containing 3,000lb of ammonal was fired under the German lines — its destruction including a German gallery — and at the same time the infantry went over the top. Unfortunately the Germans were well-prepared and quickly manned the parapet, opening up a fierce fire with rifles and machine-guns. In spite of heavy losses (partly caused by the wire being inadequately cut) the enemy

trenches were entered at several points and some of the attackers even went beyond the German front line. Stiff fighting occurred; German bombers gained the upper hand and the attackers were gradually forced back.

Right: British positions at Givenchy, north of the La Bassée Canal. This picture was taken in 1920 and it emphasises the flat, bleak landscape of this sector. The village of Givenchy was of vital importance in 1918 and was a pivot of the British defences following the German breakthrough north of this area. [IWM]

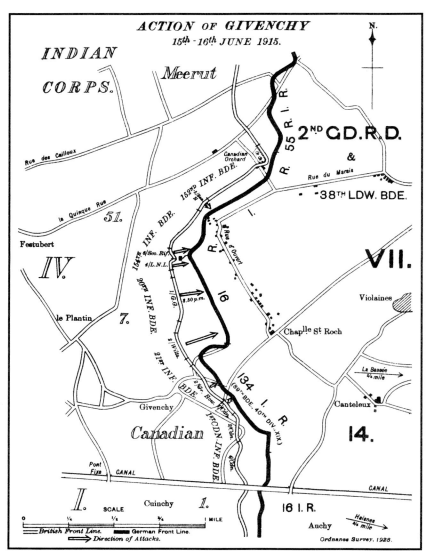

The outcome was the same when at 4.45 p.m. on the 16th the assault was repeated. Men of the 154th Brigade secured a lodgement in the German front line but were forced out again by a fierce counter-attack. Consideration was given to yet another attempt being made, but after a meeting between General Robertson, Chief of the General Staff, and General Haig it was agreed that consolidation should be the paramount objective. On the 19th Sir John French became aware that Général Foch had brought the Second Battle of Artois to an end, so there was no point in incurring further losses for any limited gains that might be

made in the Givenchy sector. Casualties in the IV Corps during the period 15th–21st June amounted to 3,811, most of which were incurred on the 15th and 16th.

Right: Béthune Clock Tower in modern times. The original belfry was built in mediæval times and, despite being badly damaged during the German offensive of 1918, it still stood defiantly whilst much of the town was destroyed around it. Béthune was an important rear base for British troops and was never captured, although it came close to being taken in 1918.

The Clock Tower, Béthune, 1919. [IWM]

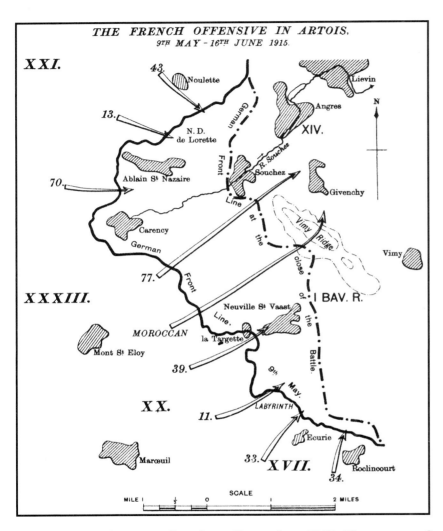

THE FRENCH OFFENSIVE IN ARTOIS,
9TH MAY - 16TH JUNE 1915.

Right, top to bottom: Souchez, November 1915. The scene of bitter hand-to-hand fighting in May–June 1915, Souchez was recaptured by the French on 26th September. [IWM]

Life and happiness: there could hardly be a greater contrast.

The village of Souchez — once almost obliterated — as it is now.

A wartime photograph of the extreme slope of Notre Dame de Lorette Ridge — its lofty eastern spur won by the French on 9th May 1915, after terrible fighting. A Gallic legend declares that victory in every war will fall to whoever becomes conqueror of this chain of hills. [IWM]

The eastern spur of Notre Dame de Lorette, covered with French graves; looking towards the mining areas of Lens. This enormous cemetery, which is almost opposite Vimy Ridge, contains the remains of 40,000 French soldiers, many of whom died in the fierce fighting for this vital hill in 1915. [Photo: John Thompson]

Aerial picture of Notre Dame de Lorette French National Military Cemetery. [Author/WFA]

East of Souchez. Zouave Valley — below the western slopes of Vimy Ridge and scene of particularly bitter fighting in 1915 when the French failed in their attempt to capture these vital heights. Relics of trenches are in abundance here and on the right is Zouave Valley British Military Cemetery. This area also became well-known to the Canadians, ninety-three of whom are buried in the cemetery.

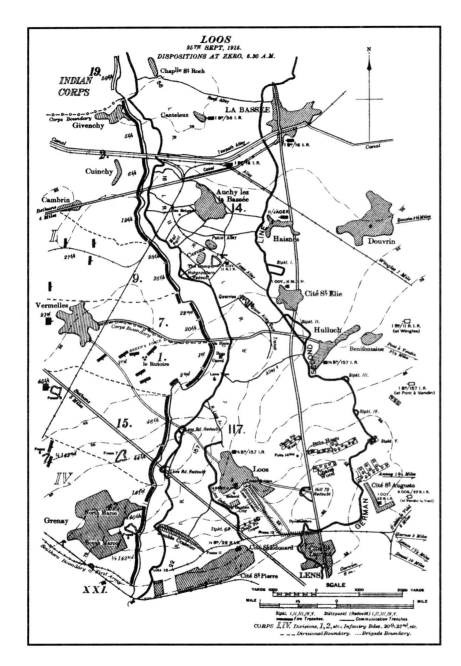

Photograph of a watercolour (artist unknown) of an attack by the 2nd Battalion of the Royal Munster Fusiliers at Loos, 1915. [National Army Museum]

THE BATTLE OF LOOS

25th September—8th October 1915

The Battle of Loos was actually something of a disaster. But it was a disaster which stemmed mainly from the insistence of Général Joffre, supported by Général Foch, in choosing the ground over which the British First Army was to attack in co-operation with major French offensives in the Champagne and Artois areas. Both Sir John French and the First Army commander, General Sir Douglas Haig, were strongly against the plan, which they believed to be ill-considered owing to the nature of the terrain in the British sector, which was flat, provided very little cover, and was dominated by huge slag-heaps from the coal mines within the area. These not only gave the Germans superb observation but afforded them ideal means with which to sweep the ground with machine-gun fire. Mine machinery was also used for observation purposes, including the lattice iron-work at Loos itself — 'Tower Bridge' as it was called.

The French plan was to assault a huge bulge in the Allied line simultaneously from the south, in the Champagne district, and in the northern (Artois) sector towards Vimy Ridge, with the British First Army in between, the objective being to cut off three German armies within the bulge, or to force their retreat back towards the Meuse, and thus possibly bring the war to an end. Neither Sir John French nor General Haig accepted the strategy, as apart from the difficult terrain in the Loos/Lens area there was a shortage of guns (especially the heavy type) and ammunition was far from plentiful at that time. Both preferred to wait until the spring of 1916 when many more men and much more war material would be available for a major offensive. General Haig also believed that it would be far more advantageous for the British to attack further north, including the Ypres/Messines sector, and both he and Sir John French envisaged that the proposed French plan would result in heavy British casualties. Sadly this forecast proved to be correct, with the French also suffering huge losses.

In spite of repeated strong protests by both French and Field Marshal Lord Kitchener, the British Secretary of State for War, Joffre refused to give way, and following a visit to France Lord Kitchener agreed to the plan being given the go-ahead. He was swayed not just by Joffre's eloquence, but by the overall strategic situation, the Russians having suffered a serious defeat in the East and the Italians (who had come into the war on the side of the Allies in May 1915) also being hard hit on their front. Also, the Gallipoli campaign had proved to be a failure. Sir John French reluctantly accepted the inevitable and promised Joffre all possible co-operation, although he initially attempted to contain it to mainly artillery support — a move which Joffre would not agree to. Six British infantry divisions of the First Army were to be involved in the offensive over a front of six miles (plus three divisions in reserve, and cavalry) and gas was to be used by the British for the first time. Unfortunately the release of this

Looking north-west across the Loos battlefield from near Hill 70. Centre right, the cooling towers of the power station at Cuinchy (close to the former site of the brickstacks); extreme right, the now-flattened (but previously conical) slag-heap of Fosse 8, on this side of which was located the notorious Hohenzollern Redoubt.

gas was a partial failure: the wind was uncertain and a number of British troops were themselves gassed. Another factor of some importance was that the Germans had forseen that the Allies would be taking the offensive and instead of a single main trench line (with support and reserve trenches) which had been the general practice up to that time, a second heavily wired defensive system was hurriedly prepared from two to four miles in the rear, so that even if a breakthrough occurred there would still be another major obstacle to overcome before cavalry could be used to break out into open country. (Later yet another 'third line' even further back, and with its own support and reserve trenches, became the norm — as British troops found to their cost during the Somme offensive of 1916.) Only 10,000–11,000 German troops initially opposed the 75,000 British committed to the battle.

Preparations for the assault went ahead, but owing to problems met with by the French the date of the attack was changed to the end of August and then subsequently amended twice more. It was finally decided that the offensive would begin on 25th September.

On the southern flank of the British sector two divisions were employed, these being the 47th and the 15th (Scottish), the latter consisting mainly of Scottish battalions of which the 9th Black Watch (44th Brigade) was one. The immediate objectives of 15th Division were the village of Loos and Hill 70 beyond it, the intention being to press on to the German second position. Their route lay just to the north of the Lens–Béthune road.

After a preliminary artillery bombardment of four days and nights, which was intensified on the eve of the assault, the gas was released at dawn on the 25th, and at 6.30 a.m. the infantry clambered out of the trenches and headed for the German positions. Few casualties occurred at first, but then machine-guns opened up from the 'Loos Defences', causing heavy losses. Eight officers and 150 other ranks of the 9th Black Watch fell in No Man's Land.

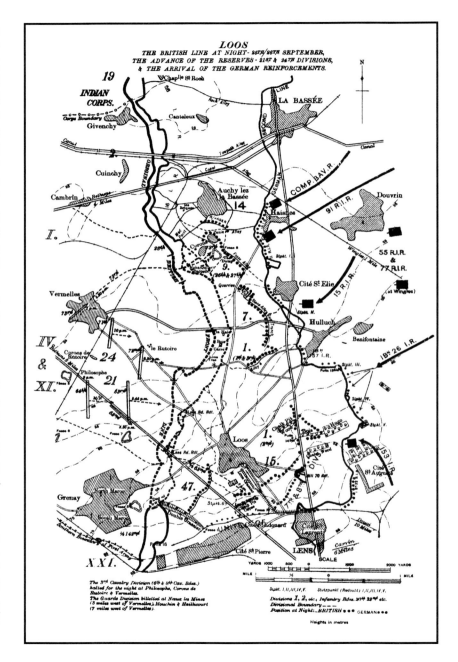

By 7 a.m. the main Loos defence line had been reached, but thick barbed-wire entanglements temporarily held up progress, which enabled two German machine-guns to inflict further casualties. The rush of several hundred Highlanders caused the Germans to flee from Loos village — the advance of the Black Watch being 'irresistible'. A group of enemy soldiers tried to stem the attack in a small square by the church, but bayonets were used freely to wipe them out. By 8 a.m. Loos was in the hands of the British, with a great gathering of Scottish units occurring near the eastern exits of the village. Then began an ascent of Hill 70, the leisurely pace of which apparently gave the appearance of a Bank Holiday crowd rather than an attacking force. On the crest of the hill a strong redoubt was captured and eight or nine hundred Scottish troops streamed down the other side. It was then that a tragic error occurred which had an important bearing on the outcome of the battle, for instead of continuing straight on, as intended, the leading company of the Black Watch veered right in the general direction of Lens, which was not included in the plan of attack. Others

Top right: Looking south towards the crest of Hill 70, with the road to Lens (which is just over the hill) on the left.

Above right: Dud Corner Military Cemetery, which contains the graves of 1,772 men from the United Kingdom and 28 from Canada. The name of the cemetery stemmed from the seemingly large number of dud shells fired in this area. It is located on the north side of the Lens–Béthune road.

Below right: Within the cemetery. On the walls at the rear are engraved the names of 20,693 'Missing' who fell during the Battle of Loos in 1915 and others who died and were never found during the nearby fighting in 1918. One of the names is that of Captain the Hon. F. Bowes-Lyon, brother of Her Majesty Queen Elizabeth, The Queen Mother. He was in the 8th Battalion The Black Watch, of 26th Brigade, 9th (Scottish) Division which attacked the Hohenzollern Redoubt, Fosse 8 and The Dump at Zero Hour on 25th September 1915.

The Loos battlefield from Dud Corner Military Cemetery, looking north-west, with the Lens–Béthune road on the left. Béthune is about five miles away. The trenches of the 15th (Scottish) Division were to the right and left of the road near where the cars are seen in the centre. The 47th Division was further to the left of the area shown here.

followed and they then came up against strong opposition, upon which the assault wavered and then ground to a halt close to the German wire, the men being pinned down by heavy fire. Many became casualties, and wounded slowly began to work their way back up the hill. The Germans, sensing a change in their fortunes, promptly counter-attacked towards the crest of Hill 70, where they eventually recaptured the redoubt. Many of those of the original British force that had gone beyond the summit of Hill 70 were killed, with only about fifty being captured unwounded.

With the summit of Hill 70, including the redoubt, once again in German hands, the survivors of the 44th Brigade on the hill were relieved and withdrawn, the brigade having suffered a total of 2,250 casualties, including 69 officers. Of these, 680 — of which 20 were officers — were incurred by the 9th Black Watch, this being a very large proportion of the battalion who had gone into action at Zero Hour.

The task of the 47th Division, on the right of the 15th Division, was to form a defensive flank between and including Loos Crassier (Slag-Heap) and what was known as the Double Crassier, south-west of Loos. In this sector the

View towards Loos (centre) from Dud Corner Military Cemetery. The gently rising ground of Hill 70 is beyond the village. A peaceful scene very different to that on 25th September 1915.

Another view of the battlefield from the cemetery, with the slag-heap of Fosse 8 on the right and, in the extreme left distance, Cuinchy power station.

gas was more successful than elsewhere and a smoke screen also helped the advance of the two brigades involved — with men of one unit actually dribbling a football in front of them! In spite of heavy enemy fire, the objectives of this division were reached, although several companies inadvertently became mixed up with the 15th Division. The 47th Division sustained 1,200 casualties.

To the north of the 15th Division was the 1st Division, whose northern boundary was the Vermelles–Hulluch road. On that front, in No Man's Land, was a famous landmark known as Lone Tree which once had been an attractive flowering cherry tree, since mutilated by shellfire. The southern part of Hulluch was one of the objectives of the division, with the assault to be continued to the German second position and beyond. In this sector the gas badly

Loos from the top of Hill 70 in the 1970s, looking in the opposite direction to the 1918 picture. The winding gear towers have since been dismantled. As in Britain, a number of the coal mines in this area have now ceased to function.

A photograph taken in 1918. Beyond the wire entanglements are the ruins of Loos. Fosse 15 and the Loos Crassier are on the right. At this end of the crassier is what was left of a pair of iron winding towers known to the British troops as 'Tower Bridge'. Before the Battle of Loos they were used as observation posts by the Germans, and British gunners attempted to destroy them, without success. One of the towers was subsequently wrecked in the fighting of September 1915 and the other was shot down by the Germans a few months later, when that part of the crassier was within the British lines. [IWM]

A somewhat similar view to that of the 1918 picture, with the Loos Crassier to the right of the village. The twin towers are the replacements for those of Tower Bridge. In 1915 thick barbed wire entanglements were sited this side of the village, with two major strongpoints to the left and right which were stormed by men of the 15th (Scottish) Division in their headlong rush to the village, and Hill 70 beyond.

121

Loos Church and the square where the Germans temporarily held up the 9th Black Watch with a barricade before being overwhelmed by the irresistible rush of the Highlanders, who made free use of the bayonet to clear the enemy away.

Ground to the east of Loos Crassier (on the left), with part of Loos village to the right. Traces of old German trenches still existed in the foreground when this picture was taken in the 1970s. The 9th Black Watch reached this point on 25th September 1915 — with some men going beyond — before they were forced back by German counter-attacks. The British lines were about half-way down the hill at the end of the battle.

affected the attacking troops and a machine-gun near Lone Tree enfiladed the men as they advanced. In spite of setbacks the Lens–La Bassée road was reached and a trench near Hulluch captured. A German counter-attack was beaten off but the division's casualties were very heavy for the ground gained.

Beyond (i.e. north of) the Vermelles–Hulluch road were three divisions of I Corps under Lieutenant-General Gough (those to the south of the road being of Lieutenant-General Sir Henry Rawlinson's IV Corps). These three northern divisions were, first, the 7th Division and, to the north, the 9th (Scottish) Division, with the 2nd Division covering ground astride the La Bassée Canal.

The 7th Division's attack was partially successful, with fierce fighting taking place at the Quarries, but there too initial success turned into disappointment. The 9th Division faced the very powerful defences of the Hohenzollern Redoubt, behind which was the flat 20-foot-high slag-heap of Fosse 8 which commanded the whole area. In spite of this major obstacle the assault by 7th Seaforth Highlanders, 5th Cameron Highlanders, 8th Black Watch and other Scottish troops was highly successful — the Redoubt, Fosse 8 and its slag-heap (The Dump) all falling fairly quickly, and follow-up troops advancing some way beyond.

Sadly, subsequent German counter-attacks recovered most of the hard-won ground in that sector, but it had been proven that the German line could be broken. Had sufficient reserves been to hand, it is highly probable that the story of Loos would have been different. Unfortunately, however, in spite of strong protests from General Haig and others, Field Marshal French had kept the reserves, consisting of two New Army divisions (the 21st and 24th who had only recently arrived in France) too far back. Their eventual appearance on the battlefield was too late to be of benefit at the crucial time, especially as they were inexperienced, already exhausted by long marches and inadequately fed, and this had a major bearing on the course of the offensive. It also led to the replacement of Sir John French as Commander-in-Chief of the British Expeditionary Force.

Fierce fighting continued in the Loos sector throughout the closing days of September and part of October. The offensive officially ended on 8th October, although from 13th–19th there was further fighting in the Hohenzollern Redoubt area.

On 4th November General Haig informed the Commander-in-Chief that the onset of winter compelled an abandonment of any hope of continuing the offensive, and the sector quietened down again. Losses were heavy — a total of 2,013 officers and 48,367 other ranks. Of these, some 800 officers and 15,000 men were killed, or missing and never heard of again.

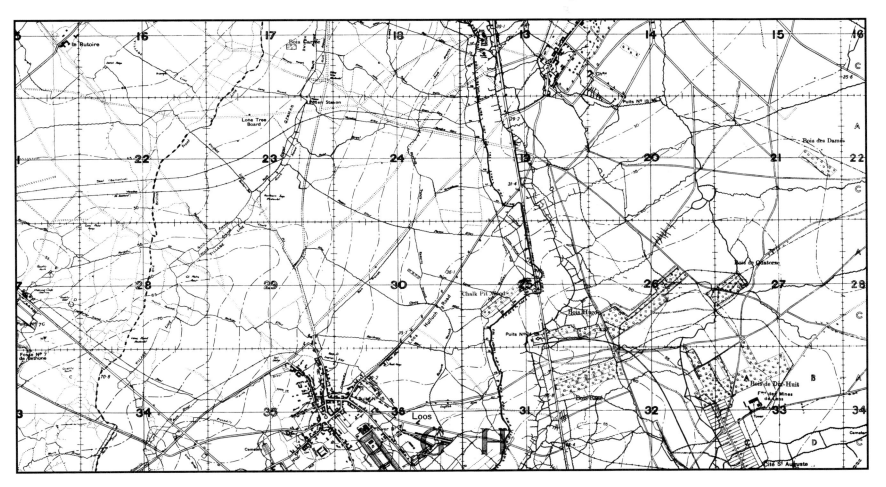

Detail from a Trench Map sheet 36C N.W. 3, Edition 7A of the Loos Area.

The once-ruined and famous Rutoire Farm, which was just behind the British lines before the battle began.

British pill-box situated behind Rutoire Farm in what is now a lovely setting.

Dead horses and damaged transport pictured beside the muddy Loos–Vermelles road during the early stages of the attack in September 1915. [IWM]

St Mary's Advanced Dressing Station Military Cemetery on the Vermelles–Hulluch road. The cemetery is at the approximate centre of the Loos battlefield and lies to the south of the former position of the Hohenzollern Redoubt. It contains 1,761 United Kingdom and 19 Canadian graves apart from special memorials. Two other cemeteries are nearby. It was mainly in this area that many casualties were caused to British troops by their own gas blowing back into their trenches.

An aerial photograph taken in 1915 of the ground west of Auchy, showing the powerful German trench system (on the right) of the Hohenzollern Redoubt area and the numerous mine craters that were the work of British and German tunnellers burrowing out from their respective lines to place their explosives beneath the positions opposite. The first British tunnelling companies (170th and 178th, RE) were formed in February 1915. [IWM]

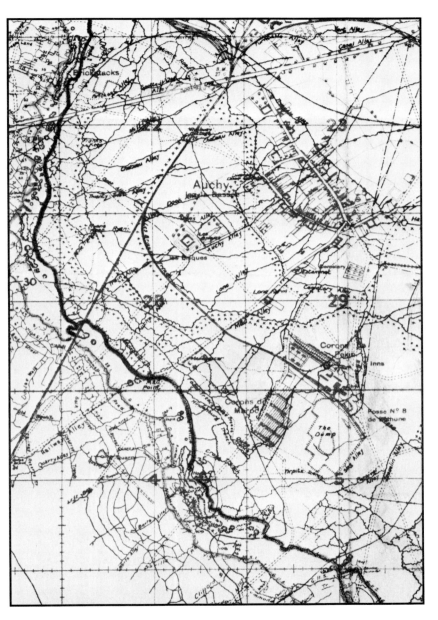

Trench map of the Auchy/Hohenzollern Redoubt area.

15th October 1915. A cloud of smoke and gas drifts overhead as shells burst along the German positions during an attack on the Hohenzollern Redoubt by the North Midland (TF) 46th Division, who captured trenches behind the Vermelles–Hulluch road and the main trench of the Redoubt. Fosse 8 is in the centre and the Redoubt this side of it; the strips of chalk indicating British trenches. [IWM]

Looking towards the site of the Hohenzollern Redoubt from the Vermelles–Hulluch road, with the slag-heap of Fosse 8 centre right. Once a field of battle; now a field of cabbages.

Desolation — the fate of coalmines and mining towns and villages all over the Loos area. Looking north-west of Hulluch, in the direction of Cité St Elie. [IWM]

Looking in the direction of Hulluch and Cité St Elie (beyond the buildings of Puit 14) from the base of Hill 70, with the Lens–La Bassée road on the right. At the end of the Battle of Loos the lines formed a salient at this point (see map opposite).

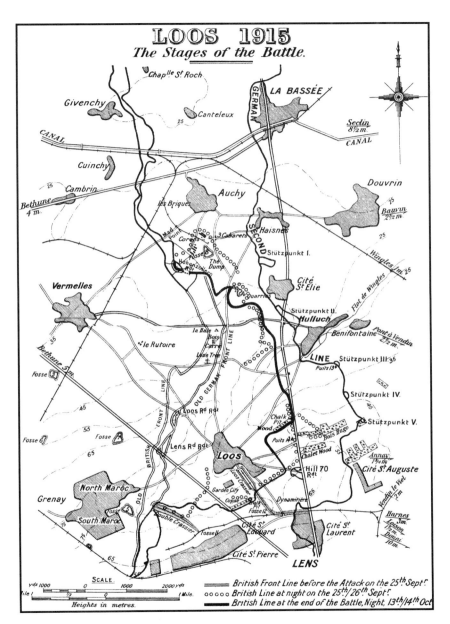

LOOS 1915
The Stages of the Battle.

Chap.lle St. Roch
LA BASSÉE
GERMAN
Givenchy
Canteleux
25
Seclin
8½ m.
CANAL
CANAL
Cuinchy
Douvrin
25
Cambrin
Auchy
Bauvin
2½ m.
25
Bethune
4 m.
Les Briques
Mad Point
3 Cabarets
SECOND
Haisnes
25
Corons
Stützpunkt I.
Fosse 8
The Dump
Hohenz. Redt.
Wingles 1 m.
25
Vermelles
Quarries
Cité St Elie
Stützpunkt II.
Flot de Wingles
Hulluch
Bénifontaine
Pont à Vendin
2½ m.
la Baie
Bois Carré
le Rutoire
LINE
Stützpunkt III. 35
Lone Tree
OLD GERMAN FRONT LINE
Puits 13.
Stützpunkt IV.
45
FRONT LINE
Loos Rd Rdt.
Chalk Pit Wood
Stützpunkt V.
Bois Hugo
Puits 14
BRITISH
Chalet Wood
Annay
1½ m.
Cité St Auguste
Lens Rd Rdt.
Loos
Hill 70 Rdt.
55
Fosse 6
Fosse 7
65
Garden City
Copse
Vendin le Vieil
1 m.
North Maroc
Dynamitière
65
Harnes
3 m.
Lesson
1½ m.
Grenay
OLD
Fosse 5
Double Crassier
Fosse 12
Cité St Edouard
Harnes
Donai
10 m.
South Maroc
75
75
Fosse 11
Cité St Laurent
65
Cité St Pierre
LENS

SCALE.
yds 1000   0   1000   2000 yds
½ mile   ½   0   1 Mile.
Heights in metres.

═══ British Front Line before the Attack on the 25th Sept.r
ooooo British Line at night on the 25th/26th Sept.r
━━━ British Line at the end of the Battle, Night, 13th/14th Oct

Right: old mine craters of the Hohenzollern Redoubt area.

1st Cameronians preparing for a gas attack. The early type of mask indicates that the photograph was taken in 1915. [IWM]

Right: Major Winston Churchill, with Général Fayolle, at HQ French XXXIII Corps, Camblain L'Abbé in 1915. The liaison officer third from the left is Captain Edward Spears. In November 1915, after resigning from Asquith's Coalition Government, Churchill rejoined his regiment, the Oxfordshire Hussars, and left for France. He commanded the 6th Battalion of the Royal Scots Fusiliers until in May 1917, as a result of the amalgamation of several battalions owing to heavy losses in the Scottish regiments, he had to give way to a more senior officer and was granted permission to return to England, re-entering politics. He was invariably to be seen wearing a poilu's helmet presented to him by the French, rather than the British version or a glengarry, because he thought it suited him better. [IWM]

Left: French front line on Vimy Ridge, November 1915. This trench was blown up by a mine in February 1916. [IWM]

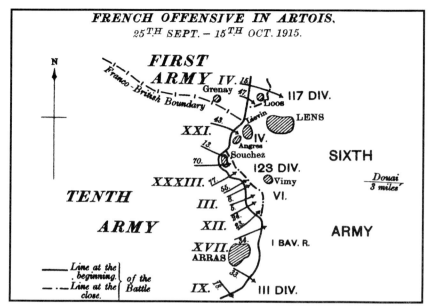

ALLIED PLANS FOR 1916

On 6th December 1915 an Inter-Allied conference was convened at Chantilly with the principal objective of co-ordinating the actions of the Allies. It was held under the presidency of Général Joffre, who on 2nd December had been promoted from Commander-in-Chief Armies of the North-East to Commander-in-Chief of the French Armies.

The situation facing the Allies as 1915 drew to a close was not a very satisfactory one in spite of several offensives having been launched by the French (Second and Third Battles of Artois and Second Battle of Champagne) and others by the British (Neuve Chapelle/Aubers Ridge, Festubert, and Loos), all of which took a heavy toll in casualties. The Second Battle of Ypres, during which the Germans nearly broke through by their surprise use of poison gas, had also inflicted heavy casualties on the Allies and some ground had to be abandoned to the enemy. On the Eastern Front, things had gone badly for the Russians and Bulgaria had joined the Central Powers. The Gallipoli expedition had proved to be a failure and elsewhere other reverses added to the discouraging outlook (a ray of hope in May having been Italy's joining the Allies). Yet the Germans too had failed to achieve the decisive results they had expected, and the advantages gained from their pre-war preparations were no longer a predominant factor. True, Great Britain was not yet able to pull her full weight but, given time, that unsatisfactory state of affairs would change. General Sir Douglas Haig took over from Field Marshal Sir John French on 19th December and Lieutenant-General Sir William Robertson became Chief of the Imperial General Staff four days later. These changes engendered more confidence throughout the British Army, it being considered by many that the right men had taken over the military direction of the war effort.

The Plan of Action submitted by the French at the Chantilly conference proposed that simultaneous attacks should be mounted by Great Britain, France, Italy and Russia

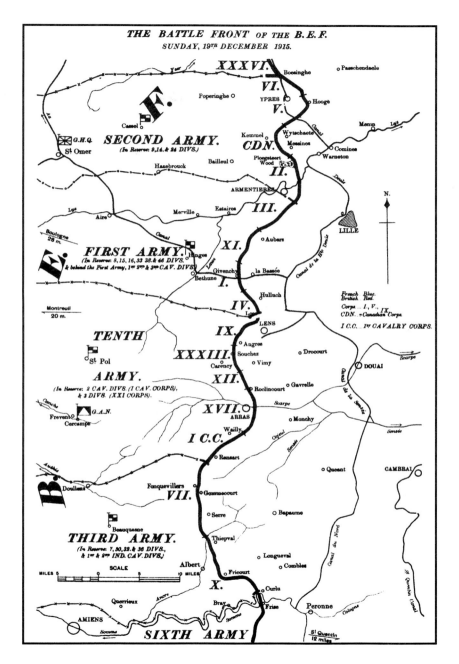

THE BATTLE FRONT OF THE B.E.F.
SUNDAY, 19TH DECEMBER 1915.

as soon as the time was suitable to do so. This was considered to be the main aim for forcing a decision, and meantime vigorous action should be taken against the Austro-German forces by those Allies with reserves of man-

Général (later Maréchal) Césaire Joffre, the French Supreme Commander.

power (i.e. Great Britain, Italy and Russia). Secondary objectives were also discussed and laid down for future implementation.

On 29th December 1915 Sir Douglas Haig attended a further conference at Chantilly, and on the following day Général Joffre wrote to him proposing a powerful combined Franco-British offensive astride the Somme. He also requested the British to take over a further part of the line then held by the French Tenth Army — a course of action agreed upon by Sir Douglas Haig. Early in January 1916 Joffre amended his plans to include several offensives by his armies at other points, plus wearing-out attacks by the British, but on 14th February he abandoned such ideas in favour of the combined Somme offensive, to begin about 1st July (a date that was to be changed more than once). This conflicted with Haig's own preference for an assault in the Ypres sector, where he believed the chances of success were more likely and the strategic advantages more positive. However, when he advocated such action to the French Commander-in-Chief it met with strong opposition and had to be abandoned — or rather postponed for a year, by which time the German defences in that area were greatly strengthened and therefore presented a far more formidable obstacle than would have been the case in 1916. General Haig did, though, instruct General Sir Herbert Plumer, who commanded the British Second Army, to give consideration to schemes for offensive action in the Messines sector.

It also became apparent that what Général Joffre had in mind was 'a war of attrition' rather than a decisive victory and that this burden should be chiefly borne by France's allies — in other words, Great Britain, Russia, and even Italy. (An attitude which may perhaps be more understandable when the fact is taken into account of the French having incurred a total of 1,932,051 casualties on the Western Front, including 49,509 officers, up to 31st December 1915, of which 1,001,271 were dead or missing. The British losses to the same date were 21,747 officers and 490,673 other ranks.)

1916

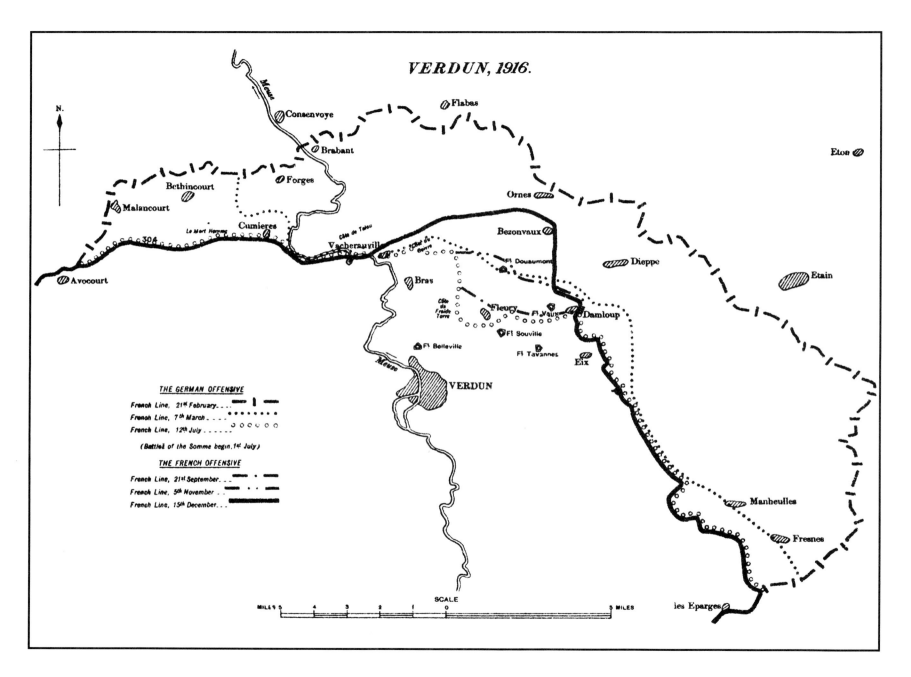

VERDUN, 1916.

N.

Consenvoye

Flabas

Eton

Brabant

Forges

Bethincourt

Ornes

Malancourt

Le Mort Homme

Cumieres

Côte de Talou

Bezonvaux

Dieppe

304

Vacherauville

Côte du Poivre

Ft Douaumont

Avocourt

Bras

Etain

Côte de Froide Terre

Fleury

Ft Vaux

Damloup

Ft Souville

Ft Belleville

Ft Tavannes

Eix

Meuse

VERDUN

THE GERMAN OFFENSIVE

French Line, 21ˢᵗ February.......
French Line, 7ᵗʰ March......
French Line, 12ᵗʰ July.......

(Battles of the Somme begin, 1ˢᵗ July)

THE FRENCH OFFENSIVE

French Line, 21ˢᵗ September.....
French Line, 5ᵗʰ November.......
French Line, 15ᵗʰ December.....

Manheulles

Fresnes

MILES 5   4   3   2   1   0   SCALE   5 MILES

les Eparges

132

THE STRUGGLES FOR VERDUN

Just seven weeks into 1916 the initiative was taken from the Allies when on 21st February the Germans launched their strong attack on Verdun. This had been a quiet front since September 1914 and at the beginning of February it was manned by only two divisions of the French XXX Corps and two Territorial regiments. The defences of the fortress had been allowed to fall into decay, the forts themselves having been denuded of heavy guns. Some reinforcements were sent during February but only three divisions were in position on the eastern, or right, bank of the Meuse to meet the initial thrust of nine enemy divisions in that sector (no attack being mounted by von Falkenhayn on the left bank). Two of those French divisions put up a spirited defence which caused delays to the German plans, but by the third day all of the French first position was in the possession of the enemy, who had been greatly helped by the crushing fire of his 850 guns, including a number of 420mm monsters. In contrast to this massive weight of firepower the French were able to muster only 270 artillery pieces.

On 24th February Général Joffre (who had earlier insisted that the Germans had no intention of attacking Verdun) agreed to his Chief-of-Staff, Général de Castenau's, recommendation that the entire French Second Army be transferred to Verdun from the reserve, to defend the left bank. Its commander was Général Pétain. Général de Castenau himself moved briefly to Verdun and quickly began to re-animate the defences on the right bank: there would be no retreat to the left bank, and Pétain was to take over the right bank as well. Général Pétain also arrived and immediately began to organise a line of resistance on the forts, especially those on Bois Bourrus Ridge. The French artillery fire was co-ordinated and the little road that represented Verdun's lifeline for supplies and reinforcements was organised and maintained to carry a constant

The famous road south of Verdun known as the 'Voie Sacrée' (Sacred Way). In 1916 this now-minor road was a vital artery for the defence of the beleaguered city. During the week commencing the 28th February over 25,000 tons of supplies and 190,000 men were brought in over it, and during June the number of vehicles travelling in either direction reached a peak of one every fourteen seconds. In the course of the battle, something like two-thirds of the entire French Army passed along it.

stream of lorries. French morale improved everywhere and by the end of February the main German offensive was beginning to grind to a halt. Nevertheless, extremely fierce fighting continued unabated; and in the course of it, the mighty Fort Douaumont fell like a plum to a handful of the enemy (the village itself holding out until 4th March after changing hands several times in desperate fighting).

With the offensive bogged down, and French guns on the Mort Homme heights enfilading his troops, von Falkenhayn agreed to what others had previously urged as essential to the Verdun operation — an attack on the left bank of the Meuse. The attack was set for 6th March: the main objective on the left bank the Mort Homme, with an attempt the following day to capture Fort Vaux, on the right bank. The attack on the left bank went in as planned (the other being delayed forty-eight hours), with very violent actions occurring during March, but with comparatively limited German gains. Then, on 9th April, five German divisions attacked Mort Homme and in extremely bloody fighting succeeded in capturing one of its two summits at the cost of many German dead, but not the higher one, a few hundred yards away, and during April the French prised it back.

Meanwhile, the French guns continued to give enfilade fire from Mort Homme's western twin, Hill 304, which the Germans had so far been unable to reach. On 3rd May over 500 German heavy guns concentrated their fire on that target. Hill 304 fell to the Germans on 23rd May, being recaptured by the French on the 24th. It was subsequently cleared by the Germans after heavy fighting; by the end of May, after a renewed attack on Mort Homme, they could claim the heights as wholly theirs. The struggle had been without respite or quarter: it is estimated that some 10,000 French soldiers died endeavouring to defend Mort Homme. The Germans had reached almost to the foot of the Bourrus Ridge, west of Verdun, and it marked the end of the offensive on the left bank.

There had since been a change of command, for on 30th April Général Pétain had been appointed to command the Central Army Group (in which the Verdun sector lay) and Général Nivelle became Second Army commander.

On the right bank, on 2nd June Fort Vaux was taken and on the 23rd the Germans attacked yet again with 70,000 troops after using Green Cross gas (Phosgene) for the first time. This was one of the deadliest gases of the war and it knocked out many of the French guns, enabling the enemy to punch a deep hole in the French defences. Terrible struggles occurred in and around Fleury, with that devastated village (which, like eight others, was never rebuilt) finally falling to the Germans, but this major effort to break through past Fort Souville to Verdun was blocked.

This was the climax and crisis point of the Verdun battle, with a real danger of the city being lost to the Germans. In desperation Joffre appealed to General Haig to advance the British offensive on the Somme, and the opening date of the assault was brought forward to 25th June but then postponed to 1st July.

On 24th June the heavy British bombardment from nearly 1,500 guns opened up on the Somme and continued pounding the enemy defences for a week. On that same day General Falkenhayn urged that the expenditure of men and ammunition on the Verdun front should be restricted, and on 1st July a further limitation of ammunition was ordered. On 2nd July heavy batteries began to be withdrawn from the Verdun sector, and on 11th July Falkenhayn issued instructions for the fighting at Verdun to be strictly on a defensive basis as 'the serious crisis in the Somme battle did not permit of a continuation of the attacks against Verdun'.

The German bid to take Verdun was effectively coming to an end, while French counter-attacks had retaken most of the German gains of 23rd June. Yet, ironically, on 12th July, during a German push on Fort Souville, the enemy came the closest he was ever to get to Verdun. For a short time, until they were dealt with by the Souville garrison, elements of a Bavarian regiment found themselves looking at the twin towers of Verdun cathedral from the roof of the fort.

The bitter fighting continued to sway back and forth during the hot summer of 1916 in a campaign which, in the words of von Falkenhayn, was aimed at 'bleeding the enemy white'. However, attrition happens to work both ways: the losses of both combatants rose inexorably as the weeks passed. In October the French launched a major counter-offensive which continued for two months, during which Forts Douaumont and Vaux were recaptured together with the remains of numerous villages lost in the early stages of the original German offensive.

Technically the Battle of Verdun ended in December, although fighting continued to flare up into 1917. The line was then quiet for several months as the French began to build up their strength for a new offensive. This took place in August 1917, with Mort Homme and Hill 304 again under French control by the end of that month. The French line advanced to the Forges stream, the front returning almost as it was before February 1916, the threat to Verdun removed.

Verdun was a battle which neither of the combatants won outright. It was in effect a watershed of the war, for it marked the point where the main burden of the war passed from French to British troops.

According to the French Official History, published in 1936, French losses for the ten months of 1916 were 377,231, of which 162,308 were killed or missing. The German losses for the same period were assessed at about 337,000, of which over 100,000 dead and missing were admitted. Some sources put the overall casualties as being much higher and certainly, when the later fighting of 1917 is taken into account, the final figures of losses greatly exceed those detailed above — a French estimate putting the combined French and German dead at 420,000.

So near yet so far. View of Verdun from just below Fort Souville. In July 1916 about thirty Germans managed to reach the glacis of the fort before being driven off when the garrison realised they were there. They had the dubious distinction of probably being closer to the city than any other enemy soldiers apart from prisoners-of-war.

1917

1916 IN RETROSPECT AND PLANS FOR 1917

The bloody battles of Verdun and the severe fighting on the Somme dominated the operations of 1916, with only minor British actions taking place on other parts of the Western Front.

On 15th November 1916 representatives of the Allied armies congregated at the Chantilly headquarters of the French Commander-in-Chief, Général Joffre, for a two-day conference. The meeting was attended by the Chief of the Imperial General Staff, Sir William Robertson, and General Sir Douglas Haig, and included representatives from Italy, Russia and Serbia. The purpose of the conference was to consider the happenings of the past year and to discuss plans for 1917 with a view to co-ordination of efforts, as had been the objective of a similar conference between 6th and 8th December 1915. The mood of the participants was optimistic and some satisfaction was evident at the course of events during the year, including the German failure to capture Verdun, the British offensive on the Somme (in which the French involvement had also been quite considerable) and General Brusilov's successful offensive on the Russian front in June. A useful contribution by the Italians was also noted. All of these actions had resulted in extremely heavy casualties but, even so, these were considered to be endurable in what had become a grim battle of attrition against the common enemy, whose losses had also been severe. The German Chief of the General Staff, General von Falkenhayn, had been dismissed and replaced by Field-Marshal von Hindenburg and General Ludendorff on 29th August and there was a belief amongst the Allies that the capacity of the Central Powers to wage war had been much reduced. There was even hope in the Allied camp that the war might be brought to a successful conclusion in 1917, though it was accepted that the path to victory would not be easy. It was agreed that France and Belgium were to constitute the principal front and that a decisive victory should be sought early in 1917 based on a renewal of co-ordinated offensives.

A French town's memorial to its dead — at St Leger, south-west of Croisilles. A more personal touch is invariably added to such memorials by a display of individual photographs, as on the shield here.

An event that happened in mid-1916, and which came as a blow to British morale, was the loss at sea of the Secretary of State for War, Field Marshal Lord Kitchener of Khartoum. He was aboard the cruiser 'Hampshire', on his way to Russia, when it struck a mine off the Orkneys and sank on the evening of 5th June, and was last seen standing calmly on the cruiser's deck as she began to settle in the rough seas which prevented escape. Within fifteen minutes of striking the mine, only about one and a half miles off shore, the 'Hampshire' plunged below the waves, carrying Lord Kitchener (whose body was never found) and his Staff, and almost the entire crew, to a watery grave. News of the disaster severely shocked the British people and led to a feeling of great loss. Various rumours of the possible causes of the tragedy abounded and continued for a long time, one theory being that the Germans had deliberately planned Kitchener's death. In fact, the German press was quite temperate in its announcement of the incident and mostly refrained from making capital out of what was seen even by them as the death of a renowned soldier.

Other items of some importance as the year came to an end were the resignation of the British Prime Minister, Mr Asquith, on 4th December, and Lloyd George's succession to the Premiership on 7th December. A War Cabinet was formed in Great Britain on 9th December and ten days later the British Government decided to institute National Service.

In France, Général Joffre was removed as Commander-in-Chief of the French armies on 12th December. He was created Marshal of France on 26th December and became Technical Military Adviser to the French War Cabinet. Général Nivelle became Commander-in-Chief of the French Northern and North-Eastern Group of Armies.

On 12th December the Central Powers made tentative peace overtures and on 18th December President Wilson of the United States of America issued a Circular Note suggesting negotiations. On 30th December the Entente Governments rejected the German peace proposals and in a joint reply to President Wilson's note outlined the Allied War Aims.

The war was to continue, and sadly the high hopes nurtured by the Allied representatives at the Chantilly conference were not to be fulfilled: 1917 was destined to be yet another year of bloody confrontations, bitter disappointments and heavy casualties. Some successes would be achieved, but the end of the conflict was still a long way ahead.

Field Marshal Lord Kitchener, died at sea, 5th June 1916.

THE GERMAN WITHDRAWAL TO THE 'HINDENBURG LINE'

25th February–5th April 1917

At the start of 1917 there was not much cheer to be had for the German higher command as it took stock of the situation following the costly defensive battles of the Somme. A worrying factor was that a deterioration had been noted in the troops, and doubts had arisen about their capability to withstand similar long spells of defensive fighting during 1917. Offensive action was dismissed as impracticable, for there were not enough men available, and the conclusion was reached — albeit reluctantly — that on the Western Front the German Armies would have to stand entirely on the defensive. Hopes were pinned on unres-

tricted submarine warfare having a decisive effect on the course of the war, although Ludendorff did not go along with the idea put forward by the German Admiralty that this could be achieved within six months. Reaching an understanding with Russia was also contemplated, but an effort made with that in mind broke down. In fact, it was to be the impending Russian Revolution which was to free Germany from the encumbrance of that front.

Meanwhile strenuous efforts had been made by the Germans to build a massive new defensive system, the Siegfried-Stellung, some miles to the rear of their main positions. Known subsequently by the British as the Hindenburg Line, it stretched from near Arras down to St Quentin and onwards to Cerny-en-Laonnois on the Chemin des Dames Ridge. It had been begun at the end of October 1916, although its full extent was unknown to the British and French until the actual German retirement in February/March 1917 (the German Air Force having made vigorous

Up it goes! Demolition by the Germans before their retreat on the Somme, 1917. [IWM]

February 1917. A German machine-gun crew at the time of the retreat to the Siegfried Line. [IWM]

139

efforts to prevent Allied reconnaissance aircraft from photographing these new fortifications). Russian prisoners, Belgian civilians and German specialist troops were used in its construction, and an extension was also constructed which became known to the British as the 'Drocourt–Quéant Switch'. This system branched off at Quéant and ran across the River Scarpe, then east of Lens and on to Armentières.

The first notification of a specific enemy withdrawal occurred on 22nd February when a bold reconnaissance by a subaltern of the 7th Royal West Kents (55th Brigade of the 18th Division) ascertained that there were no longer any Germans on the crest south of Petit Miraumont. Other patrols elsewhere confirmed the absence of German troops and, after some incredulity at these reports, orders were issued for operations to commence for regaining touch with the enemy. Between Le Transloy and Serre (a distance of over ten miles as the crow flies) it was found that the enemy had vanished. Pys was occupied in the early morning of the 25th. An attempt to enter Irles was repulsed by shellfire and German rearguard resistance. Serre was occupied by men of the 91st Brigade (7th Division). At another point many casualties were inflicted upon Australian troops by heavy machine-gun fire as they advanced prematurely against determined enemy opposition; on the 26th, however, they met with success and drove the Germans out of Le Barque and beyond Ligney Thilloy. Hand-to-hand fighting occurred on the 7th Division's front at Puisieux, which was cleared

Top right: The church at Quéant, south-east of Bullecourt. Quéant was well-known for its association with the German Drocourt–Quéant Switch Line — a powerful trench system which ran north–south between the two towns. Quéant was not captured until September 1918.

Right: Athies, south of Mons-en-Chasée, on the Amiens–St Quentin road. The vast mine crater was blown in the centre of the village to impede advancing British forces during the German withdrawal to the Hindenburg Line in March 1917. [IWM]

after hard fighting with a German rearguard in the church. Gommecourt was found to be empty by a two-man patrol of the 18th Durham Light Infantry.

Further local gains were made during the next few days and on 10th March a fresh attack was mounted on Irles with the aid of powerful artillery support and an overhead machine-gun barrage. This and associated operations met with success: the enemy was overwhelmed and a number of prisoners were taken. On the night of 12th March British patrols found the German defence line between Bapaume and Achiet-le-Petit had been evacuated, but at Bucquoy other patrols ascertained that the German positions were strongly held. A night attack on the village by the 91st Brigade of 7th Division failed with heavy loss, for the thick wire had not been cut.

Before dawn on the 17th it was discovered that the enemy had retired along the whole of the Fifth Army's front, and also on the right wing of the Third Army. The real retreat had thus begun. In accordance with detailed plans already prepared by the Germans, the Allies were to be denied the satisfaction of an unhampered advance by the systematic destruction of all buildings and other places of shelter. Roads were to be cratered and everything possible done to hinder the advancing Allied troops, including the cutting down of fruit and other trees and the filling-up or pollution — but not the actual poisoning — of wells. The abandoned ground was in fact to be turned into a desert — a policy of devastation to which the German Crown Prince objected, and which he correctly considered would reflect on the name of Germany throughout the world.

On the French front, as on the British, instances of villages, railways and much else being destroyed confirmed the enemy's intentions, and by 18th March even the defences north of Soissons had been evacuated. All civilians were also moved to the rear. Regardless of these moves, Général Nivelle decided not to alter the basic lines of his forthcoming offensive, which, according to Ludendorff, the

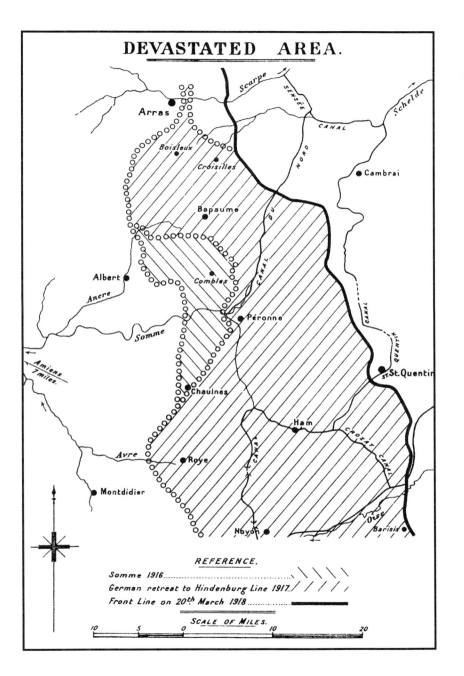

DEVASTATED AREA.

REFERENCE.

Somme 1916...........................

German retreat to Hindenburg Line 1917.

Front Line on 20th March 1918..............

SCALE OF MILES.

Germans already knew about from having captured an order relating to a great attack to be carried out on the Aisne.

Between the 17th and 24th March the advance of the British Fourth Army was fairly rapid in spite of the German demolitions. The marshy ground of the River Somme, though, presented a formidable obstacle, with all the bridges having been blown by the enemy and causeway crossings also destroyed. Magnificent work by the Royal Engineers and divisional troops overcame this problem and at the

Péronne, entered by British troops on 18th March 1917. 'Entry Forbidden' says the German sign. [IWM]

important crossing at Brie, where the Amiens–St Quentin road was carried across the Somme, engineers of the 1st Division worked all through the night to successfully bridge six gaps blown in the causeway by the retreating Germans.

On the evening of 17th March the once-beautiful city of Péronne, which had been badly damaged by the enemy, was entered by a company of the Royal Warwickshires after they had been ferried across the river on pontoon rafts, and by 3.30 a.m. on the 18th a new bridge was completed by the Royal Engineers on the site of the old one.

On the Fifth Army's front, Bapaume — that tragically unattainable goal of the 1916 Somme offensive — was entered by Australian troops of I Anzac Corps. The devastation in the town was even more appalling than elsewhere. Other Australians advanced rapidly on Vaulx Vraucourt, near the Bapaume–Cambrai road, where they surprised an enemy rear party, some of whom were caught shaving. Numerous German booby traps were encountered all along the front of the advance, and on the night of 25th March one that had been overlooked blew up Bapaume Town Hall, killing a number of Australians and two French Deputies. Other booby traps of various types claimed the lives of some unwary soldiers, but numerous lives were also saved by the bravery of the Royal Engineers in defusing many of the devices.

As the days passed, the advancing troops gradually came up against stiffer opposition from Germans holding outpost positions. Attacks were mounted on these strong-points and fierce fighting occurred at various locations, including Croiselles and Henin-sur-Cojeul, both of which were captured after furious close-quarter engagements. By 8th April most of the outpost villages had fallen all along the front of the Fifth and Fourth Armies, with the enemy securely installed behind the massive belts of barbed wire of the Hindenburg Line.

The stage was now set for the next phase of the overall struggle: the Battle — ultimately, Battles — of Arras.

German military cemetery on the Arras–Béthune road, near Neuville St Vaast — the tower of the village church being just visible in the centre. The cemetery contains the remains of over 36,000 German soldiers collected from the nearby battlefields and concentrated here after the war. It is situated on the site of a former powerful German trench system known as the Labyrinth. A few years ago a large mass grave near the road had to be moved in order to make room for a new car park!

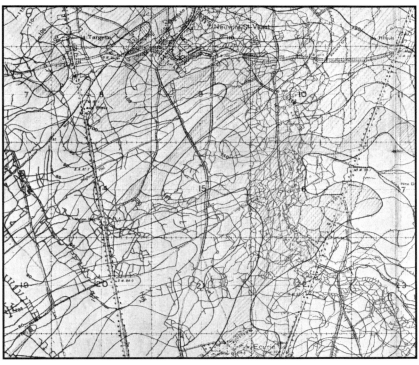

Above: The maze of trenches that once covered the Neuville St Vaast area, including those of the Labyrinth. The Arras–Béthune road is on the left, with La Targette at the top. Ecurie, which was just within the British lines, is at the lower right. Neuville St Vaast was very heavily fortified by the Germans but was partially captured during the French offensive of May/June 1915, when in one day over 300,000 shells were fired into the Labyrinth sector.

Left: Aerial view of Mont St Eloi west of Neuville St Vaast. The twin towers are of a ruined seventeenth-century abbey and were used for artillery observation, particularly by the French in 1915. They were also a target for German gunners, who were partially successful in their attempts to destroy them. Mont St Eloi was the centre of several battles in earlier French wars. The British took over this sector in the spring of 1916 and an RFC aerodrome was subsequently established here. [Author/WFA]

143

THE ARRAS BATTLEFIELD, 1917

Only main roads & railways are shown
British Line before Attack, 9th April.
SCALE.
Miles ½ 0 1 2 3 4 5 6 7 8 Miles.

THE BATTLES OF ARRAS
THE CAPTURE OF VIMY RIDGE

At 5.30 a.m. on Easter Monday, 9th April 1917, in foul weather, four divisions of Canadian infantrymen of General Horne's First Army went 'over the top' on a front of 7,500 yards in one of the most successful attacks of the war. Their objective was the crest of Vimy Ridge. Since its capture by the Germans in October 1914, this had been converted into a veritable fortress which dominated the Douai Plain and its rich coalfields. Two major attempts by the French to recapture the four-mile-long whaleback heights in 1915 had ended in failure at a total cost of around 150,000 casualties.

The attack was being made in conjunction with a major assault by eight infantry divisions of General Allenby's Third Army south of the ridge, their task being to thrust eastwards from the ancient city of Arras, on each side of the River Scarpe, with three cavalry divisions and more infantry divisions to follow up after the anticipated breakthrough. The main assault was supported by about 2,000 guns (many of them heavy pieces) and 70 tanks, covering a frontage of about 7,000 yards, which was to be widened by flank attacks including that against Vimy Ridge. Something like 350,000 men were concentrated in an area about thirteen miles square, and the offensive — which was to become known as the First, Second and Third Battles of the Scarpe — was one of the heaviest blows to be struck by the British on the Western Front.

The offensive was launched in compliance with the earlier agreement between Général Joffre and Sir Douglas Haig (with some amendments to the overall plans). Général Nivelle, the new Commander-in-Chief of the French Armies of the North and North-East, was convinced that the German front could — and would — be broken by the concerted action of the two Allies, and with the British attacking at Arras the French would be launching their own main offensive some days later in the Aisne sector, with a subsidiary attack on the Champagne front. Nivelle was certain that the plan was bound to meet with complete success. However, because the Germans had captured details of the impending French assault, they had been able to take adequate counter-measures to meet the threat.

Aerial view of Vimy Ridge, looking north-east towards the coalfields of Lens, with the impressive Canadian Memorial in the centre. This memorial, located on Hill 145, commemorates the highly successful capture of this most important feature by the Canadian Corps in April 1917. It is also a memorial to the 60,000 Canadians who died whilst fighting overseas during the First World War. Shell-holes and mine craters are in abundance here and sections of the opposing trenches have been preserved in concrete. [Author/WFA]

Consequently when those attacks did go in they met strong opposition and resulted in only limited gains at a heavy cost in casualties. What was worse, the failure of the French assault caused a breakdown in the morale of their troops and led to serious discontent which on 3rd May erupted into open mutiny. Nivelle was dismissed and Général Pétain took over command of the Armies of the North and North-east, with his place as Chief of the General Staff going to Général Foch. Nivelle was appointed Commander-in-Chief in Northern Africa, outside the theatres of war.

These latter events were, of course, still some weeks ahead as the British and Canadians went into action on their respective fronts. On the right of the four divisions that made up the Canadian Corps (commanded by Lieutenant-General the Hon. Sir J. H. G. Byng) was the British 13th Brigade (of 5th Division), which was temporarily attached to the 2nd Canadian Division. On the left of the corps was the 24th Division.

Very careful preparations had been made by the Canadians, who had constantly rehearsed their roles for the forthcoming battle. Raids made by them on the German positions helped to acquaint them with the obstacles confronting them and good use had been made of the numerous deep tunnels which led from the front to some miles in the rear to bring up men, ammunition and stores under cover. A plasticine model of Vimy Ridge was made for study at First Army headquarters and all ranks received a thorough grounding on the objectives of the assault. Artillery fire was to be a predominant feature, with a creeping barrage to precede the advancing infantry — over 900 guns and mortars being deployed on the corps frontage. In the air the Germans enjoyed a temporary superiority but in spite of this drawback the enemy defences had been well photographed and mapped. Harrassing fire at night was undertaken by 280 guns of the Canadian Machine-Gun Corps. Over 1,000,000 shells were hurled at the Germans on the ridge during the preliminary bombardment which went on for two

Taken from Sir Douglas Haig's Despatches this detail from sheet 3 covering the Battle of Arras shows the Battle for Vimy Ridge.

weeks, this massive weight of metal destroying trenches, barbed wire and strongpoints and turning the terrain into a wilderness of torn earth and mud; and also seriously interfering with the supply of food and water to the defenders. Deep dug-outs, spaced about 120 yards apart, sheltered the Germans from the hurricane of fire, and it was planned to capture these in the first rush of the assault. It was estimated that about 5,000 Germans were available to meet the initial blow from 15,000 Canadian troops, a second Canadian wave being ready to debouch from the shelter of the tunnels soon afterwards. Although aware of an impending attack, but not its strength or timing, the Germans were confident of being able to repulse any assault on their fortress position.

By 4 a.m. on 9th April, fifty-two battalions (30,000 men) had assembled on the Canadian front of about four miles and so carefully had the forming-up process been organised that the leading companies had got to within a hundred yards of the German outposts without any alarm being raised. Squalls of sleet and snow drenched the shivering men as they waited in the darkness, and just before zero hour a strange stillness encompassed the battlefield. Then, at precisely 5.30 a.m., two mines were exploded beneath the German front line and at the same time all the batteries opened fire, saturating the enemy defences with high-explosive and gas shells. A smoke barrage was laid by Stokes mortars in front of the dominant Hill 145 and other places, including Thélus, and 150 machine-guns created a zone of bullets four hundred yards ahead of the first wave of attackers as they swept forward behind the creeping barrage.

Surprise was complete, and the Canadians were upon the dazed defenders before they had time to emerge from their deep dug-outs. Frantic efforts were made by the Germans to call down a counter-bombardment to break up the assault, but when it came it was weak and mainly ineffective as many of the enemy batteries had already been pinpointed and then destroyed by the preliminary bombardment. In most cases No Man's Land was crossed with few casualties and, shortly after 7 a.m., the 1st Canadian Division on the right, supported by the 51st (Scottish) Division, had captured its second objective. The story was similar elsewhere, with La Folie Farm falling quickly to the 3rd Canadian Division and the shattered Bois de la Folie being entered after some initial resistance had been encountered. The 2nd Canadian Division halted about 500 yards short of its third objective.

Shells burst on German positions at Vimy Ridge during the bombardment preceding the attack in April 1917. [IWM]

The twin pylons of the Canadian Memorial pierce the horizon in this picture taken looking towards Vimy Ridge from the Arras–Béthune road. A motorway now runs across the ridge this side of Hill 145.

Because of its commanding position, Hill 145, the highest part of Vimy Ridge, presented a more difficult task for the 4th Canadian Division. With the enemy fortifications at that point being particularly strong, coupled with a more aggressive stand by the defenders, a hold-up in that sector could not be avoided. That hiatus apart, the whole German front line defence system had been captured by 7 a.m. and, as heavy clouds swept across the ridge, the new line was consolidated and isolated enemy pockets in the rear were 'mopped up'. At 9.35 a.m. a fresh attack was made at the southern end of the ridge and Thélus was taken by the 2nd Canadian Division, with the nearby Hill 135 also being outflanked by units of the British 13th Brigade.

Owing to the adverse weather the troops experienced a somewhat miserable night, but the sky then cleared as preparations were made by the 4th Canadian Division to continue the attack on Hill 145. By mid-afternoon, and following a brilliant action, the summit was in their possesion, as was another important enemy position on the steep slope beyond known as the 'Hangstellung'. Thus the original objectives of the division had been achieved.

The final stage of the battle for Vimy Ridge began at 5 a.m. on 12th April against the feature known as 'The Pimple' and the Bois de Givenchy, north of Hill 145. In bad light and falling snow, together with a strong wind and deep mud making conditions extremely difficult, the Canadians

Opposite page: Men of the Canadian 29th Infantry Battalion advancing across No-Man's Land under fire from the German guns. Vimy Ridge, April 1917. [DND Public Archives of Canada]

Above: German prisoners making their way through their own barrage. [DND Public Archives of Canada]

rushed these positions and by 5.45 a.m. it was all over. German trenches north of The Pimple and on the Lorette Ridge were then attacked and captured by the 73rd Brigade of the British 24th Division, after which all the enemy trenches below the ridge were completely dominated, and the approaches to them exposed to the new masters of Vimy Ridge. A German withdrawal became inevitable and an enemy move to a new line (known as the Oppy–Mercourt Line) was in fact confirmed on the 13th and 14th — those defences being two to three miles east of the ridge.

Without doubt the capture of Vimy Ridge was a brilliant success, and the total casualties of the Canadian Corps during the period 7th–14th April were only 11,297. It was a victory that fully justified the careful preparations undertaken by the Canadians. It also became a symbol of Canadian nationhood.

German prisoners captured at Arleux being searched. April 1917. [DND Public Archives of Canada]

Canadian troops of the 19th Infantry Battalion consolidating positions on the ridge. April 1917. [IWM]

Almost like the waves of a sea. Overlapping shell-holes on Vimy Ridge which emphasise the fury of the guns.

A grass-covered trench meanders across the former battleground.

Former Canadian trenches lined with concrete sandbags and preserved for posterity. The entrance to the famous Grange Tunnel is nearby.

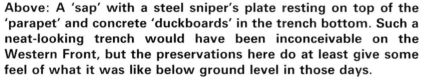

Above: A 'sap' with a steel sniper's plate resting on top of the 'parapet' and concrete 'duckboards' in the trench bottom. Such a neat-looking trench would have been inconceivable on the Western Front, but the preservations here do at least give some feel of what it was like below ground level in those days.

Above right: The German front line, complete with a concrete machine-gun position.

Middle: A well-trodden path down into a mine crater. Looking towards the former Canadian front line from the German one.

Right: Looking towards the crest of Hill 145, crowned by the Canadian Memorial, from one of the mine craters. Standing here, it is difficult not to marvel at how this beautiful vista, framed with trees, could have sprung from a pulverised and barren wasteland.

The commanding view the Germans lost. Canadian soldiers look out over the town of Vimy. April 1917. [IWM]

View from the Canadian Memorial beyond the figure of 'Canada in mourning': looking north-east towards the coalfields of Lens, with Vimy Church in the centre.

The striking twin concrete pylons of the Canadian Memorial on Hill 145 which can be seen for miles around.

Trenches and mine craters in the Thélus area. [IWM]

Looking towards Thélus over ground no longer scarred by war.

An unusual French memorial at the crossroads of La Targette, north-west of Arras. Beneath the memorial and in the vicinity are numerous caverns which were well-known to the Canadians when they occupied this sector. Close by, on the other side of the Arras–Bethune road are large British and French cemeteries. La Targette was the scene of exceptionally fierce fighting in 1915.

ARRAS
ATTACK OF VII CORPS
9th – 12th April, 1917.

REFERENCE.

British Line, Night 9th April ++++++   British Line, Night 12th April ••••••
"   "   "   10th April ○○○○○○   Germans

SCALE OF YARDS
0   500   1000   2000   3000   4000   5000

THE FIRST BATTLE OF THE SCARPE

9th–14th April

Easter Monday 1917 witnessed the most formidable assault by British troops to date. It began after careful preparations had been made and with divisions of the British Expeditionary Force being better trained and more confident of success than ever before. Although the offensive was subsidiary to the much bigger French effort on the Aisne, it made an important contribution to what might have developed into a decisive victory. The Germans had of course become aware of increased British activities on this front, including an expansion of road and rail traffic and the appearance of many more artillery batteries. German counter-measures had been put in hand: reinforcements of men, guns and aircraft were brought up and large dumps of ammunition strategically placed behind the lines. The preliminary British bombardment, which began in earnest on 4th April, greatly interfered with these defensive measures and harrassing fire on enemy communications was particularly effective. The strain on enemy troops was very severe, especially as great difficulty was experienced in bringing up their rations. Many German guns were knocked out, which resulted in the reply to the British bombardment being feeble and generally ineffective. Incredibly, when the actual British infantry assault began it still came as something of a surprise to the German military leaders. Also, the main German reserves were kept well back from the front, a factor which inevitably had a bearing on the early course of the battle. (Shades of the British failure at Loos in 1915.)

The main blow of the British offensive materialised from the eastern suburbs of Arras, with supporting operations on the two flanks. As has already been described, the left, Canadian, assault went well and practically according to plan, but on their right the 51st (Highland) Division, commanded by Major-General G. M. Harper (known as 'Uncle'

Preparation for the Battles of Arras, 1917. 12th Division artillery officers observing fire and RE field telephonists passing back results. Cuthbert Crater, two and a half miles north-east of Arras and one mile due north of Blangy. [IWM]

Part of the Arras battlefield.

Photograph taken from the present-day Roclincourt airfield, looking in the direction of Vimy Ridge. Gone are the trenches, the shell-holes, the wire, the detritus of war.

Aerial picture taken by the author in 1982, with the Arras–Cambrai road in the centre. The strategic hill of Monchy-le-Preux is in the top left-hand corner.

Above: Aerial view of Arras, 1982. The Hôtel de Ville is in the centre, on the Place des Héros, formerly the Petite Place. The Cathedral is on the extreme right. The Grande Place is in the foreground. Arras was occupied by the Germans for only a short time in September 1914. After being compelled to withdraw by the French, they dug in on the outskirts of the town, from where they subjected it to numerous heavy bombardments (in one of which, on 9th July 1915, some 6,000 shells were fired). Massive cellars beneath the houses and the Grande Place provided shelter for those inhabitants who did not flee from the constant shelling, and for the British troops, particularly before the Battle of Arras in 1917. A car park has now been built beneath the Grande Place. [Author/WFA]

Arras in flames. A contemporary postcard showing the destruction of the Hôtel de Ville in October 1914 after a bombardment by German guns. The ancient Belfry (1499) collapsed on October 21st 1914, a few days after the Hôtel de Ville had been destroyed; it had been struck by more than 60 shells.

Right: Another section of Arras (north-west of the station), with the Fauborg D'Amiens Cemetery and Memorial to the Missing centre right. This large British cemetery records 2,395 United Kingdom and 250 Commonwealth burials, and also includes 1 Russian and 28 Germans. The memorial records 35,928 'Missing' who fell in the Battles of Arras; Vimy Ridge; 1st, 2nd and 3rd Battles of the Scarpe; Arleux; Bullecourt; and Hill 70, 1917. It also incorporates the Air Services Memorial commemorating all the 'Missing' of the Royal Flying Corps, Royal Naval Air Service and Royal Air Force 'Missing' on the Western Front. Not far from the memorial is a grim reminder of the Second World War — the Mur des Fusilées, where some 200 members of the French Resistance were shot by the Germans. [Author/WFA]

The Place des Héros, as the Petite Place was renamed. On the walls inside the Hôtel de Ville are various plaques, and on the wall outside is a memorial to members of the Resistance of the Second World War.

Ruined seventeenth-century houses in the Grande Place, Arras. September 1917. [IWM]

The Grande Place in more recent times.

Harper) ran into trouble and received a serious set-back due, it was said, to the divisional commander failing to comply with the corps plan of attack. (A similar problem was to arise with this division during the Battle of Cambrai later that same year.)

Nearer the centre and north of the River Scarpe the story was different. The 34th and 9th Divisions of XVII Corps emerged from cellars and trenches and drove forward to their final objectives without too much difficulty; the 4th Division then passed through and seized Fampoux. A large hole had been punched in the German front line and the Hindenburg Line had been breached. Everywhere in that sector it appeared that the Germans were fleeing from the advancing British troops, and a great opportunity arose for the cavalry to take advantage of the opening thus offered. Unfortunately the nearest cavalry was some miles way, unable to reach the scene before the next morning. The gap remained open for several hours, with no sign of any serious counteraction by the Germans apart from some resistance at the eastern edge of Fampoux.

South of the River Scarpe, similar success had also been achieved by VI Corps, whose troops had made good use of the covered approaches to the front, and kept pace with the men of XVII Corps. There were high hopes that Monchy-le-Preux, which crowned a hill that dominated the terrain for miles around, could be captured by the end of the first day. However, numerous trenches and vast belts of barbed wire had yet to be overcome before that vital feature could fall into British hands. A twenty-foot high railway embankment known as Railway Triangle (where three rail tracks converged), and which was studded with machine-guns, also constituted a major obstacle, as did several other hills on the British line of advance.

Strong German resistance occurred at Railway Triangle, where the 15th (Scottish) Division's attack ground to a temporary halt under devastating fire until a tank called 'Lusitania' came to the rescue and shot up the German

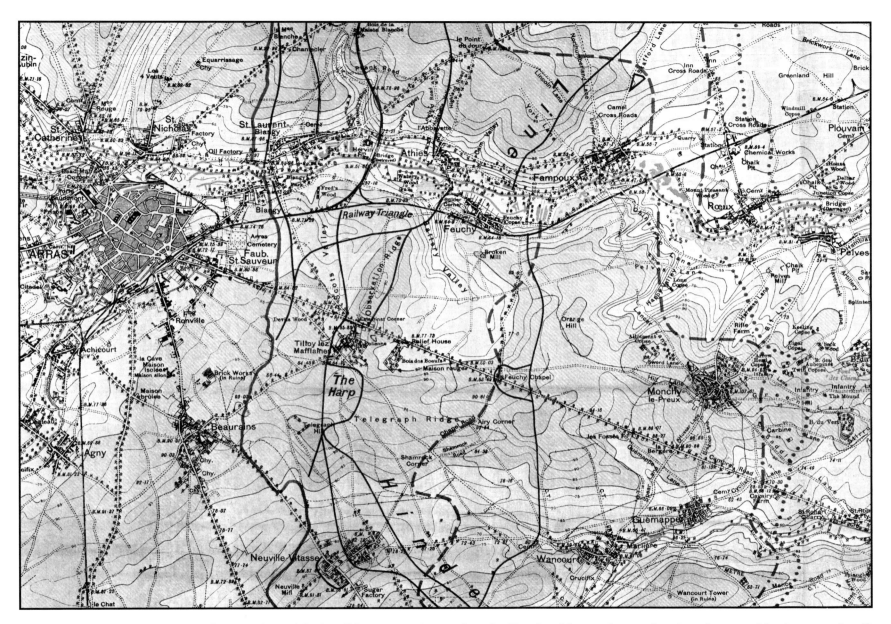

Taken from Sir Douglas Haig's Despatches, this detail from map 3 covering the Battle of Arras shows the situation outside the town itself.

Blangy, 14th April 1917. Stretcher-cases lie beside the road waiting to be taken into a dressing station. [IWM]

A quiet road in present-day Blangy.

machine-guns. Similar problems befell the 12th (Eastern) Division, with fierce, close combat, bomb and bayonet fighting taking place before the advance could be continued. Subsequently, after a further British barrage was called down on the enemy defence positions, German guns in a feature called Battery Valley (behind Observation Ridge) were charged by the Scottish troops. The sight of the surging Scotsmen was too much for the German gunners, who mostly fled, leaving many artillery pieces behind in their haste to distance themselves from the attackers. Tilloy fell to the 3rd Division, aided by tanks, and the entire German front line had then been well and truly breached. The way was open for follow-up operations, and Monchy-le-Preux lay only just over a mile away and practically undefended. However, by then the light was failing, and with the advent of darkness the vigour went out of the advance. Apart from a minor — but comparatively successful — cavalry action at Fampoux, the bulk of the cavalry had not taken part in the day's actions and, as had so often happened in the past, an opportunity to exploit a favourable situation was lost.

South of Arras, the front of the assault was broadened by the 14th, 56th, 30th and 21st Divisions of VII Corps (from north to south in that order), with the timing of their attacks being staggered (the 21st Division did not jump off until 4.15 p.m., which added to their difficulties, the enemy having been thoroughly alerted by the operations further to the north). Initially the 14th Division met with success and, aided by tanks, captured Telegraph Hill and an enemy position called The Harp. Several German machine-guns created problems but in the main enemy resistance was limited, and numbers of Germans readily surrendered to the advancing British troops. On the 56th Division's front serious opposition was encountered at Neuville Vitasse; uncut wire created a major obstacle until a tank arrived on the scene and assisted in making paths through the vicious barbs. Uncut wire and machine-gun fire also held up the 30th

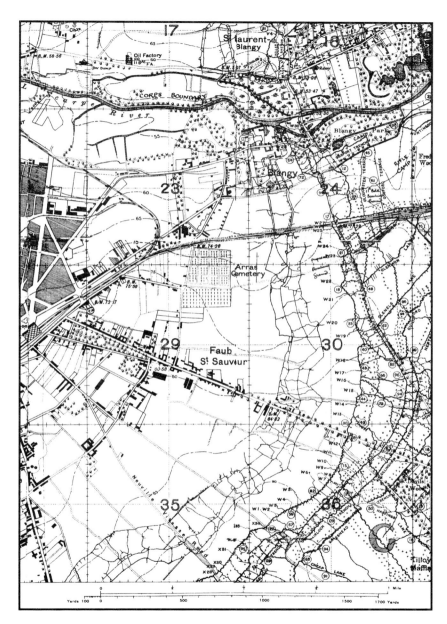

Detail from Trench Map sheet 51B N.W.3, Edition 7A, Arras.

A pile of old shell-cases in a scrap-yard at Arras. This gives a good idea of what is collected from the battlefields.

Near Blangy: Gourock Trench Military Cemetery — set in a sea of wheat this year; once a sea of death and destruction. At Blangy the German trenches were only about 2,000 yards from the centre of Arras.

9.2-inch howitzers in the ruins of Neuville Vitasse. The mound in the centre is probably all that remained of the church. Neuville Vitasse was strongly fortified and was captured by the 56th Division of VII Corps on 9th April 1917. Just beyond the village were the powerful trenches of the Hindenburg Line. [IWM]

Rebuilt Neuville Vitasse Church. After the German Spring Offensive of 1918 the front lines once more ran across this ground as a result of the British withdrawal.

Division, preventing objectives from being reached. A similar situation prevailed on the extreme right, where the 21st Division's efforts were also thwarted by growing German resistance in strong, well-wired positions.

At the end of the day, and in spite of the set-backs on the right flank, a major success had been achieved along the whole front of the overall assault: a wide breach had been made in the German defences from Vimy Ridge down to south of the Arras–Cambrai road. As a result of the German error of holding their reserves too far back from the front a splendid opportunity had arisen for a continuance of the British advance beyond Monchy but, as was so often the case, the Germans quickly recovered from their dilemma, and when at last the British cavalry did arrive it was too late for the initiative to be retained. Bad weather, with freezing conditions and snow falling on the battleground, did not help matters and added to the miseries of the troops.

At midday on the 10th, the 3rd and 12th Divisions again surged forward towards Monchy, which was under heavy fire from British guns. The 37th Division was also now on the scene to help exploit the gap. At one stage units of the 8th Cavalry Brigade moved forward north-west of Monchy but were driven back by heavy machine-gun fire with some losses of men and horses. Other cavalry continued to wait in the rear. Within the next few hours German infantry reserves began to arrive on the battlefield together with fresh gun batteries which promptly unlimbered and came into action.

At dawn on the 11th, over ground carpeted with snow, three surviving tanks crawled forward into Monchy and attacked the Germans still in the village. Two of the ironclads were knocked out and the third was hit by a British barrage which crashed down on the village. Soon afterwards elements of the 37th and 15th Divisions forced an entry, and then two cavalry regiments arrived at full gallop against heavy enemy fire, which caused numerous casualties to men and animals. German guns then concentrated their fire on the village, wreaking carnage among the horses.

A wiring party taking up corkscrew supports, crossing the railway line between Arras and Feuchy, May 1917. [IWM]

Dead German outside a dug-out near Arras, April 1917. [IWM]

A pretty area once known as Battery Valley, south-west of Feuchy. Fierce fighting again took place in this area during the German offensive of 1918, when the line was pushed back to west of Feuchy and most of the ground won in 1917 was relinquished.

Old trench positions south-west of Feuchy.

163

The capture of Monchy-le-Preux was an outstanding feat which resulted from the gallant action of the tanks coupled with the advance of the 37th and 15th Divisions and the exploits of the cavalry. Without the latter it is doubtful whether the village could have been secured owing to the utter exhaustion of the infantrymen, only a handful of whom remained from those that had stormed the hilltop fortress position earlier. What might have been meant as a German counter-attack against Monchy-le-Preux was beaten off by the effective machine-gun fire of the 8th Machine-Gun Squadron, for which Lance-Corporal H. Mugford received the Victoria Cross.

The road into the village of Fampoux as it is now. North of the Scarpe, Fampoux was captured by the 12th Brigade of the 4th Division, and the front line on the night of 9th April 1917 lay just beyond the church. This was one of the most successful and furthest advances of the day — about three miles.

More trenches south of the Arras—Feuchy railway line.

April 1917. On the newly-captured Fampoux road, a ditched tank seems as good a place as any to halt for a while. [IWM]

Right: A striking memorial to the 37th Division atop the hill at Monchy-le-Preux.

11th April was the last day on which exploitation of the victory at Arras was attempted. On that day the 4th Division was ordered to advance towards Roeux and, although a party of Irish Fusiliers got to within two hundred yards of the railway station, the attack broke down against strong German resistance; losses of the 2nd Seaforth Highlanders were particularly heavy from machine-gun fire. Relief of the divisions engaged in the offensive was now necessary and any hope of employing cavalry to capitalise on the early success was abandoned.

Total casualties of the Third Army to 11th April were surprisingly light at 8,238, and about 7,000 prisoners had been captured together with 112 guns. When added to the casualties of the First Army the total came to around 13,000: with an advance of over four miles in places, the rate of casualties to ground captured could be taken as very satisfactory.

On 12th April the Germans evacuated about 1,000 yards of the Hindenburg Line in front of the 21st Division, and both Héninel and Wancourt were taken by the 56th Division with very little resistance. Guémappe, though, was still in the hands of the enemy. Roeux, including the station and the Chemical Works, was attacked by the 9th Division without success and at a heavy cost in casualties, with the South African Brigade being violently shelled as it assembled in Fampoux. Weather conditions were abominable, with snow falling steadily and no shelter being available for the infantry (two men actually died of exposure in the 34th Division).

For 13th April General Allenby had ordered a continuance of the advance but attempts by 21st and 50th Divisions (the latter having relieved 14th Division) made little

Right: The bronze Caribou Memorial of the Royal Newfoundland Regiment at Monchy-le-Preux: one of five of these distinctive monuments to be found in France and Belgium.

Aerial view (looking south) of the important village of Monchy-le-Preux, which was captured on 11th April 1917 by the 37th Division, aided by the 15th Division, plus at least four tanks and cavalry. As it was situated on a hill which gave excellent observation all round, its capture was one of the most notable successes of the battle, and although all the tanks employed were knocked out, their involvement in this fighting was of paramount importance, especially in dealing with heavy enemy machine-gun fire. The cavalry too played a decisive role in the capture and retention of the village. Relief of the exhausted troops of 37th Division and the cavalry was carried out in a blinding snowstorm.

Monchy-le-Preux was relatively undamaged before it was captured, but it then came under terrific German artillery fire which turned it into a charnel house, with dead horses piled everywhere. Intense machine-gun fire also held up further attempts to advance east of the village for the time being.

When on 14th April the Germans counter-attacked from the woods east of Monchy, had it not been for an incredible stand by the Commanding Officer of the Royal Newfoundland Regiment (Lieutenant-Colonel J. Forbes-Robertson), together with a mere handful of his men, Monchy would have fallen. The losses of the 1st Newfoundland Regiment (88th Brigade, 29th Division) during the fighting at Monchy were very high — a total of 468 killed, wounded and missing. Those of the 1st Essex were even higher, at 585. Monchy remained in British hands until the German offensive of 1918. (see also page 214.) [Author/WFA]

progress. An important German observation post called the 'Wancourt Tower' (actually a former windmill) was a centre of resistance which caused an attack by the 9th Brigade of 3rd Division to be broken off after it had suffered heavy casualties. Meanwhile, in the north, Bailleul, Willerval, Vimy and Givenchy-en-Gohelle were evacuated by the Germans and then occupied by British troops. Gavrelle was still strongly held by the enemy.

On the 14th fresh attempts were made to push forward but these were mainly repulsed with heavy casualties, and at the end of the day the situation was practically unchanged. During the course of that morning the Germans formed up for a counter-attack on Monchy-le-Preux and only an incredible stand by a mere handful of men from the Royal Newfoundland Regiment prevented the now-ruined village from falling into the hands of the enemy. A further, more determined, German attack later in the day was also repulsed, mainly by heavy fire from the British artillery. Thus ended what was known by Third Army as the First Battle of the Scarpe, and by First Army as the Battle of Vimy Ridge. The first phase was over; but much more fighting was to occur before the Battle of Arras finally came to an end. Sir Douglas Haig still felt committed to his support of Général Nivelle and he became personally involved in drawing up plans for the next phase of the offensive.

On 16th April a conference was held by Field Marshal Haig at St Pol with the commanders of the First, Third, and Fifth Armies. From this meeting emerged plans for the Second Battle of the Scarpe. On that same day the 'Nivelle Offensive' was launched on the Aisne front but, as has already been indicated, the result was very disappointing and led to serious repercussions in the French Army. Also on the 16th (and 17th) fierce fighting occurred around the Wancourt Tower. The ruins changed hands several times until it was finally taken and consolidated by units of the 50th Division, thus giving the British troops valuable observation over much of the terrain in that area.

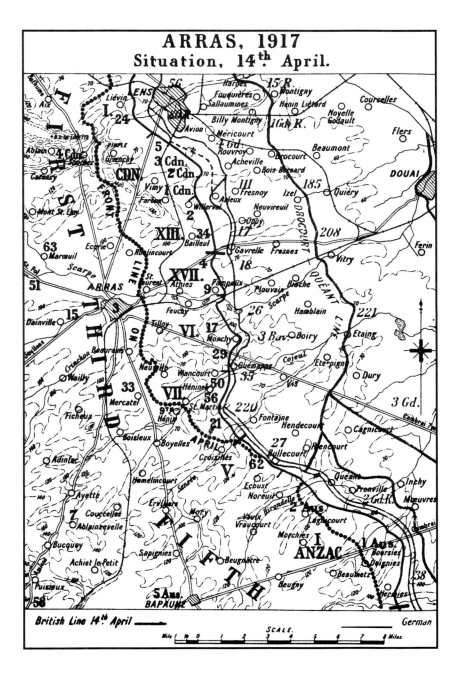

ARRAS, 1917
Situation, 14th April.

British Line 14th April ———   German

SCALE.

167

THE SECOND BATTLE OF THE SCARPE

At 4.45 a.m. on 23rd April (St George's Day) units of VII Corps, supported by twenty tanks, renewed the battle, with extremely fierce fighting taking place. These actions, which were continued on the 24th, became known as the Second Battle of the Scarpe. Guémappe was taken by Scottish troops of 15th Division (VI Corps) and lost again, but further north some success was achieved by the 33rd, 30th, and 50th Divisions. A tank reached Roeux and with its 6-pounder shells blasted the German defenders out of the houses they occupied, and the village was cleared by the Argyll and Sutherland Highlanders. Another tank, supported by the Gordon Highlanders, entered the Chemical Works against fierce opposition; in desperate fighting the station was also occupied. Strong German counter-attacks pushed back the attackers, heavy machine-gun fire preventing further advance in that sector. The important flank village of Gavrelle was attacked and captured by the 63rd (Naval) Division of XIII Corps, but any further progress east of the village was found to be impossible owing to the fierce enemy fire. On the morning of the 24th several strong German counter-attacks were made on Gavrelle but these were repulsed with heavy losses to the enemy. Guémappe was recaptured by the 15th Division, the Scottish troops digging in just beyond the village, and some progress was made east of Monchy-le-Preux and elsewhere.

On 26th April Sir Douglas Haig was summoned to Paris, where he had a discussion with the French Minister of War, M. Painlevé, about the unsatisfactory situation of Nivelle's offensive. It was evident that the French were harbouring thoughts of that offensive being brought to a close, and of Nivelle being replaced by Général Pétain. Sir Douglas Haig accordingly decided to continue the Arras operations in support of Nivelle until a clearer picture emerged of French intentions.

In Sir Douglas Haig's absence, Lieutenant-General Sir Launcelot Kiggell, his chief of staff, chaired a meeting at GHQ attended by Generals Horne and Allenby, who were told that two limited operations were to take place on 28th April, one being to capture Roeux and the Chemical Works, and also Greenland Hill and ground east of Monchy-le-Preux; the other being the capture of Oppy and Arleux by First Army. In the event the 2nd Division failed to take Oppy (Oppy Wood being a major obstacle), while Arleux fell to the 1st Canadian Division in a well-executed attack. At Roeux the inevitable fierce fighting ebbed and flowed: the 15th Royal Scots of 101st Brigade entered the village and actually dug in beyond it before German counter-attacks forced a retirement, some British troops being surrounded and captured.

Third Army casualties for the month of April amounted to just over 52,000, and those arising from First Army's involvement in the Battle of Arras were estimated at around 24,000. Something like 18,000 prisoners had been captured in total by First, Third and Fifth Armies during the month.

The Hindenburg Line trenches at Héninel, south-east of Monchy-le-Preux, from the air.

THE THIRD BATTLE OF THE SCARPE

The third, and last, stage of the Battles of Arras was launched on 3rd May on a sixteen-mile front extending from north of Arleux down to Bullecourt, with the latter village, plus Riencourt and Hendecourt, the objectives of Fifth Army. Third Army attacked on a line Fontain-les-Croisilles—Bois du Sart—Pelves and Plouvain, and First Army's task was to continue clearing-out tactics against local objectives in order to keep the enemy guessing, wear him down and also to make him believe that Arras was still the main battleground, whereas Field Marshal Haig's mind was very preoccupied with Flanders. Haig also considered it necessary to keep the Germans engaged in view of the alarming state of the French Army, available evidence confirming the French were incapable of undertaking any further large-scale actions. Indeed, only two days later the final attack of Nivelle's offensive took place and the main burden of keeping up the pressure on the Western Front then passed to the British.

The First Army's attack went in at 3.45 a.m. and in darkness, and in the north Oppy Wood again presented a major obstacle to the 31st and 2nd Divisions, and little success was achieved. The Canadians, however, once more fought their way forward and succeeded in taking Fresnoy after hard fighting. It subsequently fell into German hands again after a major counter-attack several days later in which a Flammenwerfer was used by the enemy. Roeux and its Chemical Works, attacked by the 4th and 9th Divisions of XVII Corps, continued to present an unsurmountable obstacle, many casualties being caused by fierce German fire. South of the River Scarpe, the 12th, 3rd and 56th Divisions of VI Corps faced a similar situation — uncut wire, together with heavy artillery and machine-gun fire, causing havoc in some units, especially 1st London and 7th Middle-sex of 169th Brigade. The 36th Brigade of 12th Division had more success in capturing a part of the German front line but heavy machine-gun fire stopped any further advance. Third Army's VII Corps experienced the same sort of difficulties and had very little to show for its efforts: the 21st, 18th and 14th Divisions all failed to reach their main objectives and the advance lost all cohesion. Only one tank got forward and that turned back, adding to the confusion of the infantry.

Overall, the Third Battle of the Scarpe was a failure; and attacking in darkness, but with the nearly-full moon waning behind the British troops, had proved to be a disaster which the Germans had taken full advantage of. Fighting nevertheless continued on 11th May on both sides of the Scarpe, with the 56th Division chalking up some success. Roeux was finally captured on 14th May after the Chemical Works had been taken by the 4th Division, and in spite of ferocious German counter-attacks remained in the possession of British troops.

Part of the deep skein of barbed wire that stretched in front of the Hindenburg Line near Héninel. Shellfire has made only this tiny impression on it. 3rd May 1917. [IWM]

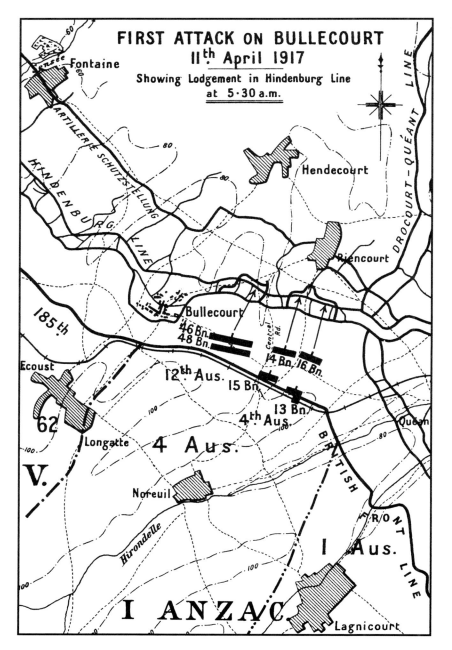

FIRST ATTACK ON BULLECOURT
11th April 1917
Showing Lodgement in Hindenburg Line
at 5·30 a.m.

THE FIRST BATTLE OF BULLECOURT

The First Battle of Bullecourt stemmed from Sir Douglas Haig's plan for General Gough's Fifth Army to assist the Third Army offensive at Arras by pressing the Germans back to the Hindenburg Line and then attacking between Quéant and Bullecourt. In the event of a breach being made in the enemy lines, 4th Cavalry Division was to push through and link up with the Cavalry Corps advancing from Arras. General Gough was enthusiastic about the plan, which he himself had suggested as an aid to General Allenby's Third Army. Bullecourt was to be in the centre of a thrust to be made by I Anzac Corps and V Corps on a front of 3,500 yards; a second objective was to be Riencourt and a third Hendecourt. It was proposed that twelve tanks should make a surprise attack on a limited front prior to the artillery opening fire, and this scheme was accepted by Gough. The 4th Australian Division was to attack behind the tanks, take the Hindenburg Line and capture Bullecourt. Zero Hour was to be 4.30 a.m. (i.e. before dawn) on April 10th.

The Australians were ready at the appointed time, with a number of men lying in the open within 400 yards of Bullecourt. Dawn was approaching but the tanks had not turned up — they had been caught in a snowstorm! The attack was postponed, but next day (April 11th) the Australian infantry took up their positions again on snow-covered ground. They went over at 4.45 a.m. and initially the attack was very successful in spite of the fact that only two tanks survived heavy shelling by the enemy. It meant, though, that the assault occurred without the necessary aid from the tanks, with the wire being insufficiently cut and with no proper barrage being fired to support the troops in order to allow the entry of the tanks. It was a disastrous combination, yet the Hindenburg Line objective was achieved in places — although at the cost of heavy casualties. Riencourt, however, was not reached, although at one time it was thought to have been captured. Gough thought that the attack was proving to be a success (it was also believed that British troops were in Bullecourt itself) and on the strength of it he ordered the cavalry forward. They were, however, driven back by fierce machine-gun fire and took no further part in the operation. Lack of proper artillery support and the failure of the tanks caused the assault to collapse, and the survivors were forced to withdraw. Casualties were heavy. The 4th Australian Brigade was almost destroyed after losing 2,258 out of 3,000 engaged in the action; the 12th Australian Brigade lost 909. The Germans claim to have lost only 750.

The Australians considered the disaster to have been avoidable and they never really forgave Gough for what they considered to be bad planning.

The entrance to the now attractive, once shattered, village of Bullecourt. Part of the powerful Hindenburg Line defences ran across the foreground.

Tablet on a memorial just outside Bullecourt.

East of Bullecourt and south of the Bullecourt–Riencourt road, with the church just right of centre. When the trenches of the Hindenburg Line traversed this now-peaceful, open landscape, it was swept by ferocious fighting.

Three chancel walls. The ruined church at Bullecourt.

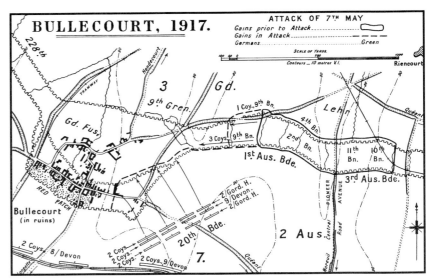

BULLECOURT, 1917.

ATTACK OF 7TH MAY
Gains prior to Attack
Gains in Attack
Germans............Green

SECOND BULLECOURT

Ever since the failure of the first attack at Bullecourt, General Gough had in mind a further attack in that sector. The Australians, however, had not forgotten what had happened and they had no trust in the tanks. The Third Battle of the Scarpe having also proved to be a failure, by May 3rd Sir Douglas Haig had more or less decided to close down the Arras offensive. He did, however, favour another assault at Bullecourt, and as a result a further fierce and bloody struggle took place over a fortnight, six British divisions being involved overall. Unlike that for the first attack, planning was more thorough; also a far greater concentration of artillery was prepared.

For the initial assault I Anzac Corps and V Corps were employed, with 2nd Australian Division attacking at 3.45 a.m. on May 3rd. Fierce fighting occurred in the Hindenburg Line trenches but on the extreme right flank something of a débâcle occurred. Heavy casualties were also suffered by elements of 62nd Division in front of Bullecourt,

but men of the 2/5th West Yorks actually fought their way right through the ruined village and for a time established posts, including one near the church.

Three tanks got into Bullecourt (one being set on fire) and others penetrated the Hindenburg Line north-west of

An unusual Australian memorial outside the church at Bullecourt.

Bullecourt. The 62nd Division was hard hit, sustaining almost 3,000 casualties, and the 7th Division was then ordered forward.

The battle ebbed and flowed during the days that followed, with furious fighting taking place everywhere and Flammenwerfers being used by the Germans. Slowly the attackers edged their way forward and on 17th May, after terrible and continuous struggles, the totally devastated village was cleared by men of the 2/5th London Rifle Brigade and 8th Post Office Rifles. Apart from local encounters over the next few days, the battle came to an end. Dead were everywhere and Second Bullecourt had the unenviable reputation of being a 'killing match' typifying trench warfare at its most murderous.

The British losses were extremely heavy: those of I Anzac Corps 292 officers and 7,190 other ranks, and those of V Corps 300 officers and 6,500 other ranks — the overall total of the divisions engaged in the battle being over 14,000. The Germans had employed the equivalent of four divisions in the Second Battle of Bullecourt and although their actual losses were not revealed it is known that theirs too were very heavy.

The Battles of Arras had been fought over a period of six weeks and Sir Douglas Haig's loyalty to the French could not be questioned. Over 20,000 prisoners had been captured by the three armies involved, together with 254 guns. It had, however, been at the cost of around 150,000 British casualties — a high price to pay, especially for the Third Army, whose own casualties from the overall total amounted to more than 87,000. Had, though, the Germans been in a position to turn their undivided attention to the weakening French front, who can tell what the end result might have been for the Allies.

German casualties for the overall period of the offensive were thought to be equal to the British, although verification is difficult owing to the different methods employed in listing such information.

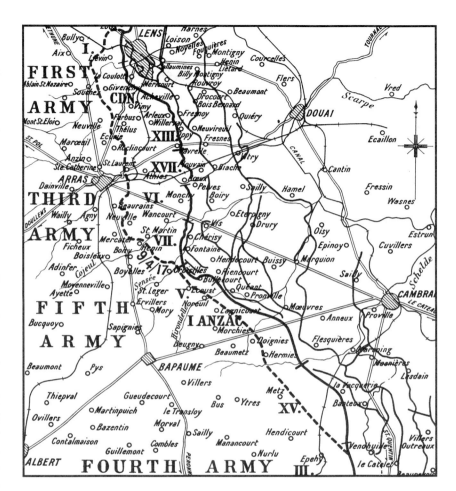

Map showing the situation at the close of the Battle of Arras.

Unfortunately, the offensive also took up much valuable time, a factor that was to have significant repercussions on the forthcoming battles in Flanders. The tragic irony too was that, as with the British Somme and Flanders offensives of 1916 and 1917 respectively, practically all of the ground won at such enormous cost was to be relinquished during the German Spring Offensive — Operation 'Michael' — of 1918.

173

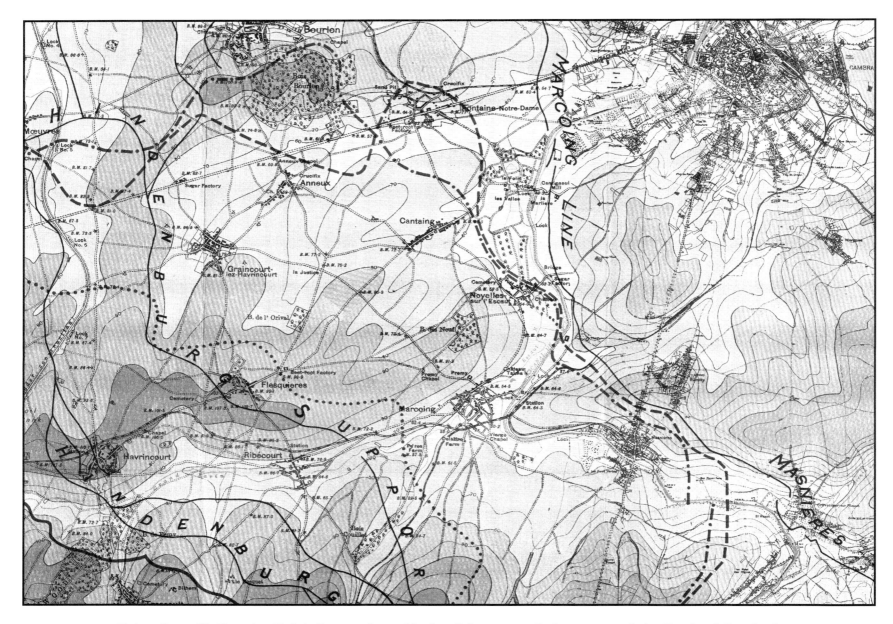

Taken from Sir Douglas Haig's Despatches, this detail from map 5 shows part of the Battle of Cambrai.

THE BATTLE OF CAMBRAI

The Battle of Cambrai, which began at 6.20 a.m. on 20th November 1917, was the first time that tanks had been used en masse. Initially it was a great success, and even caused the premature ringing of church bells in Britain, but, as with so many offensives on the Western Front, it ended as only a partial victory. It also very nearly reverted into a disaster. Nevertheless it was one of the really momentous battles of the First World War and had total success been achieved it might have shortened the war. The use of large numbers of tanks without a preliminary bombardment also introduced a new concept in warfare.

The seeds were sown at a meeting between Field Marshal Haig and the French general, Nivelle, in the early part of 1917, when the British Commander-in-Chief indicated that it was his future intention to break through the mighty Hindenburg Line fortifications protecting Cambrai with a view to capturing that city and exploiting the breach with cavalry. However, at that time the terrible Third Battle of Ypres had yet to be fought, and Nivelle's fall from grace — following the débâcle of his Aisne offensive which led to serious mutinies in the French Army — still lay in the future.

Haig again raised the subject in September of that year with General Sir Julian Byng, Commander of Third Army. Three months previously a plan had been formulated by Lieutenant-Colonel J. F. C. Fuller, GSO1, Tank Corps, for what was in effect a large-scale tank raid in the Cambrai area, where the ground appeared to be eminently suitable for such a purpose. Unlike the morass of Flanders, the terrain west of Cambrai was open and the going was good and comparatively free from the myriads of shell-holes that were associated with other parts of the battlefields. Another — independent — plan for an attack in the Cambrai area was also formulated by Brigadier-General H. H. Taylor, who commanded the artillery of the 9th (Scottish) Division, and this was submitted to Lieutenant-General Sir Charles

British Mark V tanks taking German trenches. This picture is said to have been taken in 1918, but it does serve to illustrate what the Germans must have been confronted with during the Battle of Cambrai in November 1917. [IWM]

Havrincourt Château, which was a German HQ. The château grounds were the scene of bitter fighting in November 1917.

175

The Spoil Bank north-west of Havrincourt and below Lock 7 on the Canal du Nord, which was still under construction when the war broke out. This strong German defence point was captured by the 36th Ulster Division. Thermite was used by the attackers.

Lowrie Military Cemetery, near Havrincourt. All 251 of its graves come from the fighting here in 1918. A motorway passes close by.

Woollcombe, commander of IV Corps, for consideration. Eventually, after various revisions, a master plan was collated and approved by Haig, with modifications, and this was outlined at a meeting of General Byng's corps commanders on 26th October.

It was an ambitious plan, based on a three-stage battle in which the Cavalry Corps had an important part to play, which depended on surprise for its success and the use of the whole of the Tank Corps. It also had to take into account the lack of reserves brought about by the bitter fighting of Third Ypres and the need for British troops to be sent to Italy following the disaster at Caporetto in which the Italians were thrown back with enormous losses. It was received with enthusiasm by Brigadier-General Hugh Elles, the 36-year-old commander of the Tank Corps, who was both very popular and a good soldier. He would lead the tanks into action with his flag flying on a tank named 'Hilda' in a manner since reminiscent of the tank commanders in the desert battles of the Second World War. To him the final outcome of the battle — and in spite of its setbacks — was a vindication of the method of attack previously proposed by Lieutenant-Colonel E. D. Swinton, who became known as 'the father of the tanks'.

The British Commander-in-Chief had stressed in his modifications to the plan that the town of Cambrai itself was not to be considered as a main objective of the assault but would need to be isolated by the cavalry to protect the flank of the anticipated advance to the River Sensée, about ten miles to the north, and, it was hoped, well beyond that feature. The capture of Bourlon Ridge, on which were situated the large wood and the adjacent village of that name, was of prime importance to the whole scheme as it overlooked wide stretches of the enemy rear areas in that sector. Should a breakthrough not be achieved within forty-eight hours, the offensive would be closed down. (He was subsequently to change his mind on this once the assault was under way.)

The task confronting the Third Army was a formidable one. It called for the tanks and infantry to smash through the powerful Siegfried Stellung (the Hindenburg Line to the British) which had been prepared by the Germans prior to their strategic withdrawal of March 1917 on the Somme front. Extremely deep trenches, vast belts of barbed wire, hundreds of yards deep, and numerous well-sited strong-points, with excellent fields of fire for the omnipresent machine-guns, covered the battle zone, which consisted of a well-wired outpost system, then a heavily wired and wide fire trench, with a similarly wired support trench two hundred yards behind. About a mile to the rear was the Hindenburg Support Line, with similar matching excavations and seemingly impenetrable masses of barbed wire. A third position, not yet completed, and called by the Germans Siegfried II, was located about two miles behind the main defences and that again was protected by acres of barbed wire. Doubtless convinced in their own minds of the invulnerability of these massive fortifications — plus the fact of having suffered heavy losses during Third Ypres — the Germans manned the sector lightly, with only two divisions and part of a third in the line. Other troops, though, were in the process of being transferred from the Eastern Front following the Russian revolution, and elements of these divisions had already arrived at Cambrai.

Together with the Tank Corps, the initial British assault force was to be spearheaded by five infantry divisions from III and IV Corps, these being, from north to south, 62nd (West Riding) Division, 51st (Highland) Division (both of IV Corps), 6th Division, 20th (Light) Division and 12th (Eastern) Division of III Corps. In the north the 36th (Ulster) Division was to advance after the main assault had commenced. The attack covered a front of six miles along which about 1,000 guns were deployed in well-camouflaged positions. About 300 aircraft, several squadrons of which were to be used in a close support role, were to take part in the operations. The number of tanks available amounted to 378 battle tanks plus

After the Cambrai offensive — the old British front line at Trescault, 10th December 1917.

The Cambrai battlefield, looking back towards Havrincourt and Havrincourt Wood from the site of the Hindenburg Line. What was known as the Grand Ravine, but which was actually a comparatively minor depression, is in the foreground.

A 6th Tank Battalion Mark IV 'Female'. Although this photograph was in fact taken on a training ground, it gives an excellent idea of what these steel monsters must have looked like from a German trench. Unlike 'male' tanks, which had 6-pounder guns, the 'females' were armed only with machine-guns, one of which can be seen protruding from its sponson. [IWM]

Below: The Flesquières Ridge from the Trescault–Ribecourt road: the ground across which the battle raged in November 1917. The strongly held village of Flesquières dominated the ridge and its capture was vital to the success of the offensive. However, in spite of a two-mile smoke screen, the attack on the ridge by the 51st Division was held up, and this in turn affected the cavalry operations. The initial failure at Flesquières had a detrimental bearing on the course of the battle.

98 for supply purposes and wire clearing, etc. (grappling hooks being used for dealing with the wire).

To overcome the problem of crossing the wide enemy trenches, huge fascines of brushwood, nearly two tons in weight, were secured to the top of each fighting tank by chains. These were to be dropped into a trench and used as a filling over which a tank could cross. A special 'Tank Battle Drill' had been formulated and practised to ensure close co-operation between the tanks and infantry. Two cavalry divisions were to pass through the infantry after crossings had been effected over the Escaut Canal at Marcoing and Masnières, and a bridgehead secured. They were then to proceed north-eastwards to cut off Cambrai from the east, although the town itself was not to be occupied at that stage. Other cavalry units were to assist in the capture of Cantaing and Fontaine before wheeling north-eastward to capture Bourlon. Great care was taken to camouflage the noise of the tanks moving forward to the start point in Havrincourt Wood and nearby villages, with low-flying aircraft and machine-gun fire masking the sound of the engines.

On the 18th a German raid against positions held by the 36th Division resulted in six prisoners being taken; from them the Germans learned that an attack on Havrincourt was in preparation. This, and other pointers towards an impending assault, caused the Germans to be put on the alert, but owing to the lack of any preliminary bombardment they were misled as to its scale. Consequently the offensive came mainly as a surprise when at the appointed hour the massed tanks crawled forward and the heavy British bombardment began. The all-important Flesquières Ridge was covered by a two-mile smoke screen which blinded the German defenders, and Nine Wood, north-west of Marcoing, was also screened off with smoke.

The sudden avalanche of shells crashed down on the German forward defences and the outposts were soon overrun. Along the whole front the fierce bombardment burst in a hellish fusion of noise and flame as a mixture of high-explosive, shrapnel and thermite shells rained down on the dazed defenders. Those who risked the flying metal and raised their heads were horrified to see dozens and dozens of huge ironclads crawling towards them out of the mist with guns spitting fire and the fearsome wire being crushed beneath their vast bulk, or pulled aside by grapnel hooks. Close behind came the infantry, plodding forward with fixed bayonets and following the tracks of the tanks through the barriers of wire with an ease not previously witnessed in that war. Fierce fighting occurred in Havrincourt village, and especially around the château, which had been converted into a strongpoint, with some enemy pockets holding out for several hours before being mopped up. Elsewhere terrified Germans streamed forward, hands aloft, only too ready to surrender and be taken prisoner. The so-called Grand Ravine, which in actual fact amounted to no more than a comparatively shallow depression in the ground, was full of Germans endeavouring to escape towards Marcoing, many of them having abandoned their weapons in their haste to get away from the terror confronting them.

By about 8 a.m. the Hindenburg front position had fallen — or was about to fall — on the whole of the IV Corps sector, and at 8.35 a.m. the barrage lifted on to the Hindenburg Support system on the Flesquières Ridge. The spoilbank on the west bank of the empty Canal du Nord was taken without much difficulty by the 36th (Ulster) Division, with Thermite being used in the process and numbers of the defenders running away. On the III Corps front Ribécourt was captured by 9.30 a.m., although snipers were still active in the village some five hours later. Just after 10 a.m. the 29th Division moved into the battlefield with the task of seizing a bridgehead over the St Quentin Canal between Masnières and Nine Wood for the cavalry to pass through. They reached Marcoing and Nine Wood by midday. Several tanks received direct hits from enemy field guns during this advance, and one tank which attempted to cross a damaged bridge at Les Rues Vertes caused the broken structure to collapse and fell into the canal — its crew fortunately managing to escape unhurt. Later some of the cavalry managed to cross over a nearby footbridge, as did elements of the Hampshire Regiment, but heavy fire held up the advance in this sector, with the hoped-for cavalry break-through failing to materialise.

In the north the important bridge on the Bapaume–Cambrai road over the waterless Canal du Nord was blown by the enemy, but south of that main road Graincourt was captured at about 3 p.m. by the 62nd (West Riding) Division with the aid of tanks, three of which were knocked out by field guns located on the outskirts of the village. Across to the north-east could be seen the dark bulk of Bourlon Wood, the capture of which was so vital to the success of the whole operation. Before that could happen Flesquières had to be taken; but it was there that a major hold-up occurred, with well-sited enemy guns on the ridge causing havoc to the tanks and advancing infantry. However, at least one tank managed to get right through Flesquières before becoming the victim of a German gun. The failure of the 51st Division to take this objective was claimed by some to have been because the division's commander (Major-General G. M. Harper) had decided to vary the Battle Drill for co-operation between tanks and infantry, but whatever the reason it had a serious effect on the overall assault and was instrumental in the cavalry being held back. Another factor, though, was that the massed enemy guns at Flesquières were commanded by a German general (Lieutenant-General Freiherr von Watter) who had trained his men in anti-tank warfare after having studied the problem of tanks during the Somme battles. The Germans abandoned the village during the night, but by then the opportunity for the immediate capture of the Bourlon Ridge was lost, in spite of the fact of several tanks actually getting into the almost empty wood but then having to retire because of the lack of infantry support. Had fresh infantry been available the story would doubtless have been very different.

As daylight faded on 20th November heavy rain began to fall on the exhausted troops, who had gone as far as they could. There had been an advance of over four miles that day and about 5,000 yards of the Hindenburg system had been taken. Only the lack of fresh reserves had prevented an even greater success from being achieved — but no such reserves were available. Casualties had been incredibly light and amounted to about 4,000 (as compared to over 57,000 on the first day of the Somme). Slightly over half of the fighting tanks that started had been lost, 65 of them to artillery fire; the remainder having been ditched or having broken down. In spite of strenuous efforts Bourlon had not been taken — though the opportunity had been there earlier, for at 1.40 p.m. aerial reconnaissance had ascertained that Cantaing was undefended, with nothing to stop the cavalry from advancing on Bourlon Wood. When they did eventually charge at 3.30 p.m., German machine-guns were in position and the attempt was defeated. Some of the horsemen got almost as far as Fontaine before being forced back, with the loss of some men and horses.

At dawn on the 21st Flesquières was occupied by the 51st Division and Cantaing was also captured by the 154th Brigade with the aid of twelve tanks. Fontaine was entered by tanks in the afternoon and consolidated by infantry, and Anneux was captured by the 62nd Division. In the north the Germans counter-attacked at Moeuvres, which had been entered by the 36th Division, and drove the Ulstermen out of the village. Exhaustion was now taking its toll on the troops; the momentum of the advance slowed down. That evening Sir Douglas Haig ordered III Corps to cease its operations on the right flank but at the same time decided to continue the thrust towards Bourlon in spite of his 48-hour time limit having been reached. On the 22nd he visited 51st Division HQ at Trescault, then went forward on horseback and from a suitable vantage point studied the battlefields in the direction of Flesquières. Fontaine was recaptured by the Germans that day in a fierce counter-attack.

'Hyacinth' of 'H' Battalion lay stranded in a German second-line trench in the 6th Division's sector 'at side of road one mile west of Ribécourt' according to the original caption to this photograph taken on 20th November 1917. In the trench are men of the 1st Leicesters. [IWM]

Exactly one mile west of Ribécourt (measured by the author), beside the Trescault–Ribecourt road. The village church can just be seen.

Ribécourt, 20th November 1917. The original caption to this photograph states: 'Taken immediately after capture, the camera being grazed by a machine-gun bullet.' [IWM]

The entrance to present-day Ribécourt.

On the 23rd the 40th Division (V Corps) attacked in the direction of Bourlon Ridge at 10.30 a.m. with the support of around 100 tanks and intensive artillery fire plus low-flying aircraft. Terrible fighting took place in the wood, with the crest being reached against bitter enemy opposition and at the cost of heavy casualties. More German reinforcements were being rushed into the Cambrai sector and that day too Richthofen's famous 'flying circus' arrived on the scene. An

Left: Aerial view of Flesquières (looking north-west), with the château centre left. The village, and the château, were turned into an immensely strong fortress by the Germans, who also massed guns on the ridge which were commanded by a general (General-leutnant von Watter) who had trained his men in anti-tank operations. One tank actually managed to get right through the village before being hit by German artillery. The Germans withdrew during the night of 20th/21st November and the village was occupied at dawn on the 21st by men of the 51st Division. [Author/WFA]

Men of the 235th Brigade (47th Divisional Artillery) look towards the camera whilst watering horses in shell-torn Flesquières, 24th November 1917. [IWM]

Two gendarmes stand where the horses slaked their thirst.

In front of the château at Flesquières: open ground across which tanks trundled under fire from German guns.

Close-up of the château at Flesquières, the Château de la Retraite, which was heavily fortified, as was the château wall.

The Lone Stand legend. This is a copy of a much-enlarged photograph the author was shown in Flesquières village school. It shows a memorial commemorating a stand reputed to have been made by a German who single-handedly manned a gun and took on British tanks as they topped the Flesquières Ridge after his battery had been destroyed. Some controversy surrounds this legendary event: the number of tanks said to have been knocked out by this gun varies between seven and sixteen; some accounts suggest that the lone defender was a German NCO, others that he was a Major. There is nothing official to substantiate the details.

The owner of Château de la Retraite, Monsieur de Valicourt (on the right), with his son, marking the spot where the 'lone stand' gun was said to have been positioned in the château grounds at the time of the battle. It is indeed a superb vantage point, and the slow-moving tanks would have presented excellent targets as they topped the ridge here.

183

Copy of a German photograph in the possession of Monsieur de Valicourt which was taken when the battle was in progress. Helmeted German soldiers can be seen lower right, and an aeroplane flies overhead, above the exploding shells.

The château wall, which was loopholed by the Germans for machine-guns and snipers.

New life for old. Monsieur de Valicourt standing by an interesting relic of a shrapnel-scarred tree in the château grounds.

Remains of a German strongpoint in the château grounds.

Aerial view, looking north-east and in the general direction of Cambrai, with Graincourt in the centre, Anneux beyond and Bourlon Wood upper left. Graincourt was captured in the after-noon of the first day of the battle but was lost again in the German counter-attack. Anneux was captured by the 62nd Division and also lost later. [Author/WFA]

View from the Bapaume–Cambrai road, looking south across the Cambrai battlefield, with Graincourt upper left.

The author's wife plus rural accompaniment near Graincourt: a scene far removed from that of bursting shells and of tanks rumbling towards Bourlon Wood, over in the background. The British front line was established approximately at this point after the German counter-attack of 30th November 1917.

The unfinished Canal du Nord near Moeuvres, 28th November 1917. A clearance job awaits the working party formed up on the canal bed facing the blown-up bridge. [IWM]

The Canal du Nord in use, with Moeuvres Church tower on the right; picture taken from the Bapaume–Cambrai road. The 36th (Ulster) Division fought over this ground and captured most of Moeuvres but were then forced out again. This area was also the scene of bitter fighting during the German counter-attack. Bourlon Wood is to the right of where this photograph was taken.

attempt by the 51st Highland Division to recapture Fontaine failed after hand-to-hand fighting, and dismounted cavalry were used as infantrymen in order to stiffen the front line. Part of Bourlon village came into British possession but was subsequently lost. Most of Moeuvres was overrun by Irish troops, only for them to be forced out again by fierce German counter-attacks. At nightfall Bourlon Wood was an inferno of shell-bursts and falling trees, to which was added the constant rattle of machine-guns and rifle fire. In the early hours of the black and rainy night the 51st Division was relieved by the Guards Division.

For several days the battle raged back and forth, with Bourlon village again being entered and then relinquished after fierce German counter-attacks. A number of Highland troops and others from the 13th East Surreys were cut off in the village, some of the Highlanders being surrounded and captured. Survivors were extricated with difficulty just before a fresh British barrage crashed down on the very location they had been defending. On the night of the 26th/27th a blizzard swept across the battlefield to add to the tribulations of men and horses.

At 6.20 a.m. on the 27th what proved to be the last of the British attacks went in, supported by a heavy bombardment and aided by thirty tanks. By then the enemy had been much reinforced with fresh divisions and many guns, and plans had even been formulated by the German High Command for a counter-stroke on the 30th. Meanwhile the 62nd and Guards Divisions encountered severe opposition as they endeavoured to push forward. Once again Fontaine was partly overrun, as was a portion of Bourlon village; once again both were lost in fierce German counter-attacks. Casualties were heavy both in men and tanks, and with the failure of this latest attempt Sir Douglas Haig decided to close down the offensive. Reliefs were carried out, the cavalry went into winter quarters, and the Tank Corps issued instructions for withdrawal of the tanks to the Somme area. In the nightmare conditions of Bourlon Wood men of the

View towards Bourlon Wood from near Cantaing. A pleasant pastoral scene which belies the horror of what once happened here. Savage fighting occurred over this stretch of ground and in the wood itself.

Looking towards Fontaine-Notre-Dame from close to Anneux, with the south-east portion of Bourlon Wood on the left. Fontaine was taken on 21st November after tanks broke into the village under intense fire from field guns. The village was consolidated by 7th Argylls and 4th Seaforths but a strong German counter-attack forced these troops out on the 22nd. Hand-to-hand fighting occurred in and about the village as the 51st Highland Division endeavoured to retake this stronghold, but to no avail.

Cantaing, very much the worse for shellfire. German soldiers stop for a chat near the church, its stump of a tower holed by large-calibre shells. [IWM]

Two young ladies in a very different Cantaing, near the rebuilt church. Cantaing was captured on 21st November with the aid of twelve tanks but was lost again in the German counter-offensive.

Pilot's eye view of Bourlon Wood and the village of Fontaine-Notre-Dame, where so much bitter fighting took place in November 1917. There was also much aerial activity here, and on 23rd November Baron Manfred von Richthofen arrived on the scene with his 'flying circus'. The wood was finally taken on 27th September 1918 when it was again stormed by the Canadians (see also pages 218–219). [Author/WFA]

47th (London) Division, who had relieved the 62nd Division, endeavoured to consolidate inadequate defensive positions along the crest of the wood amidst tangled undergrowth and shell-blasted trees. To add to their trials the wood was heavily bombarded with gas shells by the Germans, so that gas masks had to be worn all the time. During the night of 29th/30th November the wood was shelled very heavily, 16,000 field gun shells having been fired into it since the 28th. From dawn on 30th November an absolute storm of shells rained down on the British positions all along the front and at 11.53 a.m. the 47th Division reported dense waves of Germans attacking along the crest from east to west. The counter-stroke had begun.

The principal aim of the German commanders was the recapture of the whole of the Hindenburg system by an attack from the south to strike westwards, closely followed by one from the north directed southwards, This was intended to pinch out the British salient, and it was also hoped that an opportunity might be presented for a breakthrough. In the event neither objective was achieved, although the counter-offensive came very close to succeeding, with the British line eventually being stabilised some distance to the rear. Gouzeaucourt fell quickly but was recaptured by a brilliant counter-attack by the Guards and consolidated with the help of some tanks which had not yet left the battle zone. In the north, on the front held by the 2nd, 47th and 56th Divisions of IV Corps, the Germans attacked in force over open ground between Bourlon Wood and Moeuvres but were slaughtered in droves by the concentrated fire of many British guns, including numerous heavy pieces. One machine-gun battery of eight guns belonging to the 2nd Division is said to have fired 70,000 rounds into the flank of the attacking troops, mowing them down in heaps. An attack towards Cantaing by the German 3rd Guards Division was also smashed by intense gunfire, and the assault was contained in that sector. Except for the loss of some advanced positions, the day ended with the British line bent back but unbroken, in spite of the enormous pressure exerted by the enemy, particularly in the northern sector. Thus, what could have been a serious British defeat was averted by the gallantry of men who were already dog-tired from their previous exertions and to whom the massive German counter-stroke came as an unpleasant surprise.

Further heavy fighting took place in the south which resulted in the loss of Masnières and Les Rues Vertes on 1st December and La Vacquerie on 3rd December. However, in the north the German assault had petered out and things in that sector mainly quietened down. By now Sir Douglas Haig had decided that any further offensive action by his troops was not possible and he reluctantly agreed a shortening of the line, which meant withdrawal from the Bourlon salient position and from Cantaing, Anneux and Graincourt. By 7th December the British line west of the Canal du Nord was back almost to its old pre-20th November position, but

Left: In the German counter-stroke at Cambrai, Captain C. Raymond Hulsart (left) and Lieutenant Paul McLoud of the US 11th Engineers were decorated for gallantry at Gouzeaucourt. The 11th Engineers were one of the nine regiments sent to France after the United States entered the war, to help Allied troops on emergency railway work. At the time of the German assault, the 11th Engineers were building a railway yard near Gouzeaucourt and many of them helped the British to stop the attack, with the regiment suffering 18 casualties. Gouzeaucourt was also the place where the first American soldiers were wounded whilst serving at the front with an American unit (during shelling on 5th September 1917). [IWM]

Flesquières — including the ridge which had been such an obstacle to the original advance — remained in British hands, as did Ribécourt and, of course, Havrincourt. Marcoing, though, was also relinquished and the Germans held ground which more or less balanced British gains.

British losses from 20th November to 8th December were about 45,000, of whom 20,000 were killed or missing. German casualties were much the same. An official enquiry was held into the causes of the British reverse and questions were asked in Parliament. Sir Douglas Haig accepted overall responsibility and weathered the storm, but other heads rolled. Brigadier-General Charteris and the CIGS, Lieutenant-General Sir Launcelot Kiggell, were replaced and several other commanders were sent home. Some criticism was levelled at General Sir Julian Byng (particularly after the war in Lloyd George's memoirs) but overall the Higher Command escaped major censure, the reverse being attributed to insufficient battle training and other factors.

Perhaps not surprisingly, the Germans claimed Cambrai as a victory, but in his memoirs Hindenburg admitted that a catastrophe had narrowly been avoided only by the arrival of German divisions from the East. There is no denying that the British attack on 20th November was an achievement of some magnitude, with the tanks having proved their worth as a successful and decisive weapon of war.

Louverval Military Cemetery, Doignes, east of Bapaume and on the Bapaume–Cambrai road. The cemetery contains 118 United Kingdom, 4 Australian and 2 New Zealand graves. The memorial records 7,048 'Missing' from the Battle of Cambrai 1917. [Author/WFA]

1918

The Kaiser studying maps under the guidance of von Hindenburg and Ludendorff. [IWM]

German infantry and artillery concentrating in the wrecked streets of St Quentin immediately before the launching of the German offensive in Picardy on 21st March 1918. [IWM]

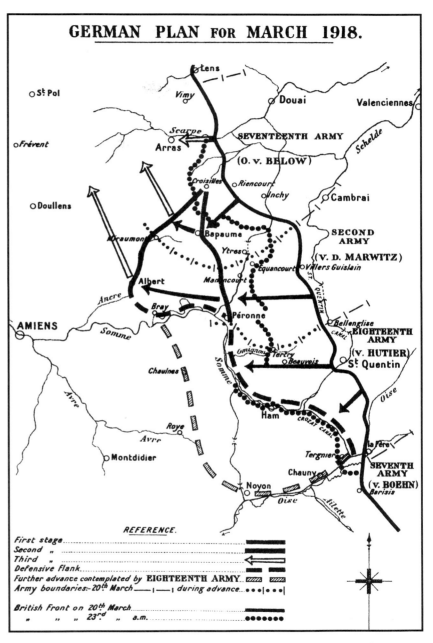

GERMAN PLAN FOR MARCH 1918.

REFERENCE.

First stage
Second „
Third „
Defensive flank
Further advance contemplated by EIGHTEENTH ARMY
Army boundaries:- 20th March ———— during advance

British Front on 20th March
„ „ „ 23rd „ a.m.

191

LUDENDORFF'S OPERATION 'MICHAEL' THE SOMME BATTLES OF 1918

Towards the late afternoon on 20th March 1918 fog began to form all along the front of the British Fifth Army (General Sir Hubert Gough) and also that of the Third Army (General Sir J. H. G. Byng) on its left. During the night it thickened, and many anxious eyes peered into the gloom of No Man's Land for unusual signs of enemy activity. The apprehension arose from the knowledge that the Germans had for some time been preparing to launch an offensive, and all the indications — including information gleaned from prisoners — denoted that a major battle was imminent. South of St Quentin, in a sector recently taken over from the French, the fog was particularly thick in the low-lying ground of the River Oise and along the Crozat Canal. The British (previously French) defences in that area were by no means as good as those north of St Quentin, where much work had been put in by General Gough's men, and those of the Third Army, in the preparation of what was known as the Forward Zone (effectively an outpost line) and a Battle Zone. A Rear Zone (later called the Green Line) had been planned, but labour shortages had prevented any real work from being undertaken on that defensive position. For his 42-mile-long front General Gough had at his disposal four corps consisting of twelve infantry divisions (eleven of which were in the line) and three cavalry divisions, whereas the Third Army, which held a front of twenty-eight miles, had fourteen divisions available for the defence of its sector (four of those being in reserve).

The Germans had built up a very formidable attacking force of three armies of sixty-three infantry divisions (plus eleven in the line). Of these, forty-three divisions were opposite General Gough's Fifth Army and nineteen opposite the centre of General Byng's Third Army. A number of these divisions had been transferred from the Eastern Front following the Russian Revolution, which had begun in March 1917 and eventually led to the Peace Treaty of Brest-Litovsk. A massive total of 6,473 guns of all calibres had been assembled by the Germans for the offensive, more than twice the number available to Fifth Army and Third Army combined. In addition, 3,532 trench mortars were on hand to lend support to the powerful German artillery bombardment. An important factor was that the German forces included highly trained storm troops, adept in the art of infiltration, their job being to take advantage of any gaps or breakthroughs in the defences and then to press on, leaving any isolated pockets of resistance to be mopped up by following troops. A very precise artillery programme had been prepared by Lieutenant-Colonel Bruchmuller, a foremost artillery expert who had been recalled from retirement. His plans were based on seven limited periods of concentrated bombardment (the first to be for 120 minutes) which would ensure saturation fire by high-explosives and gas on every possible target within the British lines — including trenches, billets, strongpoints, machine-gun positions, gun batteries, telephone exchanges and command posts, etc. It was one of the most intensive artillery programmes ever devised and it was to play havoc with the British defence and defenders.

Much was at stake for the Germans, for they knew that they had to strike before the Americans, who had come into the war in April 1917, could tip the balance in favour of the Entente with large numbers of fresh troops. Although they had forced the Russians to sue for peace, which released many troops for service on the Western Front, time was running out for the Central Powers and everything now depended on a successful outcome to what had been designated as Operation 'Michael' and had as its objective the crushing of the British prior to turning on, and defeating, the French. In this aim they were to be greatly assisted by the all-pervading fog which smothered the battlefields and effectively denied the defenders vital observation. Because of this the British artillery began intermittent fire from 3.30 a.m. on the 21st on targets that had already been registered and on localities where it was thought that the enemy could be assembling. As an added precaution the St Quentin front was also flooded by gas released from cylinders.

The blow fell at about 4.40 a.m. on the 21st when a terrific bombardment opened up on the whole of the front of the Fifth Army and that of most of Third Army. Also included in the initial intense barrage was the front of the First Army further north, this being part of the German plan to mislead the defenders as to the actual point of attack. Similar deceptive artillery fire was directed elsewhere, including on part of the French front and in the Messines sector.

The staggering fierceness and accuracy of the bombardment had an immediate effect, with many vital positions being destroyed. The immense volume of fire was overwhelming, with gas adding to the terrifying ordeal of the British troops who crouched in their trenches as the ground heaved and the air vibrated all around. Enemy trench mortars poured concentrated fire on the front trenches while field guns and heavier howitzers battered redoubts and pulverised barbed wire. Bodies and bits of bodies were blown into the air, trenches were obliterated and strongpoints became mounds of debris. Vast explosions occurred as ammunition dumps were hit, the fog adding to the general chaos in rear areas. The German artillery plan was systematically followed, each change being implemented at the appropriate time. In several places infantry clashes occurred before the main assault, and on the front held by the 18th Division the Germans captured a canal lock at 7.15 a.m. but were stopped from progressing further by a party of the 7th Buffs. Another premature attack took place elsewhere as early as 5.30 a.m.

At 9.40 a.m. the German assault began in earnest. The leading waves swept forward and burst through the Forward Zone before the British troops realised that the main attack had begun. Desperate resistance was offered by those who

A British trench after the Germans had passed this way during their 1918 Spring Offensive — a scene that was all too prevalent in those grim days. [Photo: The late Colonel G. B. Jarrett OBE, Maryland, USA]

A stack of shells collected by a farmer on the Somme in the 1980s — some of them probably relics of the Spring Offensive.

The ruined village of Vaulx-Vraucourt, north-east of Bapaume, from the air, July 1918.

The village of Vaulx-Vraucourt, 1982. The scene of fierce fighting in March 1918, now surrounded by green and pleasant fields, with no trace of war to mar its tranquility. [Author/WFA]

had survived the shelling and gassing but the fog favoured the attackers, who swept onwards leaving still-existing redoubts and other strongpoints to be mopped up by special parties of following troops. Blinded by the fog and not knowing until too late whether the figures emerging from it were friend or foe, the defenders were cut off, surrounded and either captured or bombed into submission. In a number of cases the garrisons held out for several hours and some even fought on for two days before being overwhelmed, most of the defenders by then having been killed or wounded. The loss of many vital machine-guns during the heavy shelling also had a deleterious effect on the defence, as did the inability of the British artillery to observe or direct fire where it was most wanted. A breakdown in communications between the artillery and the Royal Flying Corps, too, contributed to the overall débâcle, although much valuable information was passed on by reconnaissance planes, especially on the Third Army front, where the fog was thinner and dissipated reasonably quickly. During the assault on the 21st the Germans used nine tanks, four of them of German construction and five captured British Mark IVs.

Only in the Flesquières Salient was there no main attack, it being part of the overall German plan for that feature to be pinched out rather than undergo a direct assault. The area was, though, saturated with mustard gas, causing many casualties to the British defenders. On this sector the Germans put into operation their 'Michael 2' — an assault to cut off the Flesquières Salient and then join hands with the 'Michael 1' attackers, thus trapping the British divisions facing Cambrai/Marcoing.

By the afternoon of the 21st the German storm troops had smashed their way through the Forward Zone and well into the Battle Zone south of St Quentin, where the fog had covered their activities. Around the north of the town, however, where the fog had cleared earlier, they were fired on by the machine-guns of surviving British troops until

Wrecked artillery limbers and dead horses on the Bapaume road, 25th March 1918. [IWM]

A section of the Albert–Bapaume road in recent years.

those tenacious defenders in turn inevitably suffered the same fate as their comrades. Bloody hand-to-hand encounters occurred all along the line as the Germans pushed on; but with the sun breaking through in the morning at the junction of the Fifth and Third Armies, where visibility was better, they ran into severe British machine-gun fire and were mown down in heaps. Enemy attempts to capture a redoubt on Quentin Ridge, south of Flesquières, and which was manned by South African troops, were repulsed with heavy losses. In the Flesquières Salient the 63rd (Royal Naval) Division put up a stout opposition until they eventually received orders to retire to a new position. Just to their north the 51st (Highland) Division's front, along the Cambrai–Bapaume road, had been broken. Fierce resistance had been put up by isolated groups of Scotsmen before they too were overwhelmed by an equally determined enemy.

Further north, on the Third Army's front, the casualties from the initial bombardment had also been very severe, for in that sector the British troops were more densely packed than on the Fifth Army front. The defensive positions were also in better shape than those taken over earlier from the French in the south, but this tended to give a false impression of security and caused overcrowding of the Forward Zone, with inevitable results. Also, when gaps were eventually forced open by the German storm troops, they had a less formidable task in places as fewer British troops were manning the northern Battle Zone than in the south. Even so, they still met with fierce resistance everywhere, including from ancillary troops who had been pressed into front line service. Known to the Germans as Operation 'Mars', the attacks in that area became less vigorous and the danger to Arras receded.

As the day drew to a close the fighting died down and the night of 21st/22nd was relatively quiet apart from enemy shelling of the Flesquières Salient. Both sides had suffered heavy casualties and the German commanders took advantage of the darkness to move forward their reserves. The

British, with few reserves available, made adjustments to their positions, including pulling behind the Crozat Canal on the southern flank. Also under cover of darkness many men who had been trapped behind the German advance carefully made their way back to the British lines and rejoined their badly depleted units. Some, though, blundered into enemy posts and never reached safety.

Some thirteen German A7V tanks (they only built perhaps twenty-five at the most) took part in the attack at Villers-Bretonneux on 24th April. In designing their own battle tank, the Germans built a mobile fortress — a huge steel box on a tractor chassis with a crew of eighteen — at its best on a flat, firm surface. This one, 'Elfriede', ended up on her side about three-quarters of a mile from Villers-Bretonneux, on the Hangard-en-Sauterne road, the victim of the 6-pounder gun of a male Mark IV of 1st Battalion, Tank Corps, and a participant in the first-ever encounter between tanks. In that engagement, involving three tanks of each side, one British male and two females had been brought up to take part in the defence of the village of Cachy. The females were knocked out by a German A7V, which in turn was abandoned after being hit by the male. One of the two German tanks which then appeared was also hit by the male and abandoned, whilst the crew of the other later surrendered after coming under concentrated fire from men of the 58th Machine-Gun Battalion which caused intense 'splash' of molten lead inside. [IWM]

As night turned into day on the 22nd thick fog again hindered the British defenders and aided the German storm troops as they once more moved to the attack. Fierce fighting occurred at various places all along the line, including at Vaulx-Vraucourt, close to the Cambrai–Bapaume road, where a heavy German attack was held for some hours before the defenders were finally overwhelmed by the oncoming German masses. A breach opened up here in the British line but the enemy advance was brought to a halt by a counter-attack of twenty-five tanks of the 2nd Tank Battalion. Unfortunately only nine of these tanks survived this action, the ironclads having come under artillery fire from German guns a couple of miles away.

All through that day the battle raged. In the south, by midday the Germans had forced a passage over the Crozat Canal and were threatening to turn the southern flank, thus causing yet more withdrawals by the exhausted British troops. Units lost contact with flanking formations and every opportunity was taken by the Germans to infiltrate into the gaps created by the chaotic conditions of the battle. For good measure, machine-gun fire from low-flying enemy aeroplanes might suddenly be added to the streams of bullets that constantly covered the battlefield. In a few places discipline broke down as the morale of some British troops disintegrated under the intense pressure, and men fleeing to the rear were intercepted by military police and officers and forced at gunpoint into improvised defence positions, there to await the next enemy thrust.

By dusk the right flank of Fifth Army had been pushed right back to the Somme, but in the north the Flesquières Salient still held out in spite of the constant threat of being cut off. On the 24th, however, it was recognised by the commanders of the 63rd Division that the position could be held no longer and, to avoid annihilation — or at best capture — on their own initiative they ordered evacuation of the salient, which until then had been such a vital anchor point. Its loss, combined with the serious situation in the

An old postcard that shows what happened to Villers-Bretonneux.

south, heralded the beginning of a major retreat by the Fifth Army. This fighting retreat continued until the line eventually stabilised at Villers-Bretonneux, thirty-odd miles further west, and the Germans were about ten miles from the critically important rail junction of Amiens. By then the Germans had overrun all the ground given up by them early in 1917 and all the territory won by the British at such enormous cost in lives during the Somme offensive of 1916, plus a great deal more west of that devastated zone.

Péronne and Baupame having fallen in the early stages of the German assault, on 26th March Albert was also entered by the enemy, it having been decided by V Corps to abandon the ruins in favour of establishing the line on high ground just east of that town. The German advance petered out at that point and although several half-hearted attempts were made to emerge from the western exits these were beaten back by British machine-gun fire. North of Albert the Germans crossed the Ancre at Authuille and pushed forward a couple of miles, where they were attacked in the flank and forced on the defensive. Elsewhere too their attacks met with

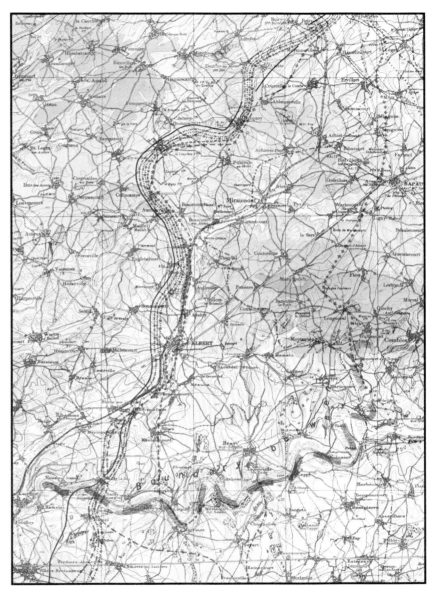

Taken from Sir Douglas Haig's Despatches, this extract from map 6 shows, day by day, German advances on the Somme, 1918.

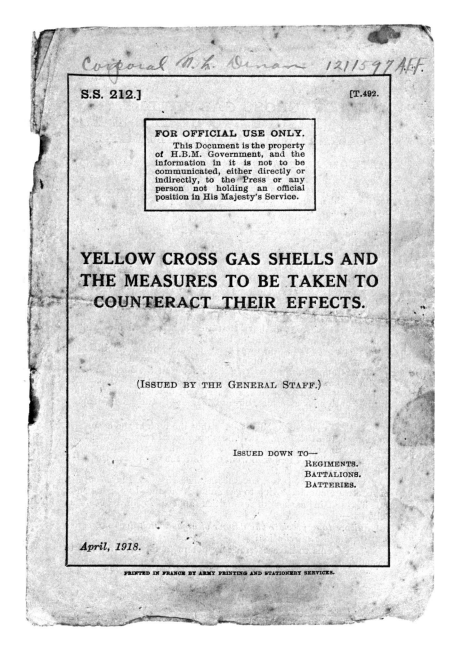

S.S. 212.]   [T.492.

FOR OFFICIAL USE ONLY.

This Document is the property of H.B.M. Government, and the information in it is not to be communicated, either directly or indirectly, to the Press or any person not holding an official position in His Majesty's Service.

YELLOW CROSS GAS SHELLS AND THE MEASURES TO BE TAKEN TO COUNTERACT THEIR EFFECTS.

(ISSUED BY THE GENERAL STAFF.)

ISSUED DOWN TO—
REGIMENTS.
BATTALIONS.
BATTERIES.

April, 1918.

PRINTED IN FRANCE BY ARMY PRINTING AND STATIONERY SERVICES.

determined British resistance and it became clear that the morale of the German soldiers was weakening, as were their physical exertions. In fact, although the enemy continued to make limited headway over the next few days, both north and south of Albert (including a belated attempt to break through at the junction of the British and French armies), the crisis point had been reached on the 26th and the victory which had been anticipated by the Germans slipped from their grasp. The British Fifth Army had been badly mauled but not broken; on the Third Army front Arras remained secure, with German successes in that area comparatively limited. One senior victim of the offensive was General Gough, who was dismissed by Sir Douglas Haig (a move which caused much controversy), Fifth Army being renamed Fourth Army and commanded by General Sir Henry Rawlinson.

Also on 26th March a high-powered Allied conference was held at Dury, three miles south of Amiens, at which a

Official pamphlet issued in 1918. Yellow Cross Gas — 'Mustard Gas' — was so called because of the yellow cross marking on the shells containing this liquid chemical (Dichlorodiethyl-Sulphide). It was first used by the Germans at Ypres in July 1917. The principal effects of this horror weapon were vomiting, intense conjunctivitis (temporary blindness) and burning of exposed skin surfaces and blistering. Death was relatively uncommon and was usually the result of septic complications. Chlorine and Phosgene (Green Cross), the other main gases used in the war, killed more speedily by flooding the lungs with oedema fluid.

Poison gas was first used on the Western Front by the Germans north of Ypres in April 1915; afterwards the Allies retaliated by adopting the use of this weapon. Deaths by gassing on the Western Front were actually less than may be generally thought. The British total was around 8,000, while there were about 180,000 non-fatal cases. About half of the deaths were as a result of Mustard Gas between July 1917 and the end of the war. Such figures aside, it was much feared by all combatants; and old soldiers continued to die from its effects in the years that followed.

decision was made to appoint Général Foch Supreme Commander of the French and British Armies, a move fully approved by Field Marshal Haig. With this development the conduct of the war took a new turn.

Officially what was designated as the First Battle of the Somme 1918 ended on 5th April, but in the Villers-Bretonneux sector much fierce fighting was to take place before the Germans finally gave up their attempts to break through to Amiens. On 4th April they had mounted a massive attack which was beaten back, and three weeks later

The results of a direct hit on an 18-pounder. Near Domart, 1st April 1918. [IWM]

The Germans having crossed the Somme, men of the 20th Division and French 22nd Division cover a road in the Nesle area from hastily-dug gun pits on 25th March 1918.

a renewed assault — during which the first tank-versus-tank battle took place — resulted in the temporary capture of that small town. That same night (24th/25th April) they were counter-attacked by the Australians, who ejected them from the ruins, and the line was again stabilised just east of the town. Eventually things quietened down all along that front as it was recognised by the Germans that they could progress no further in that area.

Meanwhile Ludendorff had already turned his attention to the next phase of his offensive based on an attack in Flanders. Operation 'Michael' had almost succeeded, but not quite. Losses had been heavy. The British had suffered over 170,000 casualties and the French (who had rushed up troops to support the British right flank) about 77,000. German casualties amounted to about the same as the Allied total.

THE BATTLE OF THE LYS
LUDENDORFF'S
OPERATION 'GEORGETTE'

Thwarted, as he had been by the restricted success of Operation 'Michael' (and the outright failure of its subsidiary, Operation 'Mars', at Arras) Ludendorff was still determined to pursue his main aim, which was to 'smash the British'. Plans had already been formulated for a new offensive, code-named 'Georgette', directed at the strategic railway junction of Hazebrouck, west of Armentières, coupled with an assault on Mount Kemmel, the objective being to cut off the British Second Army and the Belgians in the hope of bringing about a collapse in the Allied territory north of Béthune. Several larger schemes had been considered (under different code-names) but owing to insufficient troops being available it was found necessary to settle for the less ambitious scheme, with fourteen divisions of the German Sixth and Fourth Armies scheduled for the attack. Few of these troops came up to the standard of those who had fought in the recent Somme battles and some were even considered by British Intelligence to be no better than third-rate. Offsetting this possible drawback was the fact that two Portuguese divisions were in the British line near Neuve Chapelle and the fighting qualities of these men were not believed to be outstanding either by the British or the Germans. It was in that sector of the British First Army that Ludendorff anticipated an easy breakthrough.

The assault was mounted at 8.45 a.m. on 9th April after an intense bombardment of high-explosives and gas which had begun at 4.15 a.m. As on 21st March, thick fog covered the battleground as the attack went in, and on the Portuguese front success was almost instantaneous. The enemy met with little opposition apart from isolated attempts at resistance by a few of the more courageous Portuguese

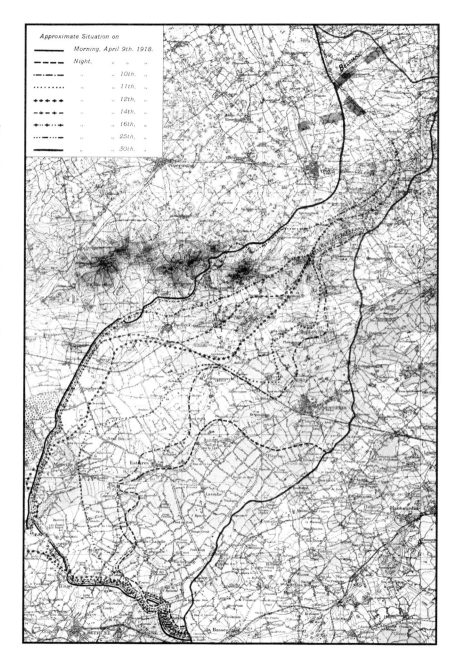

Approximate Situation on

———————	Morning, April 9th. 1918.		
— — — —	Night,	,,	,, ,,
—·—·—·—	,,	,,	10th, ,,
··············	,,	,,	11th, ,,
+-+-+-+	,,	,,	12th, ,,
—+—+—+	,,	,,	14th, ,,
+—+··+—+	,,	,,	16th, ,,
···—···—···	,,	,,	25th, ,,
———————	,,	,,	30th, ,,

Portuguese gas sentry; trenches near Neuve Chapelle, 24th June 1917. It was in this sector that the Germans broke through in April 1918. [IWM]

British casualties of tear gas at an advanced dressing station near Béthune, on day two of Operation 'Georgette', 10th April 1918. [IWM]

A front line position at Givenchy held by 1/4th East Lancs. 28th January 1918. [IWM]

Memorial to the 55th (West Lancashire) Division at Givenchy. The division put up a stout defence here during the German Flanders offensive — the Battle of the Lys — in April 1918. The line having given way on the division's left, the British defence pivoted on this point, which at that time was open country and devoid of cover.

soldiers and within hours the Germans had advanced by as much as three miles. Over the whole battle front they were supported by many aeroplanes, which gave them initial superiority over the Royal Air Force (which had come into being on 1st April by an amalgamation of the Royal Flying Corps and the Royal Naval Air Service). Both sides carried out numerous low-level attacks on opposing infantry, apart from the usual air fighting and bombing, and losses were heavy. (On 21st April the famous German air ace, Baron Manfred von Richthofen, was shot down in the Somme valley near Corbie, in circumstances that still arouse strong controversy, and his death, especially at this trying time, was a serious blow to his colleagues and the German nation as a whole.)

South of the Portuguese, the British line was held by the 55th (West Lancashire) Division (General Jeudwine) and here the Germans met with very stiff opposition. Three enemy divisions had been thrown against the Lancashire troops, who, in spite of such overwhelming odds, not only gave little ground but also inflicted many casualties on the Germans. Elements of a cyclist battalion and a cavalry outfit similarly held out until evening, by which time the 51st (Highland) Division had come up from reserve and took over the defence at that point. To the north of the Portuguese positions was the 40th Division, and in that sector the Germans managed to take advantage of the fog to infiltrate through to the River Lys, which they crossed at a point south-west of Armentières. Fortunately this was the only place where an actual enemy crossing occurred that day, but it had created a dangerous situation owing to sufficient British reserves not being immediately available to plug the gap. Sir Douglas Haig appealed to the French for assistance, but his plea was rejected by Général Foch, who insisted on keeping most of his reserves in the region of Amiens, which at that time was under fire from German long-range guns. Meanwhile two divisions were brought down from the Ypres sector to bolster the defences.

The second stage of the Lys offensive began at 5 a.m. next day when four German divisions attacked in the Armentières sector backed up by additional support and reserve divisions. Faced with such odds the British defenders had little option other than to withdraw in that area. Messines fell and on the 11th Armentières and Merville were taken by the enemy. The situation had now become very serious, and that day Sir Douglas Haig issued his famous 'Backs to the wall' order calling upon all ranks of the British Army in France and Flanders to stand firm and fight it out. He also made a further appeal to the French for help, but once again received no satisfactory response.

By now Hazebrouck was at risk and Bailleul had fallen to the enemy, as had Meteren. A dangerous gap in the British line was, however, closed by machine-gunners of the 33rd Division and a splendid stand was also made south of Hazebrouck by the Border Regiment. A less known factor, however, is that a potentially serious threat to Hazebrouck itself was averted by the 1st Australian Division being rushed up from the south to hold a vital part of the crumbling British line in front of the Nieppe Forest. By doing so, they played a major role in the overall defence of the Channel ports, and the seemingly niggardly lack of recognition of their efforts by the British authorities caused much resentment amongst the colonial troops. By 15th April the battle of Hazebrouck was officially over, although it was not the end of the fighting in that area, and the British line finally stabilised about four and a half miles east of that town. On the 16th Passchendaele was occupied by the German forces, all the ground which had been won at such tremendous cost during Third Ypres being given up voluntarily by Second Army (General Plumer) in order to shorten the line, relieve exhausted British troops and create reserves. By then the creation of reserves had been helped by the arrival of divisions from other theatres, and Foch finally allowed several French divisions, plus cavalry, to be moved up to the Ypres Salient sector.

The final blow was yet to come. In one last attempt to cut off the British and Belgians in the north — and to head for the Channel ports — Ludendorff mounted a major attack on 26th April against the village of Kemmel and its adjoining and strategic hill, Mont Kemmel. The defence of the hill had by then been taken over by French troops. This important position quickly fell to the German storm troops, who then poured over it and fought their way beyond to the village of Locre. Close to that village is a pronounced natural feature known as Mont Sherpenberg, and on 29th April this hill was also attacked. Fierce fighting raged on and around the hill but gradually the assaults diminished in ferocity and the line held at that point. The road to Ypres — and beyond — was barred.

The Battles of the Lys officially ended that day. The breakthrough hoped for by the Germans had failed to materialise. Ypres had been placed in danger, the British line withdrawn almost to its gates, and both Messines and Wytschaete were once again in the possession of the enemy. From 21st March to 30th April British casualties amounted to getting on for 240,000. But the Channel ports, which to the Germans had been tantalisingly close, were secure, and Ludendorff decided that there was no point in continuing the offensive any longer. Instead, he turned his attention once again to the south, where, on 27th May at 3.40 a.m. and after a terrific bombardment of over 3,700 guns, the Battle of the Aisne 1918 (also known as the Third Battle of the Aisne) commenced.

Along the Chemin des Dames, four British divisions (8th, 21st, 25th and 50th) which had been sent to this 'quiet' sector of the front to recuperate from a mauling they had received during March and April were hit hard in this third German offensive named by Ludendorff as Operation Blücher, which struck part of the line held by the French Sixth Army. By noon on the 27th the attackers were across the Aisne; by evening they had reached the Vesle, and by the 30th the German drive arrived at the Marne between Dormans and

An outpost of the Argyll and Sutherland Highlanders on the Lys Canal bank in front of St Floris, 9th May 1918. [IWM]

St Floris Church being shelled by the Germans. St Floris was one of the furthest points reached in the 'Georgette' offensive before it ground to a halt. [IWM]

203

Château-Thierry. Units of the US 3rd Division were inserted between Château-Thierry and Jaulgonne on the 31st, the rest arriving the following day, and, with the French, drove the German bridgehead back across the river. At Château-Thierry on 1st June a US 3rd Division machine-gun battalion took part in the town's defence, and the US 2nd Division (en route to relieve the US 1st Division at Cantigny) was diverted there to support two French divisions, which it took over from completely on 4th June. The intervention of these fresh and eager troops had helped to block the road to Paris, and on 6th June the Battle of the Aisne 1918 officially ended. Several other defensive actions were to be fought in the French sector, and one of these actions was a lesser-publicised battle known as Ludendorff's Phase 4, the Battle of the Matz, which was fought from 9th-14th June on the Montdidier–Noyon front and still aimed at Paris.

Once again after a massive bombardment and a successful advance of five to six miles the German attack faltered and ground to a halt. The fiery French Général Mangin (previously sacked after Nivelle's offensive but later reinstated) then counter-attacked vigorously with many

The Scherpenberg, a strategic hill south-west of Ypres and near Locre. Bitter fighting took place here at the end of April 1918, but, although the Germans gained a foothold on the hill, they failed to hold it or to break through in this area.

tanks and aircraft, including RAF squadrons, and drove the Germans back to their original start line. Although a costly battle (both sides lost about 35,000 men) it considerably raised the morale of the French nation as whole and greatly helped to restore the army's prestige.

One interesting outcome of this battle was the emergence of a better understanding by the Allies (who had clashed over certain aspects of the need to work together in their future overall planning), and this was subsequently accomplished under Foch's able direction. The Germans had lost the race against time and a new phase of the war was soon to begin.

THE AMERICANS IN ACTION

28th May 1918 marked the first time in the war that American troops fought a full-scale battle. The place was the important observation village and heights of Cantigny, near Montdidier, which were taken by the US 1st Division with great dash and determination. Strong counter-attacks by the Germans were beaten off and the enemy suffered numerous casualties, with about 240 prisoners also being captured. (According to the American Battle Monuments Commission the 1st Division suffered 4,111 casualties between 27th April–8th June.)

This highly successful operation was the first major 'blooding' of American troops in the European conflict. It also proved their worth in battle and showed both their allies and the enemy that they were a force to be reckoned with. It was perhaps hard luck for the 1st Division that their achievement should have been partly eclipsed by the diversion of the US 2nd and 3rd Divisions to help stem the German advance on the Marne: by the US 2nd Division's role in blocking the German drive on Paris at Château-Thierry, and by the performance of that division's 4th Marine Brigade in fighting a fiercely contested battle for nearby Belleau Wood.

The latter action and the fighting for the nearby village of Bouresches is, perhaps, one of the better known of the operations undertaken by the Americans in mid-1918.

The wood lay to the north-east of the little village of Lucy-le-Bocage amidst attractive countryside that had been

Lucy-le-Bocage, once almost totally destroyed, nestling in peaceful surroundings and where the US 2nd Division blocked the German drive towards Paris. Picture taken from the Paris-Chateau-Thierry road.

The ruins of Cantigny after its capture. [IWM]

The entrance to Cantigny as it is now.

Belleau Wood from near Lucy-le-Bocage showing some of the open ground over which men of the 2nd US Division attacked under heavy fire in June 1918.

Children play by a scarred relic of the fierce battle for Belleau Wood where men once clashed in desperate hand-to-hand struggles — vestiges of old trenches still remain to be seen today in what is once again a peaceful, leafy wood.

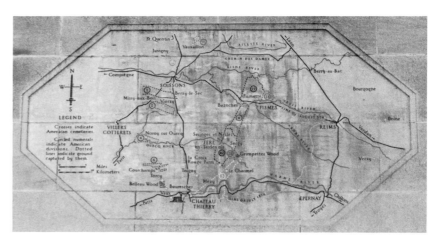

Commemorative tablet on the huge colonnaded American Memorial at Hill 304 overlooking Château-Thierry, a town where an important defensive action by the Americans took place at the end of May and beginning of June 1918. The ornamental map shows the places and ground gained by American troops on July 18th and the following weeks in the French–American counter-offensive against the German Aisne–Marne 'bulge'.

A 2nd Division marker boulder on the outskirts of Belleau Wood near the impressive Aisne-Marne American Cemetery.

American Military Cemetery, Belleau Wood, north-west of Château-Thierry. This beautifully laid out cemetery contains 2,288 graves and has an attractive chapel, on the walls of which are inscribed the names of many 'Missing'.

free of fighting since the early days of the war, a factor that may have given a misleading impression of what lay ahead for the eager troops of the 2nd Division who had been rushed up to help stem the German breakthrough towards Paris. The German High Command, which had been forcibly made aware of the American presence, gave orders that they should be refused any further successes in an attempt to reduce their importance, and at Belleau Wood the German forces did everything possible to conform with those orders. By doing so they unintentionally proved to the Americans how difficult it was to capture a not particularly large area of woodland fronted by open fields and laced with machine-guns (a lesson learned the hard way by the British during the terrible Battles of the Somme in 1916).

On 6th June 1918 the first American assault took place with French co-operation and was partially successful. Later in the day the attack was renewed at the cost of heavy casualties although the village of Bouresches was taken and held against numerous German counter-attacks of some ferocity. On the 7th, 8th and 10th further determined attacks by US troops were mounted but with little progress being made, and on the 11th yet another attack was launched against the whole wood. Violent fighting continued all day with the battle see-sawing amongst the broken trees and wrecked enemy defences but only the southern section of the wood was taken and held. Next day furious fighting continued under heavy bombardments with constant counter-attacks by both sides and casualties mounting rapidly. Eventually, after a particularly bitter struggle on 25th June the whole wood came under the control of the Americans with the Germans being compelled to acknowledge defeat at the hands of men whom they had striven to prove as being no match for their own battle-hardened soldiers.

Right: Looking across green fields in 1986 to the village of Hamel. [Photo Dr Ellen Rice]

Looking along a German communications trench towards the village of Hamel, from near Pear Trench, 5th July 1918. Hamel, north-east of Villers-Brettoneux, was both the scene of a very successful assault on German positions and the cause of a temporary rift between the Australian and British commanders on the one side and the American Commander-in-Chief on the other. Here, on 4th July, the Australian 4th Division with 62 British tanks and a token force of about 1,000 American troops carried out an attack in which, in the space of an hour and a half, the village was taken, along with some 170 machine-guns and 1,500 prisoners, for less than 1,000 casualties; but not before the American C-in-C, General John J. Pershing, keen to preserve the integrity of his forces, had strongly objected to the use of his men and a furious row erupted.

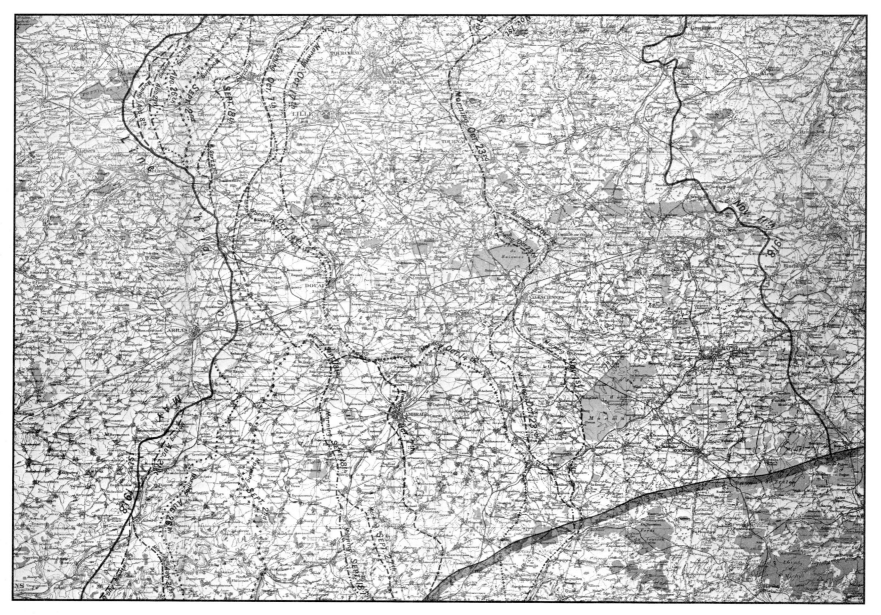

Taken from Sir Douglas Haig's Despatches, this extract is taken from map 8, showing the Final British Offensive August–November, 1918.

THE ALLIES TAKE THE INITIATIVE

By 20th July 1918 General Erich von Ludendorff had accepted that the likelihood of a final German victory over the Allies was no longer feasible following the lack of real success of his five separate offensives against the British and French over the past few months. Moreover, only two days earlier a surprise counter-stroke by the French Tenth and Sixth Armies, supported by very many guns, tanks and aeroplanes, had burst upon the Germans in the Marne salient and had met with immediate success. This carefully prepared and well-concealed counter-offensive included four American divisions (which were twice the size of the British and French ones) and four British divisions.

This unexpected set-back seriously interfered with Ludendorff's plans for a further major attack in Flanders (code-named Operation 'Hagen') which he had hoped would have a decisive effect on the course of the war. Enormous German casualties, however (calculated subsequently to be about one million), resulting from his various attempts during the first half of 1918 to force a satisfactory conclusion to the war in his country's favour, and the fact that many of the German reinforcements were now only third-rate — plus the ever-growing strength of the Americans — caused Ludendorff to abandon the proposed Flanders offensive and to recognise that the tide had turned against the Central Powers. Even Field Marshal von Hindenburg acknowledged that the initiative had now passed to the Allies.

It must have been a bitter pill for Ludendorff to swallow (and the rapidly deteriorating situation certainly had a most adverse effect on his morale), bearing in mind that the German forces had smashed their way to within about eighteen miles from Dunkirk, thirty-six miles from Boulogne and, on the French front, just thirty-six miles from Paris. They had, though, been fought to a standstill in each offensive, success almost within their grasp.

But worse was to come. On 8th August (afterwards described by Ludendorff as 'the black day of the German Army in the war') the front suddenly erupted in the Villers-Bretonneux sector as General Rawlinson's Fourth Army, in concert with the French First Army (Général Debeney) further south, opened a fierce assault which took the Germans completely by surprise. The Allied march to victory had begun.

FORMS OF PRAYER
AND THANKSGIVING
TO ALMIGHTY GOD

To be used on

Sunday, the Fourth of August, 1918,

The Fourth Anniversary of the Declaration of War

Being the Day Appointed for Intercession on behalf of the Nation and Empire and our Allies in this time of War.

An interesting leaflet — just four days later there began the offensive that was to become the advance to victory.

209

THE BATTLE OF AMIENS 1918

One of General Sir Henry Rawlinson's special instructions for the great battle which was about to be fought was the absolute need for secrecy in its preparations. Every man was made aware of this ruling (a note was pasted in every paybook) and extraordinary measures were taken to hide the activities usually associated with a major offensive from the prying eyes of the enemy. All troop movements towards the front were restricted to the hours of darkness; all ammunition and supply dumps were carefully camouflaged (and checked from the air by the RAF); sand was used on the pavé roads to reduce noise, and all civilians were evacuated from the battle zone. Any inquisitive enemy reconnaissance planes were kept at bay by the RAF.

The main effort in the assault was to be made by the Canadian Corps and the Australian Corps. Neither of these two Dominion formations had been involved in the March/April retreat and in consequence had not suffered from the extreme exhaustion and losses experienced by the other British troops during that trying period. Because the Canadians in particular were well known by the Germans for their prowess in spearheading attacks, the Canadian Corps of four divisions, commanded by Lieutenant-General Sir Arthur Currie, were not brought into the line until the very last minute, and careful precautions were taken to ensure that their transfer from the Arras sector, where they had been based, to the southern front on the right of the Australians did not come to the notice of the Germans until it was too late for them to do anything about it. The five divisions of the Australian Corps (Lieutenant-General Sir John Monash) were already located in the centre just east of Villers-Bretonneux, where they barred the way to Amiens. North of the Australians was the British III Corps, and on the right of the Canadians was the French First Army under Général Débeney.

This 19-year-old Canadian was killed on what was called by Ludendorff 'the black day of the German Army'.

A large concentration of aeroplanes (about 800 British and over 1,000 French) ensured initial Allied control of the air. The Germans, at the beginnng of the assault, had only about one-fifth of that total immediately available. As the battle progressed the latter were quickly reinforced, and the air fighting became quite savage at a later stage when the RAF endeavoured (unsuccessfully) to destroy the bridges over the Somme by bombing. One of the enemy squadrons which British bombers had to face was the famous 'Richthofen Circus', which at that time was commanded by a certain Hauptmann Hermann Göring.

On the ground the British assault was to be supported by 414 fighting tanks, 342 of these being Mark Vs and 72 Whippets, plus 120 supply tanks. The Whippets were small by comparison to the Mark Vs, weighing only fourteen tons,

A Whippet tank damaged by shellfire, Villers-Brettoneux, 17th July 1918. The Whippet's designer called it a 'chaser' — a self-explanatory name for a tank that was intended for a 'cavalry' role of exploiting a breakthrough and following up a retreating enemy. It had a top speed of 8–9 mph. [IWM]

with a crew of three and an armament of three Hotchkiss machine-guns. Nevertheless they were to play an important part in the success of the offensive. Over 2,000 guns and howitzers were concentrated on the Fourth Army's front for the opening barrage. Zero Hour for the British was 4.20 a.m. on 8th August, with the French attack due to go in forty-five minutes later. A mist began to form during the early hours of the morning and this thickened as Zero Hour approached — its existence a mixed blessing for the British and a definite hindrance for the Germans: the reverse of 21st March.

At the appropriate moment the British barrage crashed down on the unsuspecting Germans and the offensive moved under way. Everywhere, except on the III Corps front, success was immediate as the Australians and the Canadians swept forward in the mist towards their objectives. The sun broke through at about 10.00 a.m., by which time the Dominion troops were well on the way to achieving their aims, while on the left the III Corps was held up in its attempt to capture the Chipilly Spur, both the 58th Division and the 18th Division having met with strong resistance in their drive towards that important natural feature. Unfortunately this delay had serious repercussions as it enabled the enemy to enfilade the Australians with machine-gun and artillery fire, causing many casualties.

By early afternoon the main fighting was over. The Canadians had advanced nearly eight miles and reached all their objectives; the Australians, regardless of the set-back on their left, had advanced over six miles and reached most of theirs. On the right of the Canadians, the French, exhorted by Général Débeney to push forward with all speed, were slow in their advance. Their attack had taken place without the support of tanks and it became evident that some of the French troops did not have their hearts in it. The British tanks meanwhile, though suffering fairly heavy losses, did well. The Whippets in particular ranged beyond the enemy lines, taking German troops and batteries in the rear and causing a considerable number of casualties. Some armoured cars also had a field day — the crew of one of them catching a group of German staff officers enjoying a meal in what they had thought to be a safe area. Cavalry had been employed in the assault but, as had been proved so often in the past, they were no match for the German machine-guns and artillery. Even so, they were able to chalk up some successes in what had been a memorable day for the British forces. Casualties had been remarkably low — the Canadians under 4,000; the Australians even less. The Germans, though, had been hit very hard: many of their front line units had been almost annihilated; large numbers of guns had been lost and a great many prisoners taken. All told, it had been a disastrous day for the German Army and it constituted its most serious defeat since the beginning of the war.

The battle continued for three more days, enemy resistance becoming stronger as German reserves reached the crumbling front. On the second day (9th August) the Canadians still managed to advance about three miles and the 58th Division, with the aid of an American unit (131st Regiment), captured the important Chipilly Spur. Only 145 tanks were available for action that day, and this number rapidly dwindled to just 38 by the 11th. By the 12th a mere handful were left. All the crews were by then throughly exhausted after days of constant activity within the claustrophobic confines of their steel forts.

On 11th August the first phase of the offensive came to an end with British casualties of about 22,000 and French of about 24,000. German casualties totalled over 75,000, nearly 30,000 of whom were taken prisoner by the combined efforts of the British and French. At an Imperial Conference at Avesnes, Ludendorff admitted that a heavy defeat had been inflicted on the German Army and offered his resignation, which the Kaiser refused to accept. The Kaiser made it clear that he thought the 'the war must be ended'. On 14th August another Imperial Conference was held at Spa in Belgium, at which the German Secretary of State (Admiral von Hintze) was instructed to open peace negotiations, preferably through the Queen of the Netherlands. Ludendorff, however, still wanted to negotiate from a position of strength — to hold on to Belgium and parts of Russia. In the field, German reserves moving up to the front were met with jeers from the troops they were relieving, including accusations that they were 'prolonging the war'. Discipline had broken down in many units and it became apparent that the once-mighty German Army was beginning to disintegrate — a fact that the German military leaders were forced to acknowledge, although Hindenburg still retained a hope of remaining on French soil.

A lull occurred between 12th to 20th August, during which Maréchal Foch pressed Sir Douglas Haig to continue the attack with General Rawlinson's Fourth Army, in support of the French First Army, which was to aim at Roye. The British Commander-in-Chief preferred however to extend the battle front to the north to bring in General Byng's Third Army with the intention of advancing on Bapaume. This conflict of opinion led to friction between the two commanders, with Field Marshal Haig telling the Generalissimo that he

August Offensive. The road to Chipilly. German dead in the wake of an advance. [IWM]

The ruined village of Puisieux, south-east of Gommecourt, after the guns had done their work. [IWM]

(Haig) 'was responsible to the British Government and fellow citizens for the handling of the British forces'. This altercation cleared the air and actually helped to create a better understanding between the two military leaders, with Foch becoming more amenable to Haig's plans. Another problem which arose at the same time was General Pershing's insistence on withdrawing the five American divisions which were training with the British — a demand that initially met with strong disapproval from the British C-in-C, bearing in mind that the offensive was shortly due to be continued. Fortunately a compromise was reached, with three of the American divisions being transferred to American control and two remaining with the British. Further successful attacks were made by the French Tenth Army on the 18th, 19th and 20th on the Soissons front, with the Germans again incurring heavy losses.

The same spot 70 years later.

Battle of Albert. Field-guns and limbers passing a mine crater in the road in front of Warlencourt on 27th August 1918, two days after the village was taken. [IWM]

MAINTAINING THE PRESSURE

On 21st August the British Third Army attacked in thick mist — giving way later to bright sunshine — and reached its limited objectives after some hard fighting against enemy rearguards. Although successful, it prompted Sir Douglas Haig to demand that his army commanders take advantage of the disorganised enemy to press on with the utmost boldness and resolution. Albert was re-occupied by British troops on 22nd August.

On 23rd August Third Army resumed its attack, as did Fourth Army. The battle front now stretched over thirty-five miles. It was another successful day, with many prisoners being taken, particularly in the Australian sector. By now the devastated area of the 1916 battlefields had been reached and places of evil memory such as La Boisselle, Pozières, Thiepval, etc., were once again to the forefront. But, unlike in 1916, the British troops swept across that war-torn desert against only limited opposition and by the 26th had reached the outskirts of Bapaume, one of the original goals of the 1916 offensive. Three days later what became known as the

Battle of Albert (21st–29th August) ended and the Second Battles of Arras 1918 (26th August–3rd September) were fought. For this General Sir Henry Horne's First Army entered the fray; and one of its major successes was the capture, on 26th August, of the famous hill of Monchy-le-Preux by the Canadians at the cost of very low casualties. This was a remarkable achievement bearing in mind the strategic importance of that heavily fortified position to the Germans, and it accentuated the loss of morale in the enemy forces. On 29th August the New Zealand Division entered Bapaume (Battle of Bapaume, 31st August–3rd September). On 31st August the immensely powerful position of Mont St Quentin, just outside Péronne, was assaulted and captured by men of the 5th Australian Brigade (2nd Australian Division). Well under strength, the Australians had massive artillery support and by making as much noise as possible — thereby misleading the German defenders into believing they were being attacked by much larger forces — they carried this important bastion at the point of the bayonet and took some 700 prisoners. Both Sir Douglas Haig and General Rawlinson were astonished at the comparative ease with which the Australians captured this vital hill.

Battle of the Scarpe 1918. Shells bursting on Monchy just before the town was captured by the Canadians on 26th August. [IWM]

West of Monchy now, with the church surmounting the hill which was once of strategic importance.

Australian dead in the wire near Péronne, pictured on 2nd September 1918. [IWM]

Thus August ended with a remarkable tally of British — and French — successes (the French Third Army took Noyen on the same day that the New Zealanders entered Bapaume). A huge number of prisoners had been captured plus many hundreds of guns and other weapons. Casualties for the month in Fourth Army amounted to just a few short of 53,000 officers and men, and the total for Third and First Armies (including the first three days of September) came to 55,716. The French lost around 100,000 men but also took well over 30,000 prisoners and almost 900 guns. It was a most satisfactory result; but there was still a long, hard road ahead, and although the German Army had been beaten in the field it was still a formidable force and, like a dangerous animal, was constantly ready to turn on its pursuers and inflict nasty wounds.

Memorial to the 2nd Australian Division on Mont St Quentin. This statue replaced the original one (of a Digger stabbing the German Eagle with a bayonet) which was destroyed by the Germans in the Second World War.

The tranquil Somme at Péronne, with the rebuilt fifteenth-century church of St Jean in the background. The church, together with most of the town, was destroyed in the war — as depicted in the picture on page 142 taken when the town was entered by the British in March 1917 following the German withdrawal to the Hindenburg Line. Having been lost again a year later during the German Spring Offensive, the town was finally retaken on September 2nd 1918 after very fierce engagements which went on all through the previous day.

Unloading shells from lorries behind a 60-pdr battery in action on the Arras–Cambrai Road, 26th August 1918. The increased importance of artillery resulted in the number of British artillerymen rising to 526,000 — a quarter of the Army's ration strength. [IWM]

The road junction at Croiselles, a village captured by the 56th Division on 28th August 1918: a stranded Mark IV, 'Lucretia II', and a passing horse ambulance of 2/3rd London Field Ambulance. [IWM]

Above: The same road junction at Croisilles in the late 1970s.

Left: Headstones in Vis-en-Artois Military Cemetery, on the Arras–Cambrai road, south-east of Monchy-le-Preux. Vis-en-Artois was captured by the Canadians at the end of August 1918. The cemetery incorporates a Memorial to the 'Missing' who fell in 1918, 9,903 of whom are recorded thereon.

Meanwhile there was talk in high circles of the war carrying on well into 1919, with the Americans then bearing the brunt of the fighting. This, though, did not fit in with Sir Douglas Haig's own ideas. He foresaw the strong likelihood of the conflict being brought to a successful conclusion before the end of 1918 provided the Allies — including the Americans, whose First Army came into being on 10th August — co-ordinated their efforts to obtain maximum benefit from the disarray of the German forces. Perhaps not surprisingly, disputes arose over the best method of employing the American troops, with General Pershing insisting that they remain under American control and Maréchal Foch making an attempt to place many of them under French command, before eventually a reasonable compromise was reached. For his part, Sir Douglas Haig was already involved in planning to overcome the next major obstacle: the powerful defences of the Hindenburg Line.

With August giving way to September, enemy resistance was found to be stiffening all along the British front between the Scarpe and the Somme. Indeed, a number of German counter-attacks were launched, but were all repulsed without much difficulty. Meanwhile Ludendorff's aim was to hold the British on the line of the Canal du Nord north of the Arras–Cambrai road and to retire behind the Drocourt–Quéant Switch Line south of that road. The Switch was a powerful position which linked up the main Siegfried defences to the old German front south of Loos and was of vital importance to the Germans; its loss would be a serious blow to their hopes of checking the British advance. With well-known places such as Roeux, Gavrelle, Monchy, Guémappe, Wancourt, Croisilles, Vaulx-Vraucourt and Bullecourt by now all in British hands, and with the main towns of Bapaume and Péronne also having fallen, there was a real danger, from the German viewpoint, of the northern flank of the Hindenburg Line being turned. To prevent such a disaster eleven enemy divisions were deployed along a nine-mile front in that sector.

Canadian stretcher bearers advancing along the Arras–Cambrai Road, 30th September 1918. [IWM]

Mont Dury, on the Arras–Cambrai road. This gently rising ground, now so innocuous, was once covered with masses of barbed wire and trenches. It was captured by the Canadians in September 1918 and one of their distinctive memorials is located in the clump of trees centre left. The village of Dury is situated to the left of the area seen here and the trees on the right indicate the line of the Arras–Cambrai road.

Another of the destroyed bridges over the unfinished Canal du Nord at Moeuvres (see page 186) which the offensive brought back into the battle zone. This deep excavation, incorporated in the formidable Hindenburg Line defences, was crossed in the Moeuvres sector by the 63rd Division on 27th September 1918. [IWM] Below: once again, in use.

Ludendorff's anxiety was justified, for on 2nd September the 1st and 4th Divisions of General Currie's Canadian Corps, together with the British 4th Division of First Army, plus Third Army's XVII Corps (52nd, 57th and 63rd Divisions) attacked astride the Arras–Cambrai road and smashed their way through the formidable Switch Line defences, thus overcoming one of the strongest enemy positions on the Western Front. Six miles of the Switch were captured, incorporating a vast network of trenches north and south of Quéant, and several villages, including Dury together with its important ridge. Some 8,000 prisoners were also taken in what was one of the finest feats in the campaign. The flank of the Siegfried defence zone had indeed been decisively turned.

Away to the north, in Flanders, other British successes had been achieved and the French too were continuing their advances. The whole Allied front was now in a fluid state. Vast numbers of prisoners had been taken and very many guns, and German morale was clearly declining.

On 6th September General Byng's troops had reached the western end of Havrincourt Wood and on the 7th most of the wood was in British hands. On 12th September, after a short but fierce battle, Havrincourt itself was captured, as also was the village of Trescault; thus the scene was set for the forthcoming battle for the great road and rail junction of Cambrai. First, though, the wide and deep (but dry) Canal du Nord had to be crossed; so too had the immensely strong and awe-inspiring southern bastion of the Hindenburg Line Zone, the strongest part of that zone being between St Quentin and Bantouzelle, along the line of the heavily fortified Scheldt Canal.

The task of storming the Canal du Nord — the key to the way to Cambrai — was entrusted to the 4th, 3rd and 1st Canadian Divisions of First Army, and the 63rd Division of Fourth Army, with Zero Hour 5.30 a.m. on 27th September. A heavy bombardment preceded the assault and, as dawn broke, the attackers surged forward and after some heavy fighting broke through the formidable defences in the

Aerial view of Bourlon village, looking west towards Moeuvres, with Bourlon Wood in the foreground. [Author/WFA]

Moevres sector. From there the 63rd Division swung towards Graincourt, where the Germans initially put up a stubborn defence, and north of the Bapaume–Cambrai road Bourlon village was taken by the 4th Canadians, the infamous wood itself being captured by the 3rd Canadian Division. Anneux fell, and the 57th and 52nd Divisions advanced beyond the ruins towards Fontaine-Notre-Dame; further south, the Guards and the 2nd Division also made good progress. Ribécourt and Flesquières fell to the 3rd Division, with the right flank being taken care of by the 5th and 42nd Divisions. To the north of Moevres and Bourlon the 1st Canadian Division and the 11th Division captured several villages, and to their left the canal was crossed by the 56th Division. By evening complete success had been achieved: the Canal du Nord lay behind the British positions, which were then not far from the Scheldt Canal. More than 10,000 prisoners had been taken together with 200 guns, and German morale had been shaken more than ever.

A memorial to the Canadian Corps' achievements in the final stages of the war, on the edge of the rising ground of Bourlon Wood, which cost so many lives.

On 28th September Gouzeaucourt, Marcoing and Fontaine-Notre-Dame fell to the British, which meant that all the outer defences of the Hindenburg Line had been thoroughly broken. Cambrai was threatened from both north

Bourlon village in ruins, October 1918. [IWM]

Two young ladies stroll in Bourlon where artillery wagons and motor ambulances once rolled by. The Hôtel de Ville is centre left and the church just outside the right-hand edge of the photograph. Bourlon Château, which stood at the end of the road straight ahead, was rebuilt after the war but was subsequently destroyed by fire.

and south, and even the important town of Douai further north was endangered by the breakthrough. Ludendorff's cup of woe was not yet full, however, for that day Belgian, British and French troops, under the command of the King of the Belgians, attacked on a front of twenty miles in Flanders and met with immediate success. More places of evil memory fell quickly to the combined Allied forces and the limits of the terrible 1917 battles of Third Ypres were reached and passed without undue difficulty. Passchendaele, that epitome of suffering, was captured by the Belgians on 29th September, and troops of Plumer's Second Army took Wytschaete, Messines and other villages (or rather ruins) that were once well within enemy lines. Over to the east, on the Meuse–Argonne front, the French and Americans had begun a forward thrust on the 26th. The Americans had encountered some problems owing to the difficult terrain, lack of suitable roads and inadequate staff planning. However, in spite of these and other obstacles the keen but mainly inexperienced US troops fought their way forward for seven miles against very stiff opposition and captured numerous well-fortified villages, one of which was Montfaucon, located on a vital hill that gave commanding observation over many miles in all directions. Its loss was a serious blow to the Germans, who rushed forward troops from other parts of the front from where they could not really be spared — it having become clear that the American push created a very dangerous situation which called for an immediate and forceful response. To the left of the Americans the French also advanced about three miles across territory and places that had become famous in the bitter battles of September 1915. In other sectors too the French advanced successfully, while Italian troops were involved between the River Ailette and the Vesle. Everywhere there were signs of the German front cracking, and on 29th September Sir Douglas Haig delivered a further mortal blow that had the Germans reeling back as some of their strongest defences crumbled under this latest assault.

THE ST MIHIEL SALIENT

On 12th September 1918, for the first time, the Americans went into action on the Western Front as an independent army. The occasion was the attack by the recently formed US First Army under the personal command of General John J. Pershing, Commander-in-Chief of the American forces in Europe, against the St Mihiel Salient south-east of Verdun and south-west of the heavily fortified town of Metz. Ever since its creation late in 1914 this prominent salient, twenty-five miles long at its base and protruding sixteen miles into the allied lines, with its apex pointing towards Paris, had been a thorn in the side of the French. It was the scene of much bitter fighting earlier in the war and constituted a major threat to the French lines of communication, particularly during the terrible Verdun battles of 1916. Its eradication would be a welcome relief.

Soon after General Pershing's arrival in France (13th June 1917), the St Mihiel Salient was discussed at a meeting with Maréchal Pétain, who agreed that its reduction could be a likely future task for the Americans once they had sufficient troops for that purpose. Subsequently that sector of the front was used by US divisions to gain experience of front-line conditions (other US divisions received training with the British and French). Uppermost in the US Commander-in-Chief's mind was his intention to eventually see American forces in action on a completely independent basis under American control. Above all he feared that constant calls by the British and French for American troops to be used as general reinforcements for the Allied armies would result in the dissipation of his rapidly growing forces, and his determination to avoid this possibility had already been the cause of some friction between the top military leaders. He had given vital aid to the French during the crisis of Ludendorff's late-May offensive (Operation 'Blucher') in the Aisne–Marne sector during which elements of the US 3rd and 2nd Divisions did so well at Château Thierry and Belleau

Marker Stone at the south-western tip of the St Mihiel Salient which indicates the furthest point reached by the Germans in their attempt to outflank Verdun in 1914.

The southern face of the salient near the apex. This photograph clearly shows how the German positions dominated the lower ground to the south and it perhaps explains why this prominent feature remained in enemy hands for four years. In the foreground are some remains of what would have been French trenches.

Wood respectively, but the time had now come for a full-scale battle in which his men would really be able to show their mettle. Sir Douglas Haig was against the planned offensive as he believed it would be more rewarding for an advance to be made through the Argonne Forest towards Mézières to cut the lateral railway, but Pershing was adamant and insisted on the planned assault going ahead. Général Foch initially agreed with Haig but, after mediation by Pétain, Pershing got his way, although it was agreed that the assault would be limited to reaching the chord of the salient — i.e. up to what was known as the German 'Michel Line'. Previous American ideas of continuing the advance towards the strongly fortified town of Metz were abandoned in favour of a further major offensive to be launched west of the Meuse, after completion of the St Mihiel battle, in conjunction with the French Fourth Army.

Because of serious manpower problems, and also being aware of an impending assault in the St Mihiel sector, Ludendorff had in fact already ordered the evacuation of the salient. However, only the heavy German guns had been withdrawn before the American/French assault began. Seven American divisions (82nd, 90th, 5th and 2nd of I Corps, and 89th, 42nd and 1st of IV Corps — from right to left) were to attack the south-east face of the salient; opposite, on the north-west face, the US 26th Division and part of 4th Division, supported by the French 15th Colonial Division, were to launch a secondary attack to drive south-eastwards. Two other French infantry divisions, plus a dismounted cavalry division of II Colonial Corps, were to apply pressure at the apex of the salient. Nine German divisions, plus one division in reserve, held the salient. In round figures, the Americans numbered 550,000 and the

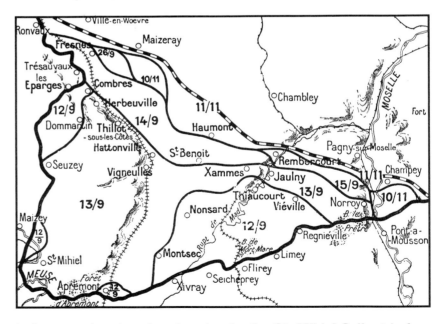

Left: map showing the situation in the St. Mihiel Salient before the offensive — that above, shows the situation at each stage.

French 110,000 (of whom about half of each were used in the actual assault). The attackers were supported by over 3,000 guns, 267 tanks (mostly light; 154 of these being manned by Americans) and almost 1,400 aeroplanes, 600 of those being a French Air Division. The British Independent Air Force under General Trenchard also supplied bombers.

The preliminary bombardment opened up at 1 a.m. on the 12th. Four hours later, in unpleasantly wet conditions (steady rain having fallen during the night), the main attack went in under a creeping barrage, to be followed at 8 a.m. by the secondary assault. Initial opposition in the south was light. In places resistance by enemy machine-guns was encountered, resulting in some casualties; in general, though, the advance proceeded in a most satisfactory manner, with objectives mainly being reached well within — or even ahead of — timetable.

Within 48 hours the St Mihiel Salient ceased to exist and the jubilant attackers overlooked the defences of the Michel Line, which the Germans were hastily trying to improve in the belief that the Americans would be continuing their advance in the direction of Metz. Somewhat to their surprise this course was not followed and the fighting then died down as the Americans began the immense task of transferring half a million men across to the Argonne Sector, forty miles away, where they were due to attack again on 26th September as agreed with Général Foch.

American casualties in the St Mihiel battle were very light and amounted to only about 7,000. Some 16,000 prisoners were taken and hundreds of guns captured, and the enemy had been very badly shaken. General Pershing had every right to be proud of the outcome and also of the conduct of his troops in action, many of whom had not previously been involved in any fighting. He was convinced that his insistence on creating a separate American Army had been fully vindicated. This force would shortly face a far more severe test among the wooded and heavily fortified hills and valleys of the Meuse-Argonne region.

Entrance to a German bunker on the St Mihiel heights.

The outstanding natural feature of Montsec (Hill 380). On its crest, the impressive American monument erected to commemorate the capture of this hill in September 1918. A French attempt to take this important position in June 1917 failed in the face of its formidable defences.

THE BATTLE OF THE ST QUENTIN CANAL

The area of attack was between Marcoing and St Quentin, the main thrust being on the front of General Rawlinson's Fourth Army. For two days the British guns pounded the German defences, forcing the enemy to shelter in tunnels and deep dug-outs and to keep his head well down. Then, at 5.50 a.m. on 29th September, General Rawlinson struck between Holnon and Vendhuile with III Corps, the American 27th and 30th Divisions of the US II Corps, the Australian Corps and XI Corps.

In front of III Corps the Scheldt Canal cutting was very deep and to their north the Americans attacked over ground where the canal disappeared into a 6,000-yard tunnel which was used by the Germans as part of the vast Hindenburg defence system and was connected by shafts to the trenches above. Where the canal emerged at the southern end of the tunnel was the village of Bellicourt; a few miles south was Bellenglise. The cutting between these two places was quite shallow; at Bellenglise itself the canal ran almost level with

The southern entrance to the St Quentin Canal Tunnel, near Bellicourt, October 1918. [IWM]

Dug-outs on the southern bank of the St Quentin Canal. [IWM]

A recent picture taken within the canal tunnel, which gave good shelter to large numbers of German troops who garrisoned the Hindenburg Line defences. Barges were used as billets.

9th October 1918. Smashed barges line the canal in the cutting at the tunnel's northern entrance, south-east of Vendhuile and west of Le Catelet. [IWM]

The St Quentin Canal at peace and in use. In 1918 the canal formed part of a complex defensive system which the Germans considered to be impregnable.

the surface of the ground. Below Bellicourt the Germans had strongly wired trenches about a mile west of the canal, whereas north of Vendhuille their main positions were on the east bank. To the rear of the canal were further masses of barbed wire covering numerous heavily fortified villages — the overall defences being as much as five to seven miles in depth. It was certainly an incredibly hard nut to crack and Ludendorff staked everything on a last hope that any Allied attack would come to grief amongst the wire and machine-gun positions of what he believed to be an impenetrable defence system. A captured enemy order stated: 'This is our winter position . . . There can be no question of going back any further.' The German High Command intended that the position was to be held; any further retreat was unacceptable.

At Bellenglise the Scheldt Canal formed an angle leading east to Lehaucourt and thence to Le Trinquoy where it turned south again towards St Quentin. The Bellenglise bend was considered to be a key point in the assault and it was there that the 46th (North Midland) Division attacked. Prior to the assault this division had carried out trials with

Looking west to the Riqueval Bridge (centre) across which men of the 6th North Staffords (46th Division) charged on 28th September 1918 led by Captain A. H. Charlton. On the right is a concrete pill-box in which a group of German pioneers had sheltered from the intense British barrage, their task being to blow the bridge in the event of a British breakthrough. They emerged too late and were shot down by the Staffords, who then successfully stormed the enemy trenches on the east side of the canal, thus making this vital supply artery secure for the troops that followed.

Men of the 137th (Staffordshire) Brigade, 46th Division, line the banks of the canal for Brigadier-General J. V. Campbell, VC, to address them from the Riqueval Bridge on October 2nd 1918. Some are still wearing lifejackets. [IWM]

Verdant foliage; the new masonry long since weathered. Riqueval bridge was of vital importance in 1918 and its capture was a stroke of good fortune.

collapsible boats, rafts and other ideas for crossing a major water obstacle, and every possible effort was made to ensure that the passage of the canal would be both successful and rapid. Even lifebelts were obtained for that purpose, 3,000 having been commandeered from leave-boats at Boulogne. Non-swimmers were to be helped by means of life-lines, and footbridges were built in advance for immediate use after the initial crossings had been made. The 46th Division's attack was led by the 137th Infantry Brigade under Brigadier-General J. V. Campbell, VC, and was composed entirely of Staffordshire troops. Their task was to destroy enemy defences west of the canal, cross the canal itself, break through the Hindenburg Line east of the canal and then capture Bellenglise, after which other brigades would pass through to continue the attack.

A thick mist hid the German lines as the assault began and all three attacking battalions of the South Staffords dashed forward on the west bank of the canal. At some points stout resistance was put up by the enemy but in the main the first line trenches fell quickly, with the Staffordshires using their bayonets freely. A German counter-barrage caused some casualties before the canal was reached, and machine-guns also caused temporary hold-ups, but nothing could stop the impetus of the attack. The east bank of the canal was quickly reached and a foothold gained in the face of bombing from above and machine-gun fire from the flanks. Bayonets were again used frequently as the German trench system east of the canal was attacked, many of the enemy seeking to escape in the mist and others giving up with little resistance. Bellenglise, which had been badly battered by the British artillery, was entered, many of the enemy machine-guns in the village already having been knocked out by the barrage. From the Bellenglise tunnel entrance around a thousand prisoners were taken. All the objectives of the British had been reached by 8.30 a.m. and in accordance with the timetable laid down, this very satisfactory situation having been helped by the unexpected

St Quentin Canal at Bellenglise, showing the defence system to the east of the canal and the German bridges. [National Army Museum]

— and courageous — capture of the vital Riqueval bridge by the Midlanders. The brigade's casualties were surprisingly light — 25 officers and 555 men: a small price to pay for such a superb achievement.

Meanwhile, on the left of the Midlanders, the two American divisions of the US II Corps had done extremely well in the sector above the tunnel. The 30th US Division (Major-General Lewis) had broken through the main Hindenburg defences, captured Bellicourt and entered Nauroy. To their north the 27th US Division (Major-General O'Ryan) had fought their way to Bony, where they were engaged in fierce fighting around that village. In their general eagerness the Americans omitted in some cases to mop up enemy

strongpoints they had overrun and so found themselves attacked from the rear by small groups of enemy soldiers firing at them with machine-guns. Other Germans came up from inside the tunnel via the main shafts (the entrance having been sealed by the Americans) and this added to the confusion, but eventually all the enemy soldiers who were found in the rear of the American front lines were either killed or captured. Serious casualties were inflicted on the attacking troops by heavy machine-gun fire from enemy strongpoints known as The Knoll (south-west of Vendhuille), Guillemont Farm (east of Lempire) and Quennemont Farm (south-west of Bony); and the 107th Infantry Regiment of the 27th Division in having 337 men killed and 658 wounded on the 9th suffered the greatest loss of any American regiment in a single day during the war. The Americans continued the attack with considerable vigour and by noon Quennemont

View from Lempire, south-east of Vendhuille, towards the former site of the Hindenburg Line defences on the American 27th and 30th Divisions' sector. Bony, Bellicourt and the St Quentin Tunnel are over the crest of the ridge. The Knoll, another area of fierce fighting by the Americans, is just outside the left-hand edge of the photograph. American casualties in this sector were severe.

View towards Bony, south of Vendhuille and just west of the St Quentin Tunnel. The village can be seen in the centre. This whole area was covered with masses of barbed wire and trenches of the Hindenburg Line system. Many American casualties were suffered at Bony, where an American cemetery now stands.

Farm and The Knoll had been captured by the 27th Division. In the afternoon the Australian 5th and 3rd Divisions took over from the Americans although some of the latter continued to fight alongside the Australians. Total casualties of the 27th and 30th Divisions amounted to over 7,500 officers and men, and several Congressional Medals of Honor were awarded to American soldiers for individual acts of exceptional bravery during the very fierce fighting. The success of these two divisions in breaking the Hindenburg Line in that sector won warm praise from General Pershing and other Allied commanders.

North of the Americans and Australians, the British 12th and 18th Divisions of III Corps advanced at Vendhuille, and on their left Third Army units also made good progress, with La Vacquerie and Masnières falling to the New Zealanders and 62nd Division respectively. The 63rd Division reached the southern outskirts of Cambrai after crossing the Scheldt, whilst the Canadians advanced to its north-west environs, thus beginning an envelopment of that important town. In the south the French, under Général Débeney, were also undertaking a flanking movement on St Quentin, and the next day (1st October) most of that city was in their hands. Fierce fighting took place in the northern and western parts of Cambrai, with the Germans rushing in reinforcements in a desperate attempt to hold back the Canadians. Crevecoeur and Rumilly were taken by the New Zealanders and the 3rd Division, and other villages fell to Fourth Army troops, with the Australians capturing the ruins of Bony, where the Americans had recently been hit so hard. By this time most of the main Siegfried Line defences had been captured.

As October came in, the whole length of the Western Front was ablaze from Flanders to the Meuse; the Allies were attacking everywhere. In the north Lille was being threatened: the enemy was falling back between Lens and Armentières, and La Bassée and Aubers Ridge at last came into British hands. The French too were advancing steadily on all sectors and on the Meuse General Pershing was preparing a fresh attack. On 3rd October the 2nd Australian Division broke through the last stronghold of the Siegfried Zone known as the Beaurevoir Line and on the 5th the village of Beaurevoir itself was captured.

Since 26th September thirty-nine German divisions had been defeated, with the British and the two American divisions capturing over 36,000 prisoners and nearly 400 guns. On 4th October Pershing's men advanced nearly three miles on the Meuse front — but not without difficulty against stubborn German resistance — and with St Quentin having fallen Général Débeney's First Army was four miles east of the Scheldt Canal. Next day the Australian Corps was withdrawn from the line for a well-earned rest, having fought constantly from 8th August onwards against mainly stiff opposition. Between 8th August and 5th October the corps had lost 5,000 killed or having died of wounds and over 16,000 wounded. Its valiant contribution to victory was undoubtedly of the highest order and General Monash's pride in his men was more than justified.

On 8th October further strong pressure was exerted by the Allies all along the Western Front — the British, French, Belgians and Americans each advancing in their own sectors. At some points the enemy tried desperately to stem the tide — and even counter-attacked with captured British tanks at one point — but by the evening Ludendorff's troops were falling back to the Oise and Selle in some disarray. That day the southern part of Cambrai had been entered by patrols of the 57th Division of XVII Corps (Third Army) and during the night the Canadians also forced their way into the town from the north. On the 9th Cambrai was completely occupied, with the Canadians then pressing on for three miles beyond the town. The battlefield of Le Cateau, where General Smith-Dorrien and II Corps made their stand in August 1914, was then just two miles from the British advance guards, and the Siegfried Zone had by then been left well behind. Also on 9th October General Pershing relinquished command of the US First Army, which was

The American Military Cemetery at Bony.

The broad, thick belts of barbed wire which formed part of the Hindenburg Line defences at what was known as the Beaurevoir Position, between Lormissel Farm and Mushroom Quarry. This section was defended by over fifty machine-guns but was stormed by the 25th Australian Infantry Battalion, with tank support, on 3rd October 1918. [IWM]

A rather dejected-looking German prisoner and two cheerful Canadian soldiers at the last milestone before Cambrai on the Arras–Cambrai road. [IWM]

The author taking it easy on the last milestone before Cambrai. The Arras–Cambrai road is on the right; Bourlon Wood is over to the extreme right, outside the photograph.

taken over by Lieutenant-General Liggett, and established the US Second Army under Lieutenant-General Bullard.

The combined Allied successes from 8th to 10th October sounded the death-knell of any German hopes of negotiating from a position of strength. Foch's master plan based on squeezing the enemy into a trap between the British, French and Belgians on the one hand, and the French and Americans in the Meuse-Argonne sector on the other, had not quite succeeded to date, but without any doubt whatever the enemy had been decisively beaten in the field. With the Allies pressing on all sides, Ludendorff could do little to change the course of events other than delay the final day of reckoning, but with most of his troops weary and demoralised, and in some cases close to breaking point, the end could not be far away. Already one of Germany's allies, Bulgaria, had withdrawn from the conflict, an armistice having been signed with the Entente Powers on the last day

of September, and on 4th October the German and Austro-Hungarian Governments had sent Notes to President Wilson proposing an armistice based on the Fourteen Points he had drawn up in January for ending the war. On 8th October the President had replied to the German Government's Note, but it had become obvious that interpretation of the Fourteen Points was going to be a problem, especially as the military situation had changed so drastically since the beginning of the year.

Dismayed by what appeared to them to be exceptionally harsh terms for a cease-fire, the Germans baulked at accepting the proposals as submitted. The Allies — and particularly the French — were, however, determined to seek retribution for the years of suffering. Correspondence passed back and forth during October between the Allies via President Wilson, who acted as an intermediary, and meanwhile the Allies continued to move forward on all fronts.

Buildings fired by German mines in the southern suburbs of Cambrai. 9th October 1918. [IWM]

Cambrai Town Hall surrounded by ruins, 23rd October 1918. [IWM]

The same spot, after more than fifty years have passed.

Neat and tidy in the 1970s.

THE ADVANCE CONTINUES

On 6th October the second and concluding phase of the British offensive had commenced with the opening of the Second Battle of Le Cateau (6th–12th October), and in spite of stiffening enemy resistance the west bank of the River Selle had been reached by 10th October. Le Cateau itself was in British hands on the evening of that day and cavalry did valuable work in harrassing the enemy and in the capture of a number of other villages in the region of the old battlefields of 1914. Troops of the US 30th Division and the New Zealand Division were also engaged in heavy but successful fighting. In the air the RAF took full advantage of the chaotic conditions behind the German lines by bombing and machine-gunning transport and troops on the choked roads. In Flanders General Plumer's Second Army, together with Belgian and French forces under the command of the King of the Belgians, resumed their attack on 14th October after having worked hard to re-establish communications in the desert acres of the old Ypres battlefield. This met with complete success against considerable resistance, and numerous towns and villages were taken.

In conjunction with the forward movement of the British Fourth and Third Armies the French First Army on their right also continued to advance east of St Quentin and cleared a major part of the west bank of the Oise–Sambre Canal. Away to the east the French and Americans pushed forward on both sides of the Argonne Forest and by 11th October it became evident to the German High Command that a further widespread withdrawal of their hard-pressed and depleted forces was necessary. Laon was in French hands by the evening of 13th October, and in the north Ostend fell to the Allies on 17th October. On the evening of the same day, Douai was entered by troops of the 8th Division of General Hunter-Weston's VIII Corps and next day Lille was also evacuated by the enemy, with the line being carried forward well east of that town by the 57th and 59th Divisions of XI Corps. By the evening of 19th October, after much severe fighting in difficult country, and following strong attacks by the British XIII Corps, which included the American 30th and 27th Divisions, the enemy had been driven across the Sambre-et-Oise Canal south of Cantillon. North of Le Cateau the fighting was also severe, the attackers coming up against heavily wired and strongly defended German positions, this opposition finally being crushed with the aid of tanks and all objectives being successfully reached. Particularly heavy fighting took place in the Bois l'Eveque and other places such as the hill-top village of Pommereuil, with German machine-gunners offering determined resistance. The twenty-four British and two American divisions engaged between 17th and 25th October in what became known as the Battle of the Selle River had taken 20,000 prisoners and captured 474 guns from the thirty-one German divisions opposing them. A major advance had been achieved against weakening — but in some cases still formidable — enemy resistance, and the rapid succession of heavy blows dealt by the British forces had a most serious effect upon the utterly exhausted German troops.

THE MEUSE–ARGONNE SECTOR

While the British and their allies were pushing forward on the painful road to victory after four long years of suffering, the Americans were also engaged in fierce battles in the Argonne, and northwards towards Sedan. Some people tend to minimise the very important American contribution to the successful concusion of the war. Although they were late in the field, there can be no doubt that the presence of these mainly inexperienced — but very keen — troops was a deciding factor in causing the Germans to sue for peace. By 30th October 1918 there were nearly two million Americans in France (actual combat strength 1,078,200) holding 79 miles of front — and more were coming. Such a massive build-up could not be ignored, and

Right: Looking west from near Apremont, in the Meuse–Argonne region, towards Hills 244 (left), 223 (centre) and 180 (right), area of operations of the 82nd Division and scene of a fierce action on 8th October 1918 in which one of its soldiers, Private First Class (Corporal) Alvin C. York won fame and later became renowned as the screen hero Sergeant York. The division's aim was to cut the German railway communications in the forest . . .

Hill 244 and the village of Châtel-Chéhéry (seen in the picture nestling below the hills) were captured by the 28th Division, operating to the south of the 82nd Division, and the latter took Hill 223 and the high ground beyond. In the ensuing fighting Corporal York's unit (G Company, 2nd Battalion, 328th Infantry) was held up by heavy machine-gun fire from a wooded slope across the valley and the 1st Platoon, in which he was in charge of a squad, was badly hit. The platoon commander (Sergeant Harry Parsons) then ordered four sections amounting to seventeen men — including Corporal York and commanded by Sergeant Bernard Early — to outflank and silence the enemy machine-guns. This move met with initial success, with prisoners being taken, but Sergeant Early was then badly wounded by machine-gun fire, as was the corporal who took over, with a number of the men also being killed. York then took command of the remaining seven privates and in spite of incredible odds eventually succeded in capturing 132 Germans (including five officers, one being a battalion commander) and thirty-five machine-guns, after having killed at least twenty of the enemy by rapid fire with his rifle and pistol. Together with his seven privates and three wounded comrades, and under heavy shell-fire, he shepherded this long column of prisoners back to the American lines. His exceptional coolness, firearms skill and daring enabled his regiment to continue its advance and subsequently led to the award of the Congressional Medal of Honor.

to the Germans — who were already struggling hard to find replacements for the very heavy losses of their 1918 offensives — the omens were clear: they had failed to destroy their somewhat exhausted British and French enemies and they now faced huge numbers of fresh troops who were eager to finish the job. The writing was on the wall, and the German High Command knew it.

Above: The ground to the west of Châtel-Chéhéry where the 82nd Division ran into difficulties and Corporal (later Sergeant) York won immortal fame. Hill 223 rises to the right, Hill 244 is away to the left. The valley beyond Hill 223 was swept with German machine-gun fire from the wooded ridge which halted the division's advance towards their objective, the important Decauville railway about three kilometres to the north-west. Corporal York's astonishing exploits greatly helped to restore a serious situation and was widely recognised as one of the outstanding feats of the war.

With German casualties since March standing at about two and a half million, Ludendorff was now in a desperate situation, with no hope of relief in sight. Hard-pressed on all fronts and with literally no reserves with which to stem the tide, his shrunken divisions dangerously short of artillery, rifles and ammunition, and with morale in many cases near to breaking-point, the end could not be far off. A negotiated peace now appeared to be the only way out; but even that promised no easy solution, for on 23rd October President Wilson sent a further Note on behalf of the Allies which made it clear that there was no room for German equivocations. The Note demanded surrender, the replacement of German militarism by civilian control and in effect the abdication of the Kaiser. Acceptance of those terms would be tantamount to a final admission of defeat in the field, and on 24th October Ludendorff resigned. On 27th October the Germans accepted the terms, to be negotiated by a people's government headed by Prince Max of Baden, who had become the German Imperial Chancellor on 4th October and had written to President Wilson that day with a view to opening negotiations and the conclusion of an immediate armistice. (A similar approach was made from Vienna on that same day.)

Events were now moving fast elsewhere in the political sphere: Turkey was on her knees; Austria was on the verge of collapse following a successful assault by the Italians on the Piave front (in which the British XIV Corps was also involved). On 30th October Turkey signed an armistice with the Entente for hostilities to cease at 12 noon on the 31st, and a few days later, on 4th November, hostilities also ceased with Austria-Hungary following the signing of an armistice the day before.

The last major attack of the Great War on the British front was designated the Battle of the Sambre (1st–11th November) and at 5.15 a.m. on the 1st began with an assault south of Valenciennes by the Canadian Corps of First Army and XVII Corps of Third Army. Heavy fighting took place

The village of Ors; the road bridge over the Sambre Canal.

The Sambre Canal from the bridge at the village of Ors, west of Le Cateau and south-west of Landrecies. On 4th November 1918, about a thousand yards along the towpath from here, the poet Wilfred Owen was killed. Lieutenant Owen fell in action as troops of the 2nd Battalion Manchester Regiment of 96th Brigade, 32nd Division, endeavoured to cross the canal at dawn under heavy machine-gun fire from Germans on the opposite bank. Owen was encouraging his men forward when he was hit. There were many killed and the attack was not a success. Thus Britain lost one of her finest poets just seven days before the guns fell silent. The Manchesters crossed the canal by a floating bridge south of Ors later in the day. Two VCs were won in the action in which Owen was involved.

against stiff enemy resistance, with the Canadians forcing an entry into the town from the west. Over on the Argonne front that day the French and Americans also successfully attacked; pressure by Général Gouraud's French troops assisted the US First Army to break out of the wooded country where it had been boxed in, the result being a very satisfactory American advance of six miles, which increased to twelve miles by 3rd November.

On 4th November the capture of Valenciennes was completed by the Canadians whilst other successes continued elsewhere, the River Sambre being crossed at various points. Fighting was heavy near Landrecies, which was taken by the 25th Division, and in the Mormal Forest V Corps of Third Army pushed its way through the tangled woodland to the eastern edge. Le Quesnoy, which had been beset by

Ors Village Communal Cemetery, where Lieutenant Wilfred Owen, MC, is buried (third from left). Ors Church is behind.

Another soldier who fought on the Sambre Canal was Private W. E. ('Josh') Grover MM, seen above with his mother and sisters while on leave from France in 1917. 'Josh' joined the army via the Derby scheme (which asked for registration of readiness to serve when called) in 1915 at the age of eighteen, volunteered for France and fought on the Somme at High Wood, at Nieuport on the coast, and in the Ypres Salient; also in the Cuinchy/La Bassée area in 1918 at the time of the German breakthrough, where he won his Military Medal. On 4th November 1918 he took part in an attack by the 2nd Battalion of the Royal Sussex Regiment (2nd Brigade, 1st Division) against a lock control-house on the Sambre Canal not far from where Wilfred Owen was killed and he narrowly missed being severely wounded, or even killed, when a German bullet struck — and rendered useless — the Lewis Gun he was holding at an angle across his chest in order to protect his body. He survived the attack and went home on leave shortly before the Armistice and later returned to take his place in the occupation of Cologne, 'Josh' died shortly before his 92nd birthday in 1989, just a few hours after the author, and the author's wife, visited him in hospital at Dover, where he had been taken following a short illness.

Note: In the Sambre Canal attack the Commanding Officer, Colonel D. G. Johnson, won the Victoria Cross.

The Battle of the Sambre Canal had been fought and mostly won as the war entered its last phase. Further fighting was still called for, however, as the Germans fought desperate rearguard actions, one of which was at the small, walled town of Le Quesnoy, southeast of Valenciennes and west of the Forest of Mormal. With its massive Vauban-built ramparts and defensive moats it was thought that it could prove to be a hard nut to crack, so plans were made to encircle the town before enforcing its surrender. The task of taking the town fell to the New Zealand Division, and on 5th November they attacked at dawn. The encirclement went off successfully. Under heavy fire from the inner and outer ramparts, the New Zealanders forced their way into the powerful defences with the aid of scaling ladders. A break was made in spite of intensive enemy small-arms fire and the ramparts were carried in a most determined manner at the cost of around 200 casualties. More than 200 Germans were killed and 700 were captured, together with many machine-guns and other weapons. Six days later the war ended.

The causeway entrance to the town of Le Quesnoy where the Germans put up a stout defence before yielding to fierce attacks by New Zealand troops.

The moat and high ramparts surrounding Le Quesnoy, which demonstrate the excellent defensive positions of the Germans.

The spot where the all-important breach was made in the ramparts at Le Quesnoy by troops of the New Zealand Division. The plaque on the wall depicts their splendid action, led by Second Lieutenant Francis Evans, who, sadly, was killed whilst making a dash to the inner defences at the head of his men.

the New Zealanders, surrendered on the 5th, a day on which 19,000 prisoners and 450 guns were captured by the British alone. Guise fell to the French on the 5th and the Belgians were near to Ghent. Pershing's Second Army, under General Liggett, was now advancing along the right bank of the Meuse, and the US First Army was closing in on the vital Metz railway and also approaching Mezières. Thus Foch's trap was rapidly closing. Nothing but a negotiated armistice could now spare the Germans from certain defeat and enable them to save some sort of face. Meanwhile rumbles of revolution surfaced in Germany and on 4th November mutiny broke out in the German fleet at Kiel. The trouble quickly spread to other ports and industrial centres, with soldiers, sailors and workers forming special councils and the red flag well in evidence. The disturbances spread to Berlin a few days later. The rot had really begun to set in.

On 7th November the Guards Division entered Bavai, scene of much confusion in 1914, and on the following day General Byng's troops were approaching the fortress of Maubeuge, which, just over four years earlier, von Kluck had attempted to use in a manoeuvre to hem in the BEF: had he succeeded in that aim the story of the war would certainly have been very different. Most of the men who had fought in those early days were either dead, prisoners or wounded, some mere wrecks of former human beings. The weather too was vastly different — wet and cold, in contrast to the hot, sultry days of August 1914. And now militarily the rôles were reversed. The all-powerful German forces that had advanced rapidly with the near certainty of victory apparently just a few months away were now close to disintegration and desperately fighting off constant attacks by what had once been a seemingly broken enemy. The wheel had indeed turned full circle: all the more poignant for the British troops that the war should be nearing its end close to the place where for those still remaining of the original BEF it had all started — the town of Mons, just a comparatively short distance away.

On 8th November Maubeuge was entered by the Guards (it was captured on the 9th) and the Canadians were advancing along the Mons–Condé Canal, the town of Condé having fallen the day before. The ancient city of Tournai was also captured on the 9th, and on the 10th Ghent was in the hands of the Belgians. A few days earlier the Americans had reached the famous city of Sedan, having advanced twenty-five miles since 1st November, and on the 8th the French had closed up to Mezières — that important town coming into their possession on the 10th.

Whilst all these successes were being chalked up by the Allies, a flurry of diplomatic activity was taking place. On the 7th a German armistice delegation headed by Herr Matthias Erzberger (Centre Party Deputy), and including the Foreign Minister, Count Obendorff, had passed through the French lines, and the next day they faced Maréchal Foch, Général Weygand (Foch's Chief-of-Staff), plus staff officers, and the British delegation headed by Vice-Admiral Sir Rosslyn Wemyss, First Sea Lord. The meeting was in a train drawn up in a siding in the Forest of Compiègne especially for the purpose of the armistice negotiations and Foch lost no time in making it clear that there was no scope whatever for bargaining. Having been presented with the Allied terms, which they found quite staggering, the Germans were given just seventy-two hours to accept the conditions as laid down, and a courier left to report the situation to the German authorities. On the 10th the Kaiser left Germany to seek sanctuary in Holland, the Crown Prince following suit.

Following a Government conference in Berlin, the German delegates were instructed to accept the terms, and at 5 a.m. (French time) on Monday, 11th November (not without protest from the German delegates) the Armistice was signed. Hostilities on all fronts were to cease at 11 a.m. That same morning the Canadians entered Mons — fighting having continued during the previous night on its outskirts — and what is believed to have been the last death by direct enemy action (Private George Price) occurred at the small village of Ville-sur-Haine, north-east of Mons, just two minutes before the Armistice came into effect.

So ended the greatest conflagration the world had ever witnessed. At least twelve million men had been killed and many more millions wounded — a great number of them crippled for life. Dynasties had been toppled, thousands of towns and villages had been destroyed and a great swathe of gas-soaked, shell-scarred earth had been cut across Western Europe which would take many years to recover.

For the British forces the end had come after 98 days of almost non-stop advance from near Amiens to Mons — a vindication of their belief in the final outcome that they had held on to even in the darkest days of the German Spring Offensive. Since the advance began on 8th August they had won seven major victories and taken about 190,000 prisoners and 3,000 guns. These operations had cost some 350,000 killed or wounded, and those who did not live to enjoy the fruits of their efforts, and who are buried across the Channel beneath a then British Empire headstone, lie like the dead of the previous four years in the quiet, beautifully-kept cemeteries dotted around the French and Belgian countryside, while others are commemorated on memorials to the missing. Their memory — the memory of all the men of the United Kingdom and their Commonwealth comrades who died as a result of the fighting on the Western Front between 1914 and 1918 — lives on.

The headstone of Private G. Ellison, the last British soldier to be killed in the war, on 11th November 1918. He is buried in St Symphorien Military Cemetery, not far from the first to die in 1914 (see page 33).

The first house on the right was the spot at Ville-sur-Haine where Private George Price was shot just two minutes before the Cease-Fire on 11th November 1918, thus making him the last Canadian soldier to die in the war. A plaque commemorating this sad event was erected on the front of the house by his comrades on 11th November 1968. Since this picture was taken (in 1984) the house has been swept away for road changes.

Armistice ceremony, Mons. Troops of the 3rd Canadian Division which captured the town marching past the saluting base. Mons was recaptured by troops of the 7th Brigade, 3rd Canadian Division, Canadian Corps (First Army). Just before midnight on 10th November units of the 42nd Battalion forced a passage into the southern part of the town and moved northwards. Soon afterwards a company of the Royal Canadian Regiment (attached to the 42nd Bn) entered the north-western environs and by daybreak on the 11th the city had been cleared of Germans. At around 7 a.m. the pipe band of the 42nd Bn played its way into Mons, but the official entry was not made by the 7th Canadian Brigade until 10.30 a.m. when, on the instructions of General Currie, GOC Canadian Corps, they were accompanied by an escort of the nearby British 5th Lancers, a unit that had been part of Brigadier-General H. de la P. Gough's 3rd Cavalry Brigade (Allenby's Cavalry Division) at Mons in 1914. This was a generous gesture on the part of General Currie who arrived in the town in the afternoon. [IWM]

The British Expeditionary Force Memorial at Mons, commemorating the two battles fought in 1914 and 1918, which now stands at La Bascule, not far from where Private Carter of the 4th Middlesex was photographed in August 1914 (see page 23). The Memorial was erected in 1952 in the garden of the Citadel (above), being inaugurated by Field Marshal Alexander, Earl of Tunis, and then moved thirty-four years later to its present location. It bears the inscription: 'Here the forces of the British Empire fought their first and last battles of the 1914–1918 war'.

At this railway siding in the Forest of Compèigne (a section of track that had been laid from Rethondes for heavy artillery firing on Noyon) the German delegation headed by Herr Erzberger were presented the terms of an armistice by the representatives of the Allied armies and navies, Maréchal Foch and Admiral Wemyss on 8th November 1918. [IWM]

The site of the siding where the Armistice was signed at Compiègne, with a statue of Maréchal Foch in the background. After the French capitulation in the Second World War, Hitler ordered the demolition of the site, and the Armistice carriage was taken to Germany, where it was destroyed by SS troops at Ohrdruf to whence it had been taken in March 1945 from Berlin. A replica coach is housed near the reconstituted memorial.

Maréchal Foch (second from right), Admiral Wemyss (centre) and Foch's Chief of Staff, Général Weygand (on Wemyss's right) and others outside the railway coach in which the Armistice was signed. [IWM]

Above: The imposing façade of Etaples British Military Cemetery, on the coast south of Boulogne, which contains over 11,000 graves, mostly from the United Kingdom. 655 Germans are also buried there. The surrounding area of sand dunes was the site of numerous hospitals and reinforcement camps and of the infamous 'Bullring' training area, which had a notorious reputation with the troops because of its bullying NCOs (known as 'Canaries'), who were basically the cause of a comparatively minor mutiny in September 1917 — an event that was hushed up by the authorities and came to light in the late 1980s through the highly controversial television programme 'The Monocled Mutineer'. The main Boulogne–Paris railway line ran right through the area and perhaps not surprisingly this and the training camps became the target of German bombers in 1917. Unfortunately, hospitals were also hit, and seriously hurt men who were so close to reaching home became victims of the bombing, as did some of the nurses, several of whom are buried in the cemetery. Many of the graves contain soldiers who died from the effects of gas gangrene. Nowadays it takes only a short time by car to reach Etaples (known to British troops as 'Eat Apples') but in 1914–1918 it represented a tiring twenty-mile route march to many of the soldiers on their way to the front. Over 100,000 men were encamped in the vicinity of the cemetery in 1917.

Funeral of Sister Margaret Lowe, of Binscarth, Manitoba, who died of wounds received during a German air raid on Etaples in May 1918. Beyond the mourners and the many crosses is the main railway which fed the hungry war machine with men, weapons and stores. The location of hospitals next to this line was the subject of controversy as it — and the nearby camps — regularly received attention from German bombers. [IWM]

Beautifully laid out and carefully tended graves at Etaples Military Cemetery as it is now. A Boulogne–Paris express train can be seen speeding by in the background.

Comrades in death, in which all are of equal rank.

An unknown soldier — one of the very many thousands who come under that heading. As the date is given as 25.11.16, it is likely that his name is carved on the immense memorial at Thiepval which records the names of 73,412 'Missing' during the Battles of the Somme. [IWM]

Temporary crosses on graves at Terlincthun British Military Cemetery, near Boulogne, where remains discovered on the old battlefields in more recent years are now concentrated. An average of twenty remains come to light on the Western Front each year. Most of them are unidentifiable but occasionally it is possible to make an identification from identity discs or other means.

Terlincthun British Military Cemetery, near Boulogne. In the centre foreground is a special memorial dedicated to 49 British soldiers and 2 Germans who were found on the site of a former trench at Ovillers-la-Boisselle (Somme) in November 1982.

Looking across Mash Valley, with Ovillers on the right and Ovillers British Military Cemetery on the left. The former site of the German front line trenches is indicated by the white chalk markings to the left of the minor road. The spot where the remains were discovered is just this side of the cemetery entrance.

Pieces of boots and other equipment, plus a grenade, where the remains of a British soldier were found by a farm worker at Rozières, south of the Amiens–St Quentin road during one of the author's annual visits to the battlefields. The soldier could not be identified but his buttons showed that he belonged to the Manchester Regiment. His water bottle had been damaged by a piece of shell and a flat-type electric torch was found by his remains.

The grave of Lieutenant-Colonel John McCrae, Canadian Army Medical Corps, at Wimereux Communal Cemetery, three miles north of Boulogne (where the gravestones lie flat because of unstable ground). He died on 28th January 1918 from illness and will forever be remembered for the poem 'In Flanders Fields' which he wrote on the banks of the Yser Canal, just north of Ypres, in 1915. A verse from that immortal poem is inscribed on a nearby special memorial seat at the entrance to the cemetery.

Arrival of the gun carriage bearing the Unknown Warrior at the Cenotaph, Whitehall, for the unveiling of the permanent memorial by His Majesty King George V, 11th November 1920. A temporary structure had previously served this purpose. [IWM]

The coffin of the Unknown Warrior in Westminster Abbey, 7th November 1920. [IWM]

The tomb of the Unknown Warrior in the Abbey today (in the foreground) with St George's Chapel behind. [*After the Battle*]

Peace Day Celebrations, 19th July 1919. Allied troops march through London. A British drum and fife band leads the Indian Detachment. [IWM]

A photograph of the Menin Gate Memorial to the Missing at Ypres taken shortly after its inauguration in 1927. Inscribed on panels within the archway are the names of almost 55,000 men of the armies of the British Empire who died on the Ypres sector of the front and who have no known grave. Through the archway, the Cloth Hall can be seen being rebuilt.

Most memorials in the United Kingdom were erected to commemorate those who died in the Great War — but not this one. It registers the names of men of the hamlet of Knowlton, near Dover, who actually returned safely. Of the thirty-nine people living in the village when war broke out, twelve men enlisted before March 1915. Each went to France: each came home alive. The sculptured column was erected in their honour and has been called the happiest peace memorial in Kent. Inscribed on the memorial are the words: 'One Crowded Hour of Glorious Life is Worth an Age Without a Name.' The names of the twelve men are also listed (a major, two captains, three corporals and six privates). A thirteenth name (of a major) appears to have been added at a later date. Most of those listed belonged to the Royal East Kent Yeomanry and the Buffs. [Research by John Holland-Hobbs]

Special ceremony of the 20,000th blowing of the Last Post at the Menin Gate, Ypres, by members of the Ypres Fire Brigade on 20th February 1988. The ceremony was first carried out in 1927 and has continued every evening since 1929 apart from the period of the German occupation of the town during the Second World War.

A SURVIVOR

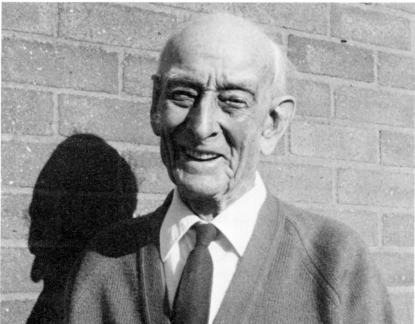

Left are two pictures of former Sergeant Archie Stanley, 1st Battalion The Buffs (East Kent Regiment), 16th Infantry Brigade, 6th Division, who [in 1990] was 98 years of age and the last surviving 'Old Contemptible' in Kent.

Archie was 22½ years old when he went to France at the beginning of September 1914 and he saw action on the Marne and the Aisne. From December 1914 to May 1915 he was in the Armentières sector. He later fought at Hill 60, where he missed being killed by an enemy shell which dropped into a trench a few moments after he left it (a friend being blown to pieces). He was in action during the Somme battles of 1916 and later fighting, but came through safely only to be wounded by one of our own shells, when he was hit by an 18-pounder nose cap towards the end of the war. He was taken to a base hospital at Etaples and then on to Charing Cross Hospital. When the war ended he was a convalescent at Brighton, having survived four years in some of the hottest spots of that era.

A lifelong non-smoker and non-drinker (he never even drank rum in France), Archie was married for 71 years until, sad to say, the lifelong union of this devoted couple was broken by the death of his beloved wife in May 1990 at a residential home in Dover where they spent their last happy years together. Remarkably well for his age — and lucid — (although somewhat frail) Archie was still able to recall some of his more memorable wartime experiences with surprising clarity. Inevitably, however, the passage of time took its toll, with memories of those days fading into the distance.

One of Archie's ambitions was to reach his 100th birthday and get the Queen's telegram. Sadly fate intervened before he was able to accomplish this aim, because following a partial hip replacement he failed to recover and died on December 29th 1990, at the age of 98.

When asked to summarise his feelings, Archie replied with modest simplicity: 'We owed allegiance to our King and our Country and we did our duty; that's what it was all about.' In saying this, Archie was speaking in effect for most of the young men of 1914. We shall not see their like again.

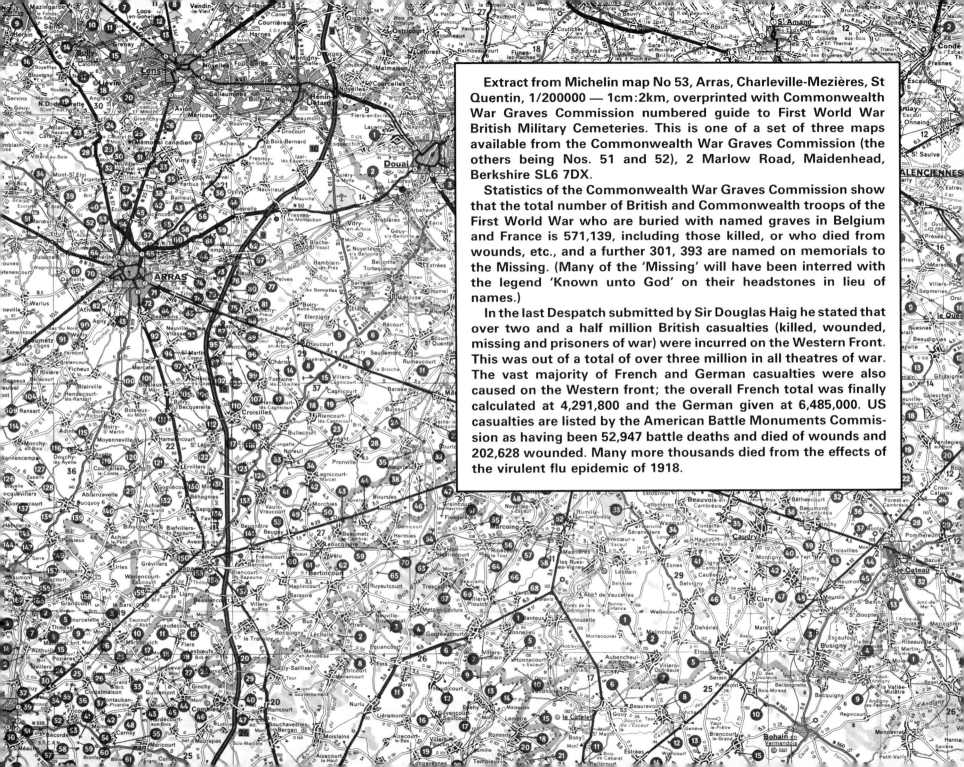

Extract from Michelin map No 53, Arras, Charleville-Mezières, St Quentin, 1/200000 — 1cm:2km, overprinted with Commonwealth War Graves Commission numbered guide to First World War British Military Cemeteries. This is one of a set of three maps available from the Commonwealth War Graves Commission (the others being Nos. 51 and 52), 2 Marlow Road, Maidenhead, Berkshire SL6 7DX.

Statistics of the Commonwealth War Graves Commission show that the total number of British and Commonwealth troops of the First World War who are buried with named graves in Belgium and France is 571,139, including those killed, or who died from wounds, etc., and a further 301,393 are named on memorials to the Missing. (Many of the 'Missing' will have been interred with the legend 'Known unto God' on their headstones in lieu of names.)

In the last Despatch submitted by Sir Douglas Haig he stated that over two and a half million British casualties (killed, wounded, missing and prisoners of war) were incurred on the Western Front. This was out of a total of over three million in all theatres of war. The vast majority of French and German casualties were also caused on the Western front; the overall French total was finally calculated at 4,291,800 and the German given at 6,485,000. US casualties are listed by the American Battle Monuments Commission as having been 52,947 battle deaths and died of wounds and 202,628 wounded. Many more thousands died from the effects of the virulent flu epidemic of 1918.

APPENDIX 1
THE AIR WAR 1914-1918
AND THE AIR 'ACES'

Half-way through the Great War, and despite the Somme Offensive and other major battles during the first two years, stalemate still existed on the Western Front from the infantry standpoint. In the air, meanwhile, considerable changes had occurred since the early days of the conflict which Great Britain entered with very few aeroplanes, including the Royal Flying Corps' unarmed 80 mph BE2a — the first British aeroplane to land in France.

Both Germany and France, however — and even Russia — had placed more emphasis on building up air appendages to their armies, and the Germans undoubtedly enjoyed superiority in the air in those early days of movement, with considerable success being achieved from accurate reports by their airmen of the disposition of enemy forces. Indeed, the Taube monoplane, with its distinctive bird-shaped wing, was to become a regular menace to British troops in the anxious days of 1914 as it hovered above them at Mons, Le Cateau, during the retreat, on the Aisne and throughout the subsequent heavy fighting of that year. British reconnaissance planes, though, also registered successes, having warned GHQ of long columns of German troops approaching the British positions along the Mons Canal (a report that was not at first fully believed) and, in the days of the retreat, confirming the unexpected and surprising change of direction of von Kluck's First Army across the face of Paris. A French aviator also reported this important development.

The RFC operated in France during the first weeks of the war (The Royal Naval Air Service being an entirely separate entity) with a mixed bag of aeroplanes, some of which — like the Bleriot monoplane and the Henri Farman biplane —

A monument on the cliffs above Dover (not far from the Swingfield radar pylons) which commemorates the departure of RFC squadrons from a nearby field to Amiens in August 1914.

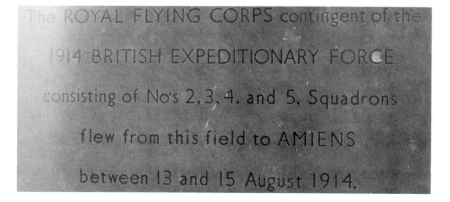

The ROYAL FLYING CORPS contingent of the 1914 BRITISH EXPEDITIONARY FORCE consisting of No's 2, 3, 4, and 5, Squadrons flew from this field to AMIENS between 13 and 15 August 1914.

A plaque on the monument which denotes the historic event.

could hardly make any headway against a strong wind. In those days, too, the aircraft were unarmed except for the revolvers — and in some cases rifles — carried by the pilots and/or observers which enabled them to take pot-shots at the enemy, without, however, a great deal of success. In those early days a chivalrous understanding of sorts existed among many — but not all — of the opposing airmen, but that charitable attitude was to change as the war progressed and the fighting in the air, like that on the ground, became more bitter and bloody, with machine-guns taking the place of side-arms, and a readiness to kill the enemy being more predominant than any humanitarian feelings.

As 1914 gave way to 1915 and plans were made by the various commanders to break the deadlock on the Western Front, the air war escalated as the Frenchman, Roland Garos, and two collegues developed a method of firing a machine-gun through the propeller arc by means of metal wedges being fixed to the wooden blades. This invention was fitted to a Morane monoplane, and in April 1915 Garos successfully shot down a German Albatros. Unfortunately, he was brought down by ground fire over Courtrai (east of Ypres) and his aircraft fell into German hands in spite of his endeavours to set it on fire. The Germans, who were delighted at such a prize, quickly began experiments based on the same method but encountered difficulties in their tests.

It is perhaps ironic that an aircraft designer of a neutral country, a Dutchman named Anthony Fokker, who had offered his product to the British without success and in consequence turned to the Germans as an outlet for his skills, was the first to come up with a successful method of firing a machine-gun mounted above the engine without shooting off the propeller. At the end of 1913 Fokker had obtained a French Morane-Saulnier monoplane, which he mainly copied, and called it the Fokker Eendekker (better known as the Eindekker), and it was with this aeroplane that in May 1915, and at the instigation of the Germans, he

The BE2a which was the first British aeroplane to land in France after the declaration of war. It landed at Amiens and its pilot was Major H. Harvey-Kelley, DSO, Royal Irish Regiment, attached to the Royal Flying Corps. He is seen here, on the ground below right of the aircraft, in a field at Lythe, near Whitby, reading a map, in August 1914. Major Harvey-Kelley was killed in April 1917 behind the German lines. [IWM]

A Fokker 'Eindekker' EI. With its forward-firing machine-gun. This type of aeroplane mauled the British and French opposition in what became known as the 'Fokker Scourge' in 1915 and 1916. [IWM]

experimented with a cam-operated interrupter-gear which, despite its crudeness, did what was needed by allowing the pilot to aim his aircraft directly at the enemy and fire through the propeller arc without damaging the blades.

Thus was born what became known to the British as the 'Fokker Scourge' which caused havoc to the lumbering Allied reconnaissance planes. It was a time that saw the air war change dramatically, with the Germans enjoying complete air superiority until new aeroplanes such as the manoeuverable French Nieuport II biplane, with a machine-gun mounted on its top wing and a top speed of 97 mph, arrived later in the year. Meanwhile, German pilots acquired fame with the seemingly invincible Eindekker, with two names in particular becoming widely known, these being Oswald Boelke and Max Immelmann. Those two more than any others were to influence the whole concept of aerial fighting tactics and were the forerunners of a band of fighter 'aces' — a term coined by the French and applying to any aviator who destroyed five aircraft, but frowned upon by the British authorities who disliked the publicity attached to it, their belief being that it eulogized men who were doing their duty like everyone else. The German criteria was eight 'kills'.

On 26th April 1915 a 27-year-old aviation pioneer by the name of William Rhodes-Moorhouse (who first flew in 1909) made history as a Second Lieutenant in No. 2 Squadron RFC when he bombed the railway station at Courtrai, Belgium, in a BE2. The attack was aimed at delaying the arrival of German reinforcements during the Second Battle of Ypres and although his mission met with success, fierce enemy small-arms fire over the target severely wounded the intrepid young pilot as he flew just 300 feet above the ground. In intense pain and only semi-conscious he flew his badly damaged aeroplane back to his base thirty-five miles away, managed to land safely and reported before being treated for his injuries. He died the next day and was posthumously awarded the VC — the first of nineteen to be awarded during that war to British and Empire airmen. His body was subsequently brought back to the family home at Parnham House, Beaminster, where he was interred in a private grave on a hill overlooking the house. The ashes of his son, a WW2 RAF pilot who was killed in the Battle of Britain, were also placed there.

Lieutenant William Rhodes-Moorhouse, the first aviator VC.

Two months later a British RNAS pilot, Flight Sub-Lieutenant R. A. J. Warneford, also made history by destroying a German Zeppelin (LZ37) above Ghent, an action which led to the immediate award of the Victoria Cross. He was given little time to enjoy his well-deserved fame, though, as he died in a crash that same month. In the French sector, a young aviator named Jean Navarre also distinguished himself when on 1st April in a Morane monoplane he brought down a German aeroplane with three well-aimed rifle shots (one of which injured the pilot), thus bringing immediate recognition and acclaim to Navarre, who went on to enhance his reputation over the bloody battlefields of Verdun early in 1916.

As 1916 dawned, the Germans still had superiority in the skies and they put this to good use during the early days of the Verdun fighting. However, by mid-April the advantages they had enjoyed so far were beginning to wane as the Eindekker became outdated and the Nieuport II quickly gained the upper hand. Navarre and another French 'ace', Lieutenant Charles Nungesser, chalked up success after success in their own individualistic ways, but on 17th June Navarre was shot down and seriously wounded in the head, an injury that afflicted him both physically and mentally and, combined with the death of his brother at about the same time, literally finished him as a pilot. (He was killed in a plane crash in 1919.) Nungesser, although sustaining various injuries, went on to score twenty-one victories by December 1916. He succeeded in staying alive throughout the remainder of the war and, although scarred by numerous encounters with the enemy, raised his total of 'kills' to forty-five, which earned him a considerable number of military honours. (He disappeared in May 1927 during an attempt to cross the Atlantic.)

Another Frenchman, Capitaine René Fonck, who was subsequently destined to become the Allied Ace of Aces with seventy-five victories (he believed the actual total to be more), was at that period employed as a reconnaissance

Capitaine Guynemer being decorated with the Légion d'Honneur by Général Franchet d'Espérey on 5th July 1917. [IWM]

The village of Poelcapelle, north-east of Ypres, which in 1917 existed in name only, the whole area being one vast sea of desolation. On the right is the memorial to the famous French 'ace' Guynemer, who is believed to have been shot down near this spot but whose remains were never found.

253

pilot in rather ancient Caudrons in the Vosges region. The skies of Verdun were also the scene of operations of the famous and much decorated Capitaine Georges Guynemer for a short time before he was shot down and injured. His squadron was one of the first to be re-equipped with the Nieuport IIs and during his enforced stay in hospital other fighter pilots of the unit, which was known as the Stork Squadron — the emblem of a stork being painted on their aircraft — continued to take a steady toll of enemy planes.

Guynemer was able to rejoin his squadron in time for the Somme fighting, with his score rising to eleven by the end of July. In September, and flying a new French machine, the Spad VII with a top speed of 119 mph, his score quickly rose and by January 1917 he had claimed thirty victims, a total which increased to fifty-four before fate took a hand. Worn out by the incessant fighting, he survived until 11th September, when, with an accompanying Spad, he attacked an enemy two-seater over Poelcapelle (north-east of Ypres) and in turn was set upon by a flight of Albatros DVs. His companion managed to escape but Guynemer disappeared and his body was never found, it being believed that it was destroyed in a British bombardment. A memorial to his memory now stands at Poelcapelle crossroads crowned with a stork with drooping wings — a symbol of one of the most famous of all French squadrons.

In 1916 a few Nieuport IIs were in action on the British front and these helped to break the hold of the Eindeckker. The German threat was also diminished by the introduction of a new British fighter aeroplane, the De Havilland DH2, a pusher type (i.e. with the engine behind, 'pushing' the aeroplane) mounting a .303 Lewis gun in the nacelle at the front. At the end of 1915 No. 24 Squadron had been formed with these machines, and in February 1916 the squadron arrived in the Somme area, at Bertangles, where the DH2s and the two-seater FE2bs quickly got the better of the Fokker E types, thus gaining mastery of the air for the British on that part of the front. This advantage was to continue during the period of the bitter Somme fighting until September, when once again the balance swung in the Germans' favour with their new Albatros and Halberstadt planes.

The commander of No. 24 Squadron was Major Lanoe G. Hawker, VC, DSO, who became the first Royal Flying Corps 'ace', with a total of nine victories, before he was shot down in November of that year by a German pilot who was also becoming a legend — Baron Manfred von Richthofen. Major Hawker had been in France with the RFC since 1914 and was awarded the DSO in April 1915 after a lone bombing expedition in a BE2c on Zeppelin sheds near Ghent. He won the coveted VC when he downed three enemy machines in one day on 25th July 1915 — the third to be awarded to a member of the air services and the first awarded for aerial combat.

On the day of Hawker's death on 23rd November 1916 his was one of four of No. 24 Squadron's DH2s which encountered five of the new German Albatros DIIs over the Somme battlefield. Two of the British planes were forced to turn for home because of engine trouble and a third was damaged in the ensuing combat, the pilot landing safely. Hawker was left alone and he and Richthofen (who had already won fourteen victories) engaged in a duel in which the German ace found that his intended victim was anything but an easy conquest. Despite trying every trick in the trade — initially with much success — Hawker could no longer outfly or outfight Richthofen's far more powerful and speedier aircraft with its two machine-guns, and inevitably the end came after a lengthy contest, when the British flyer received a fatal head wound which caused him to crash headlong into the ground.

Earlier that same year — on 18th June — the great Immelmann, inventor of the famous 'Immelmann turn' (a manoeuvre aimed at getting above and behind an opponent), died after an aerial battle with British planes near Lens. The cause of his death was subject to controversy, but whatever the actual reason — one suggestion was that his weapon synchronising gear had failed, causing him to shoot his own propeller away — his aircraft broke apart and he fell to his doom after having been credited with fifteen victories over Allied opponents.

Immelmann's death was a calamity for both German civilians and airmen alike, and this major blow to morale was repeated a few months later when another renowned German airman, Oswald Boelke, also died in unpropitious circumstances. His score up to 25th October had been thirty-nine and on that day he added yet another to his tally by destroying a BE2 near Serre. Three days later he was leading a flight of six aircraft when the wing-tip of one of his companions clipped his wing strut, which caused the top wing to collapse. As his comrades watched helplessly, Boelke's aircraft nose-dived to the ground and he was killed instantly. So passed the first of the great high-scoring German airmen of that era.

While Major Hawker was notching up his score in 1916, a shy young Nottinghamshire-born lad, who had joined the Sherwood Foresters in 1914 at the age of eighteen, was employed in flying the BE2c and single-seater Bristol Scout with No. 13 Squadron, having gained his wings in January of that year. His name was Albert Ball, and he was to become one of the most illustrious of all British fighter pilots, with a final tally of forty-four before his young life was snuffed out. An individualist, Ball thought nothing of attacking enemy formations single-handedly, and his tactics of surprise and aggressiveness, coupled with skilful timing, invariably wrought havoc amongst his startled enemies, whom he gave no time to recover before he made a quick getaway. In May 1916 he was transferred to No. 11 Squadron, where he was delighted to find himself in control of a Nieuport, in which he obtained further successes which led to his award of the MC.

After a short spell on BEs, having requested a short rest from operations, and once rested, to his disgust, having been transferred to No. 8 Squadron on artillery spotting

Max Franz Immelmann beside a British plane which he shot down in combat. [IWM]

flights, he again rejoined No. 11 Squadron and at the end of August 1916 was posted to No. 60 Squadron flying Nieuports. Early in October he was sent back to England as an instructor and was awarded the DSO and Bar, but he longed to get back into action and, following his transfer to No. 56 Squadron — formed especially to fly the new SE5 (which at first he did not like) — he was back in France on 7th April 1917 as a flight commander, where he lost no time in quickly adding to his score, and also his fame.

On 7th May 1917 Ball made his last flight in an eleven-strong patrol of SE5s and near Cambrai encountered a large enemy force. A fierce action followed, with the last glimpse of Ball by his comrades being as he disappeared into a bank of clouds. Soon afterwards an aircraft was seen by enemy ground troops near Annouellin (east of La Bassée) to come out of cloud with its engine stopped; it then crashed to the

The wartime grave of Captain Albert Ball, VC, DSO (two bars), MC, Royal Flying Corps, killed near Lens after a fight with von Richthofen's squadron, 7th May 1917. [IWM]

ground, Ball's badly crushed body being found in the wreckage. His death aroused controversy, with the British claiming that their foremost airman of the time had not died from being struck by an opponent's bullet, but through malfunction of his aircraft or anti-aircraft fire. The Germans, however, declared that he was a victim of Lothar von Richthofen, younger brother of the famous Manfred. His death occurred a few weeks before his twenty-first birthday — he was later awarded a posthumous VC.

Prior to Ball's death, 1917 began with the Allies at a considerable disadvantage in the air war owing to the superiority of the two-gunned Albatros and the overall methods employed by the enemy, including the use of large formations of aircraft. The Nieuport 17 was badly under-powered compared to the Albatros — and with its single wing-mounted Lewis gun, also underarmed — but it was the extremely vulnerable British reconnaissance machines in particular that became an easy prey to the marauding enemy fighter planes.

As preparations for the great Arras offensive continued apace, activity in the air also intensified. Following the launching of the assault in early April, the skies above the attacking and defending ground troops were filled with aeroplanes of both sides seeking control of the air. In this the Germans were initially highly successful, that month becoming known to the RFC as 'Bloody April', as indeed it was as the casualties increased rapidly. In that month alone British losses amounted to around 150 aircraft (many of them 2 seaters) compared to less than half that total for the Germans. By now, however, a number of British planes had been fitted with what was known as the Constantinesco synchronising gear which was a considerable improvement over earlier efforts at overcoming the problem of firing machine-guns through the propeller. Hydraulically operated, and named after its Romanian inventor, it was put into production by Vickers with DH4s being the first machines to arrive in France — in March 1917 — equipped with this development.

As April wore on, other new British aeroplanes made their appearance, with the SE5, Sopwith Pup and Sopwith Triplane all whittling away the advantage previously held by the Germans. At about that time, too, another young man, who had previously been a cavalryman, arrived in France. He was a Canadian Captain (later Major) named William Bishop, and he was destined to become one of the most famous of all British fighter pilots with a confirmed score of

Captain W. A. Bishop, VC, standing by his Nieuport Type 17 Scout B1566 of No. 60 Squadron RFC in 1917. He scored thirty-six of his confirmed victories in this type, which he flew until 28th July 1917. [IWM]

seventy-two, more than half of them in the ubiquitous Nieuport 17. Unlike many of his compatriots, he survived the war, having won the VC, DSO with Bar and MC for exploits which made him world renowned. He died in 1956 after a most distinguished career which included the post of Director of the Royal Canadian Air Force in World War Two. Like Ball, Bishop attacked almost recklessly but he coupled this aggressive spirit with superb marksmanship and skilful flying, all of which held him in good stead during those grim days of April 1917 when so many of his compatriots fell to earth, many of them meeting with a fiery death as their aircraft spiralled down in flames.

One particularly conspicuous aircraft over the Arras battlefields was an all-red Albatros piloted by the most famous of all German fighter 'aces' — Baron Manfred Freiherr von Richthofen, whose official final total was never exceeded by any other pilot in World War One. Towards the end of 1915 the young cavalry officer, who had joined an élite Lancer regiment in 1911, transferred to the air service and for a while acted as an observer on the Eastern Front. A chance meeting with Oswald Boelke subsequently led to his being chosen to join a new Fighter Squadron formation, Jagdstaffel (Jasta) 2 which aimed at obtaining air supremacy and he quickly began to claim victims, many being of the slow two-seater observation types. He celebrated his victories by presenting himself with a small silver cup as a trophy for each success (until silver no longer remained available later in the war).

On 23rd November 1916 Richthofen had his epic fight with Major Hawker which resulted in the death of the British fighter ace, and in January 1917 he was awarded the coveted Pour le Mérite. At the same time he was given command of Jasta 2, in which other first-class pilots abounded, including his brother Lothar. Richthofen's squadron, the aircraft of which were all painted in different colours, became known to the British as the 'flying circus'. (Jasta 2 was subsequently banded together with three other Jagdstaffeln into a new independent fighter wing subsequently named Jagdgeschwader 1.)

At the end of April 1917 Richthofen went on leave, having already been promoted to Rittmeister (a cavalry rank equivalent to that of Captain — Hauptman in German) with his score by then having risen to fifty-two. At home he was fêted as a hero and the German propaganda machine went into full swing in publicising his exploits to an adoring public. Upon his return to the front, the creation of Jagdgeschwader I had taken place, which he led into action at every opportunity. Then, on 6th July, he had a narrow escape: during an attack on some FE2ds of No. 20 Squadron a bullet shaved his head and caused him to crash-land after first having lost consciousness. By the time he left hospital, 'Bloody April' had receded into the background and new British aircraft appeared on the scene which denied the Germans their previous dominance. Sopwith Camels, Bristol Fighters and SE5s all combined to make life more difficult for the German airmen whose losses began to mount inexorably.

A contemporary German postcard photograph of the famous Baron Manfred von Richthofen.

One of the more celebrated German aces to fall later that year was the renowned Werner Voss, who had been fighting in the Chemin des Dames sector at the time of Nivelle's abortive offensive in April. Also a former cavalryman, who had enlisted under age, he had transferred to the air service in 1915 and was an observer during the Battle of the Somme. In November 1916 he had transferred to Boelke's old squadron, Jasta 2, and quickly made his reputation as a fine flyer and dangerous enemy, with his score being close to that of Richthofen by February 1917. At the end of July 1917 Voss was in command of Jasta 10 and the new Fokker Triplane had made an appearance on the aerial battlefield. Voss loved this very manoeuverable aircraft and painted a face on the engine cowling which soon became well-known and feared. His score had mounted to forty-seven by 23rd September, a day on which, having shot down a DH4 north of Ypres, the twenty-year-old German ace attacked an SE5 but was himself attacked by six machines of the renowned No. 56 Squadron led by James McCudden.

Incredibly, Voss turned and attacked the attackers with exceptional ferocity, and for ten minutes the British pilots were kept at bay before eventually one of them (Second Lieutenant Rhys-Davids) got in a long burst which raked the Fokker from end to end and it began to glide downwards. Still being fired at by Rhys-Davids, Voss's plane went into a steep dive and crashed near St Julien, disintegrating as it hit the ground. The remains of the pilot, who was identified as Voss, were buried nearby by British soldiers. Of him McCudden wrote: 'As long as I live I shall never forget my admiration of that German pilot who, single-handed, fought seven of us for ten minutes and also put some bullets through all of our machines. His flying was wonderful, his courage magnificent, and, in my opinion, he was the bravest German airman whom it has been my privilege to fight.'

In the meantime, Richthofen too was flying the versatile Fokker Triplane, which like his previous aircraft he had painted scarlet-red, and on 2nd September (during Third

Ypres) he claimed his sixtieth victory. By the end of the year his score had reached sixty-three and, with Voss having been killed, he was undoubtedly the unchallenged ace of German aces and was idolised accordingly. Then came the German offensives of spring 1918 and with the RFC once more busily engaged in helping to fight back the German infantry hordes, Richthofen steadily added to his tally, which rose to seventy by the end of March.

Three weeks later the number of his victories had increased to the astonishing figure of eighty — and one day after that he was dead, having been shot down in the valley of the Somme in circumstances which to this day remain controversial. His demise was officially accredited as having been caused by Canadian Captain A. Roy Brown, a Flight Commander of No. 209 Squadron (flying a Sopwith Camel) but disputed by Australian machine-gunners who also fired at the low-flying all-red Fokker Triplane which was chasing a Camel of Brown's squadron and was in turn being chased by Brown himself. Upon examination of his body, it was ascertained that Richthofen had been killed by a bullet, but it has never been possible to ascertain with complete certainty the origin of the fatal shot and the mystery will doubtless remain unresolved for ever, partly due to the fact that his aeroplane was quickly stripped by souvenir hunters, with possible evidence being destroyed in the process. Suffice it to say that the greatest of all German aviators was dead at a time when his country could least afford to lose such a valuable source of propaganda, but his name lived on and he is still immortalised as a legendary figure who had no equal among all the flyers of the combatant nations.

The British ace who came closest to Richthofen's total of eighty 'kills' was Major Edward Mannock whose official score was seventy-three, one above William Bishop's. (Mannock's biographer believed that his unofficial total was not far from one hundred.) Three things made 'Mick' Mannock different from most British flyers, these being his manifest hatred of Germans (developed from experiences in

Turkey in 1914 and 1915), the fact of his being a superb shot, and his absolute dedication. He was born in 1887 (the son of a Regular soldier) and was thus much older than the average airman, which may be the reason why he was extremely difficult to get on with.

A pre-war Territorial in the RAMC at Canterbury, where his parents had lived, he took a job in Constantinople where he was interned when Turkey entered the war. With a problematical left eye he was released and sent home just before the Gallipoli landings began and, having rejoined the

A display cabinet at the Kent Battle of Britain Museum, Hawkinge Aerodrome, near Folkestone, containing Richthofen mementos, including photographs, copies of technical reports and models of the various-coloured Fokker Triplanes that he flew; also his all-red crashed aircraft (right). Two unique items of this display are the fuel gauge (centre-right) stated to have been removed from his plane after the crash and which has a bullet hole (depicted by the white spot) near the centre of what had been the hand-painted ceramic gauge face, and a spark plug from the 110-hp Oberursel rotary engine, both items once having been part of a special Scottish collection. [See Acknowledgements]

Medical Corps as a Sergeant, made no secret of his feelings for the enemy, to the extent of indicating a refusal to attend wounded Germans. Not surprisingly this met with the disapproval of the authorities and, after first applying for a commission in the Royal Engineers, he decided to try aeronautics, in which (apart from poor landings) he showed promise, and qualified as a pilot in November 1916. In April 1917 he joined No. 40 Squadron, then commanded by Robert Lorraine, a pre-war actor and flyer of somewhat similar temperament to Mannock. It was not, however, until the beginning of June 1917 that he had his first real success by shooting down a two-seater at close range, to be followed by another a few days later. An unfortunate accident caused him to be sent home for a spell, but early in July he was once again in action and by the end of the year he had scored nine 'kills'. A further period at home followed, during which he joined No. 74 Squadron which was equipped with SE5s, and upon promotion to Captain became a Flight Commander. He gave lectures on tactics that subsequently proved to be of great benefit to the young pilots and constantly practised his marksmanship, particularly in deflection shooting.

A week after the start of the German 1918 Spring Offensive, the squadron was in constant action in France, where it rapidly proved its mettle as a close-knit fighting machine. Mannock was in his element and at the end of May was awarded the DSO, to which, shortly afterwards, a Bar was added. Dogfights, in which many aircraft were involved, were the order of the day at that time and the strain began to tell, with Mannock showing signs of the effects of constantly living on a razor's edge. In June he was sent home on leave — his squadron's overall score being even higher than that of the famous No. 56 — and later that month he was promoted Major and took over command of No. 85 Squadron.

Back again in France, his desire to kill Germans continued unabated (even when Richthofen had been killed he expressed pleasure) and his score was then well beyond that of another famous British ace, Major J. T. B. McCudden. On 26th July disaster struck, for on that morning, together with a young New Zealander whom he wished to give an opportunity to make a kill, he was off at dawn, passing over the German trenches near Laventie. They successfully dealt with a two-seater and in doing so lost much height, coming down as low as just a few hundred feet from the ground. Enemy ground fire hit both planes and suddenly Mannock's machine caught fire and blew up as it crashed. His companion also crash-landed, but within the British lines, and to him fell the sad task of informing his comrades of Mannock's tragic loss. More than anything else Mannock had always feared being burned to death and it is believed that he carried a revolver (like some others) to avoid such a calamity. Whether or not he managed to use the revolver before he crashed or ground fire had killed him prior to the impact will never be known because nothing was left to either confirm or dispute that fact. There is no positive record of his remains ever having been found.

Major 'Micky' Mannock, VC, DSO (two bars), MC (one bar), St Omer, June 1918 (killed July 1918). [IWM]

After the war a VC was conferred on him by the King, and a block of flats in Canterbury is named after him where the Mannock home once stood. A bed is also dedicated to him in the Kent and Canterbury Hospital (Bell Ward). Every year a small service is held in Canterbury Cathedral in his memory by the RAF Association at which a wreath is laid on a memorial tablet by the Lord Mayor.

Major James McCudden was another pre-war service-man who subsequently became a famous fighter ace. A Kent-born man who had joined the army as a boy bugler, he transferred to the RFC in June 1913 and in so doing he became a member of No. 3 Squadron, the first Royal Flying Corps squadron to have been formed. For some time he was involved in ground duties and it was not until December 1915 that he experienced his first aerial combat, at that time as a Sergeant Observer. He then became a pilot and by July 1916 (having already received the Croix de Guerre) he was flying FE2d two-seater aircraft over the Somme battlefields, being transferred to No. 29 Squadron on August 3rd, which had single-seater DH2s. At the beginning of 1917 he received his commission, having already shot down his first enemy aircraft, to be followed by two more later.

In No. 66 Squadron, equipped with Sopwith Pups, McCudden's experience rose, and with the rank of Captain he then joined the famous No. 56 Squadron (with SE5s) in August as a Flight Commander. By the end of that year his total was thirty-seven, four of those being in one day (a feat to be repeated shortly afterwards). In February 1918 he claimed his last victim before he was posted home in March as a flying instructor, but not before his total of victories had reached fifty-seven. In April 1918 he was awarded the VC, the DSO and Bar to his MC, thus making him, at the age of twenty-two, the most decorated pilot in the British flying services.

In July 1918, having been promoted to Major, and being given command of No. 60 Squadron, tragedy struck when McCudden took off from Aix-le-Château airfield in France on the way to his new posting. His engine failed and — surprisingly for a trained pilot — he apparently attempted to turn back to the airfield at a low altitude and with a dead engine instead of trying to land ahead. He stalled and crashed to his death in nearby woods and, although no-one can say for sure whether he had committed a cardinal sin in making such a manoeuvre, or if other unknown factors were to blame, this accident thus prematurely ended the life of one of the RFC's brightest stars.

Of the considerable number of flyers who came into the 'ace' category, there were Italians, Belgians (Willy Coppens, for instance, who scored thirty-seven victories), Austro-Hungarians, a Russian, and Americans (amongst whom were Edward Rickenbacker — 26 'kills', F. Luke Jnr — 18, Raol Lufbery — 17, and Elliot White Springs — 12). Many British (such as Raymond Collishaw — 60, and Anthony Beauchamp-Proctor — 54), and Germans (for example, Ernst Udet — 62, who was the second highest scorer behind Richthofen, and Lothar von Richthofen, the Rittmeister's younger brother — 40), and, to a lesser extent, French flyers

Major J. B. McCudden, VC, DSO, MC, MM, seated in the cockpit of an SE5 aeroplane. [IWM]

scored quite high figures, and very many more with less successful totals were aces within their own right even though they did not achieve the eminence of their more acclaimed compatriots. Not surprisingly, it was the fighter aces, with their daring exploits, who held the spotlight; but the pilots of reconnaissance planes (and their observers) and the light (and later the much larger heavy) bomber pilots carried out their unenviable and dangerous tasks stoically and courageously, as too did the RNAS pilots on land and sea. All played their part aimed at winning the war.

On 1st April 1918 the RFC and the RNAS were combined to form the Royal Air Force under the overall command of Sir Hugh Trenchard. Less than two weeks earlier the Germans had begun their Spring Offensive on the Somme, to be followed by the battles of the Lys, the Aisne, the Matz and the Marne, in all of which British squadrons were involved. Inevitably losses mounted quickly in the persistent air fighting in which large numbers of aircraft of both sides were engaged, and following the turn of the tide, when the British and French took the offensive on 8th August, the incessant combats continued to take a heavy toll. On the first day of the successful assault by the Allies forty-five RAF aircraft were destroyed and as many again were lost by other means. Constant bombing raids by DH4s and DH9s were made on the retiring enemy troops, together with their lines of communication, and these regular excursions called for heavy escorts of fighters, with the Germans fighting back desperately to stem the advance. Sometimes as many as a hundred or more aircraft would be occupied in aerial combats over the front or beyond the German lines, with the sky seemingly filled with turning, twisting aeroplanes combined with the roar of racing engines and the staccato rat-tat-tat of machine-guns. Every so often one would plummet down to earth with engine screaming and the pilot dead or dying in the cockpit. Others would spin down with controls shot away and, all too regularly, a machine would fall in flames with the occupant or occupants facing that most dreaded of deaths of being burned alive. In those days there were no parachutes to allow a British airman to escape (allegedly because the authorities feared that such a means of getting away would lead to premature abandonment, but more likely because no really suitable types of parachute were developed until the closing stages of the war) and quite often a pilot would jump over the side to avoid being roasted. Whatever, death was inevitable and the grim reaper claimed many young lives from the furious air battles as the war drew to a close. Some Germans though had parachutes towards the end of 1918, including Ernst Udet and Lothar von Richthofen. Udet actually saved his life with one after jumping out of a burning plane.

On 11th November 1918 the Great War ended, as did that four-year era of the fighter 'ace', many of whom did not live to see the day of victory. Those that did found life very much different to the days of constant patrols and battles in the skies, and some found it difficult to adjust accordingly. A number of them found outlets in civilian flying duties as the commercial aspect grew; others in barnstorming air circuses. Yet others became famous in the air forces of the world, and many simply faded into obscurity.

The aeroplane, the potential of which had at first not been fully appreciated, but which subsequently became a vital instrument of war, had grown from a 'string and wire' apparatus into a fast (for its time) and formidable weapon.

In 1918, though, the principal thought in everyone's mind was relief at the end of so much suffering and trial, and the weapons of the previous four years were consigned to the smelting furnaces. Aeroplanes were no exception to the disposal programme, and in the couple of years following the Armistice many thousands were discarded, mainly on a scrap material basis.

It was not until the late 1930s, with the advent of the Hurricane and the Spitfire — and in the case of the Germans the Messerschmitt 109 — that the fighter plane really came into its own again; but that is a different story.

APPENDIX 2
THE BATTLES OF THE SOMME

The Battles of the Somme began at 7.30 a.m. on 1st July 1916 and continued almost unabated for four and a half months. The offensive — at first a mainly British affair, with the French at that time heavily committed at Verdun but taking an important part later — began with high hopes of it leading to a conclusion of the war that same year in the Allies' favour. It was, however, to end in stalemate after petering out in horrific conditions and atrocious weather in November of that year after the British, French and the Germans had suffered enormous losses. (British casualties on 1st July were 57,470.)

'The Somme' was actually a series of battles spread over the period and will forever be remembered as the testing ground of the men of Kitchener's New Armies who had flocked to the colours in the early days of the war and after preliminary training had finally arrived on the battlefield to face an enemy consisting of some of the best-trained troops in the world. The fact that the combatants of both sides fought with exceptional courage throughout the long, hard slogging match is indisputable; nor can it be argued that the result was anything other than a considerable disappointment to the Allies, in spite of the Germans admitting that they could never afford another Somme bloodbath — their casualties being estimated at over 600,000.

The staggering British losses (419,654) for the capture of a comparatively limited area of ground, and the methods employed, remain the subject of controversy to this day — and will doubtless continue to be. Yet, whatever might be thought of the rights and wrongs of the offensive (initially aimed at aiding the French, who themselves lost 204,253), those thousands upon thousands of civilian soldiers from the United Kingdom proved their mettle in adversity and were not found wanting at a time of severe trial. The price paid for their bravery — and that of the regulars and territorials — was horrendous, but in spite of the tragedy which struck so many homes throughout the land, a determination to work for final victory remained paramount.

Above right: The author (on the left) with the Earl Haig OBE, KStJ, DL, and Countess Haig below the statue of the Earl's father, Field Marshal Sir Douglas Haig, in the town of Montreuil during a tour of the Somme battlefields in 1984. The Earl and the Countess were on that occasion guests of The Western Front Association, which the author founded in 1980. The statue replaced one that was destroyed by the Germans in 1940.

'Gibraltar' — a German strongpoint still standing rocklike at the western end of Pozières after its capture. [IWM]

The rock no longer stands — not above ground, that is. The entry to the base of 'Gibraltar' was uncovered in time for the 70th anniversary of the Battle of the Somme. Steps lead down below ground but lower levels have been blocked off. An Australian memorial is nearby. It is understood that further excavations and reconstructions are planned.

Much suffering had yet to be endured before ultimate success was to be achieved, and a high proportion of 'Kitchener's Men' who fought on the Somme did not survive to celebrate that victory.

The book *The Somme Then and Now*, besides being an account of the engagements that constituted 'The Somme', is also a tribute to those men of Kitchener's New Army, and a few additional photographs relating to the subject are included here.

A sad picture of the graves of a father and son in Dartmoor Military Cemetery, near Becordel-Becourt, both of whom served in the Royal Artillery and were killed on the same day, 5th September 1916. One can well imagine the shock meted out to their family when news of their deaths was passed on by the authorities. In this same cemetery is buried 68-year-old Lieutenant Henry Webber, who was killed by a shell on 21st July 1916. He was said to be the oldest soldier in the British Expeditionary Force to have been killed in the Great War.

Wrecked German light railway engine between Le Sars and Warlincourt. The Butte de Warlincourt can be seen in the distance, March 1917. [IWM]

Sir Edward Carson on the Butte de Warlincourt, September 1917. [IWM]

Memorial on the crest of the Butte de Warlincourt erected by The Western Front Association. The original German wooden cross featured in the author's book *The Somme Then and Now*, and which stood near this spot, fell into disrepair and disappeared some years ago. (Photo: Major Rodney Turner)

In 1982 the author announced to a general meeting of the WFA (of which he was then chairman) that it was his heartfelt wish to purchase the Butte on a personal basis for retention as a perpetual memorial to all those who fought in the great battles of the Somme in 1916. It was here that the British offensive ended in stalemate in that sector in November of that year. Initial steps were taken to ascertain the possibility of such a purchase but further severe illness and other factors then halted the proceedings. Subsequently this infamous hill was purchased by the WFA aided by subscriptions from members and the memorial was dedicated at a special ceremony on 30th June 1990 attended by British and French dignitaries. To John Giles that once awful mound, which cost the lives of so many of those who attacked and attempted to capture it in 1916 (and for a brief time succeeded), and for which he had a deepfelt personal affinity for over two decades, represents so much of what he believes enabled those men of 1914–1918 to carry on despite daunting odds, viz duty, honour, stoicism, courage and a capability to endure suffering (and not forgetting a perfectly natural element of fear often offset by an amazing sense of humour).

ACKNOWLEDGEMENTS

As with my previous books, I have relied substantially on the Imperial War Museum for wartime photographs, and I express my thanks for permission to reproduce those from that source which appear in this book. Specific thanks are due to Mr Mike Willis for his help during my visits to the Museum.

Several pictures emanated from the National Army Museum, Chelsea, and here too I extend my appreciation for assistance in that connection.

I am particularly grateful to Mr Winston Ramsey and his son, Gordon, Editor and Assistant Editor respectively of *After the Battle* magazine for their most valued support in the publication of this book. Their encouragement — and patience — in the face of lengthy delays on my part (caused by personal health problems) is greatly appreciated.

For the Foreword I am much indebted to Major the Rt. Hon. The Earl Haig, OBE, KStJ, DL.

Numerous maps from official sources have been reproduced including a number from *Official History of the Great War, France and Belgium*, published by MacMillan and Co., London, and *Sir Douglas Haig's Despatches, December 1915–April 1919*, Edited by Lieutenant-Colonel J. H. Boraston, OBE, published by J. M. Dent and Sons Ltd., London 1919. Thanks are expressed in that respect to The Controller, Her Majesty's Stationery Office, London, and Ordnance Survey, Southampton.

Combined thanks also go to Michelin et Cie, Paris, and The Commonwealth War Graves Commission, Maidenhead, for permission to utilise one of their special Michelin maps (No. 53) issued by the CWGC, on which are over-printed details of the locations of War Cemeteries and Memorials, and special thanks are extended to Mr Bernard McGee, CWGC Information Officer, for his assistance and information supplied.

The National Archives of Canada, Documentary Art and Photography Dept., supplied several photographs for the Vimy Ridge section of this book, for which thanks are given for permission to publish. Thanks also go to Mr Fred Gaffin, Post Confederation Historian, Canadian War Museum, Ottawa, for assistance readily given.

I am also indebted to the following who have helped me by granting permission for publication of various texts:

Associated Newspapers plc: Extract from the *Evening News* dated 11th November 1918 (rear endpaper).

Illustrated London News Group: Poem *Christmas Bells* from 1914 edition of *The Sphere* (p.82).

Institut Geographic National, France: Section of Map No. 2, Lille–Dunkirk 1:1,000,000 (p. 86).

Personal contributions, which are gratefully acknowledged, have come from:

Miss Stephanie Cross, Bagshot, Surrey: Papers relating to her grandfather, Driver/Wheeler Leonard Cross (pp. 17 and 248) and Lord Roberts' Message to the Troops (p. 21).

Mr. D. P. Brindley, Bearsted, Kent: Loan of Diaries of Captain James Brindley, DSO, MC, from which extracts have been taken by the author (pp. 65–69 and 79–80).

The late Mr (former Private) W. E. 'Josh' Grover, MM, Wootton, Kent: Christmas 1914 tin (p. 82) together with photograph and details of his involvement in the Sambre Canal action in 1918 (p. 235).

The late Mr (former Sergeant) Archie Stanley, Dover, Kent: Details of his war-time service (survivor, p. 250).

Mr (former Captain) G. B. Jameson, MC, Sidmouth, Devon: Details of his wartime exploits (p. 98).

Monsieur de Valicourt, Flesquières, France: Photograph of the Château de la Retraite (p. 183) and loan of German photograph for copying (p. 184); also for information relating to the 'lone stand' legend (p. 183), and other assistance. Thanks also to his family for courtesies extended during my visit there.

Much appreciation is also expressed to the Kent Battle of Britain Museum, Hawkinge Airfield, Aerodrome Road, near Folkestone, Kent, for giving me special permission to photograph their collection of von Richthofen mementos and additional assistance in that connection.

For additional photographs, as credited, and assistance in other directions, I express thanks to: Paul Foster, John Tanner, Dr Ellen Rice, Richard Dunning, John Thompson, Paul Goodwin, John Holland-Hobbs, Mrs N. Giles, Geoff Bridger, Terry Whippy, Mary Freeman, Jim Lucas, Howard Giles, Basil Kidd, Barry Bullock, Nicholas Bullock, Tony Spagnoly, Major Rodney Turner and the late Colonel J. B. Jarrett, OBE (Maryland, USA).

In the event of any inadvertent acknowledgement omissions having occurred, apologies are offered accordingly.

Finally, very special thanks are given to all those people who have done so much to help me fight serious illness over many years and have thus played an important part in enabling me to complete this First World War trilogy; especially my dear wife, Margery, who has been my constant companion and nurse on numerous battlefield researches and pilgrimages; the cardiac surgeons of St Thomas's Hospital, London (specifically Mr Bryn T. Williams, FRCS and Dr M. M. Webb-Peploe FRCP); the consultants (especially Dr D. J. E. Taylor FRCP) and staff of the Cardiac Department of the Kent and Canterbury Hospital, and my GP (Dr A. Hoda) of Ash.

Note: (1) IWM is an abbreviation of Imperial War Museum.

(2) Author/WFA relates specifically to aerial photographs taken personally by the author during his chairmanship of The Western Front Association.

The Evening News

London's Predominant Evening Journal. Largest Net Sale in the United Kingdom.

WAR LATE EXTRA

NO. 11,543. (Thirty-eighth Year.)   LONDON: MONDAY, NOVEMBER, 11, 1918.   ONE PENNY

THE ARMISTICE TERMS.

RHINELANDS TO BE OCCUPIED.

ALLIED GARRISONS AT MAINZ, COBLENZ AND COLOGNE.

ALL SUBMARINES TO BE HANDED OVER.

BUCHAREST AND BREST TREATIES NULL AND VOID.

The Prime Minister made the following announcement to-day:—

The Armistice was signed at Five o'clock this morning, and hostilities are to cease on all Fronts at 11 a.m. to-day.

PREMIER'S STATEMENT IN THE HOUSE.

The Prime Minister in the House of Commons this afternoon read the terms of the Armistice. The points of these terms are:—

Immediate evacuation of Belgium, Alsace-Lorraine, and Luxembourg.

Evacuation by enemy of Rhine lands completed within 31 days.

Railways of Alsace-Lorraine to be handed over.

All German troops in Russia, Rumania, and elsewhere to be withdrawn.

Immediate repatriation of Allied and United States prisoners without repatriation of Germans.

Complete abandonment of the Treaties of Bucharest and Brest-Litovsk.

Immediate cessation of all hostilities at sea.

Handing over to Allies and United States of all submarines.

Duration of the armistice to be 36 days.

5,000 guns (2,500 heavy, 2,500 field guns), 30,000 machine guns to be handed over.

BEYOND THE RHINE

FOCH CALLS THE "HALT!"

TROOPS NOT TO PASS BEYOND LINE REACHED AT 11.

"CEASE FIRE" ON ALL FRONTS.

The following messages were issued to-day through the wireless stations of the French Government:—

"Hostilities will cease on the whole front as from November 11 at 11 o'clock (French time).

The Allied troops will not until a further order go beyond a line reached on that date and at that hour.

(Signed) MARSHAL FOCH.

German Plenipotentiaries to the German High Command, to be communicated to all the authorities interested:—

Radio 3084 and G.Q.G. 2 No. 1206 received.

Armistice was signed at 5 o'clock in the morning (French time). It comes into force at 11 o'clock in the morning (French time).

Delay for evacuation prolonged by 24 hours for the left bank of the Rhine, besides the five days; therefore 31 days in all. Modifications of the text compared with that brought by Yelldorf will be transmitted by radio.

(Signed) ERZBERGER.

—Admiralty, per Wireless Press.

THE TERMS IN BERLIN.

Formally Accepted by the Government To-day.

COPENHAGEN, Monday.

It is officially reported from Berlin that the German Government in Cabinet meeting has formally accepted the armistice terms of the Allies.—Exchange Telegraph.

PREMIER'S STATEMENT.

Terms Signed After All-Night Discussion.

On Mr. Lloyd George's entry into the House he was received with loud and rousing cheers, the members standing waving their hats, while others waved the order papers on the day.

The Prime Minister, who spoke immediately, said that after a discussion which was prolonged all night the armistice was signed. He would read to the House the conditions of the armistice in so far as they had reached them up to the present.

He ought to warn the House and the public that they had only received such corrections as were rendered necessary by the new conditions. These corrections had only been received by telephone, and there was a possibility that there might be a few mistakes, but substantially the terms represented the conditions which

PEOPLE'S GREAT SHOUT AT PALACE.

THE ROYAL FAMILY ON THE BALCONY.

GUARDS' BAND PLAYS "STARS AND STRIPES."

With you I rejoice and thank God for the victories which the Allied arms have won, bringing hostilities to an end and peace within sight.—The King, at Buckingham Palace.

"We—want—King—George."

Like an American college cry the enormous crowd outside Buckingham Palace at noon shouted these words:

"We—want—King—George!" They thundered at intervals until there was no mistaking their wish.

It was a wonderful waiting. The people were massed together outside the Palace as far as the eye could see. They were on every statue and right up Queen Victoria's monument.

Overseas men in almost every instance occupied the highest pinnacles. Air officers were only on the tops of taxi-cabs! Waacs were shoulder high.

The crowd had stormed the gates of the Palace when the police attempted to shut them, after a sufficient number of people had been admitted to the forecourt.

At the changing of the guard at noon they took the eight Guardsmen, who were marching off with fixed bayonets, and lifted them shoulder high—a liberty probably never taken with the Guardsmen on duty before.

THE KING'S GREETING.

On the guns in the forecourt were seated many people well known in London—the Marchioness of Salisbury, Lady St. Oswald, Lady Gainford, Mrs. George Keppel, the Countess of Airlie, Lady Stanley and her sister, Lady Honor Ward, Lady Sandhurst, and others.

With their faces pressed close to the railings outside were the Lady Lytton's children and the children of Mr. McKenna.

"King, come!" they shouted every now and then.

A roar greeted the King and Queen as they entered the balcony—the roar of a people satisfied. Nothing was ever heard like it. No cheer could express what lay behind that roar of jubilation.

The King, who was in naval uniform, stood at the salute, and the Queen waved a Union Jack. The whole assembly swayed with one great emotion.

The crowd did not wait for the band. They began "God Save the King" as if previously arranged. The effort was wonderful.

The Allies, at every interval, fluttered in a breeze. Now under the Queen waved her flag. King and Queen and people were absolutely at one.

A MEMORABLE SCENE.

All the war songs followed "Keep the Home Fires Burning," and the children who have sung it all the long years of war joined in and the Queen beat time.

"Land of Hope and Glory" followed, and then flags were waved and a quieter feeling settled on the crowd as the band played "The Old Hundredth"—"All people that on earth do dwell, sing to the Lord with cheerful voice."

The King stood at the salute as "Stars

HOW THE KAISER ESCAPED.

RUSH INTO HOLLAND BY MOTOR CAR.

WANTED TO SURRENDER TO THE BRITISH MILITARY COMMAND.

ACCORDING to an Eysden message, shots were fired at the ex-Kaiser's train, and the Imperial fugitive thereupon made his escape across the Dutch frontier by motor-car.

There is no confirmation of his arrival at Middachten Castle, but from Amsterdam it is reported that, with the Crown Prince and Hindenburg, he is remaining at Eysden awaiting the decision of the Dutch authorities, who are expected to place a suitable residence at his disposal.

It is also reported from Amsterdam that the Kaiser at first attempted to make his way into the British Lines with a view to surrendering to the British, but was headed off by Revolutionary troops, thereupon he turned back and made for Holland.

HAGGARD AND BROKEN DOWN.

The Imperial Fugitive's Journey.

A Central News message from Eysden, dated Sunday and received to-day, says:—

Last night a German general arrived at Eysden in a motor-car on a secret mission.

Later it leaked out that he had come to notify the Dutch authorities of the imminent arrival of the ex-Kaiser.

A number of Dutch officers were immediately despatched from the Hague to Eysden, and this morning a royal train steamed into the station shortly before eight o'clock, in which were a number of officers of high rank and members of the Emperor's suite.

But the Kaiser himself was not in the train, and it became known that he had previously arrived in a motor-car via Monland.

He had decided not to travel by train because during its journey several shots had been fired at the carriage windows.

The Kaiser therefore alighted at an early stage and got into a car which shortly before the train steamed in drove up to the station platform.

The Kaiser alighted and went on to the platform.

He looked haggard and broken down, and though he maintained a stern countenance to all beholders, his nerves seemed to be not far from the breaking point.

THE CROWN PRINCE.

Mystery as to Where He Is.

AMSTERDAM, Monday.

It is rumoured here that the ex-Crown Prince has arrived at Middachten.—Reuter.

According to the Central News Eysden correspondent, nobody there is positive that he was in the train, and it is rumoured that he was held up by German soldiers, who refused to let him pass.

KING OF SAXONY GOES.

Grand Duke of Oldenburg Also Dethroned.

COPENHAGEN, Monday.

A Berlin official telegram announces that the King of Saxony has been dethroned.

It is announced from Hamburg that the Grand Duke of Oldenburg has been dethroned.—Reuter.

MORE BATTLESHIPS REVOLT.

AMSTERDAM, Monday.

According to a report from Brunsbuettel, on the Kiel Canal, the sailors of the battleships Posen, Ostfriesland, Nassau, and Oldenburg, which are lying off Brunsbuettel, have joined the revolutionary movement in Kiel.—Reuter.

LATEST NEWS

EX-KAISER TO BE INTERN

Amsterdam, Monday

It is stated on good authority that the Kaiser will be interned in Holland.

He will leave Eysden at this morning for Middachten.—Reuter.

DUTCH SENTRIES "HOLD UP" FUGITIVE KAISER

MAASTRICHT, Sunday Night (delayed)

Early this morning three German motor-cars crossed the frontier at Eysden.

The occupants wanted at once to proceed, but were prevented by the sentries.

Soon after, five more motor-cars appeared, in the last of which was the German ex-Emperor in a general's uniform.

The sentries held up the motors until instructions arrived from the H—Reuter.

THE ARMISTICE. MODIFICATIONS MAY BE EFFECTED.

When the House of Commons met this afternoon the Earl of Crawford, as Privy Seal, read the terms of the armistice in the absence of Earl Curzon, explained that messages had been stantly exchanged between London and Paris during the day, and certain modifications might be effected, but substantially the terms of the armistice were the same as the Prime Minister had read the House of Commons.

EX-EMPEROR'S RETINUE

The Dutch newspapers report the Imperial party which has arrived in land numbered 51 persons in all, included, besides the ex-Kaiser and suite, the Crown Prince, Hindenburg, fourteen gentlemen-in-waiting.

It is stated that the party left Maastricht not for Middachten but castle.—Reuter's Amsterdam Correspondent.

B.D.